ATLA Monograph Series
edited by Dr. Kenneth E. Rowe

1. Ronald L. Grimes. *The Divine Imagination: William Blake's Major Prophetic Visions.* 1972.

2. George D. Kelsey. *Social Ethics Among Southern Baptists, 1917-1969.* 1973.

3. Hilda Adam Kring. *The Harmonists: A Folk-Cultural Approach.* 1973.

4. J. Steven O'Malley. *Pilgrimage of Faith: The Legacy of the Otterbeins.* 1973.

5. Charles Edwin Jones. *Perfectionist Persuasion: The Holiness Movement and American Methodism, 1867-1936.* 1974.

6. Donald E. Byrne, Jr. *No Foot of Land: Folklore of American Methodist Itinerants.* 1975.

7. Milton C. Sernett. *Black Religion and American Evangelicalism: White Protestants, Plantation Missions, and the Flowering of Negro Christianity, 1787-1865.* 1975.

8. Eva Fleischner. *Judaism in German Christian Theology Since 1945: Christianity and Israel Considered in Terms of Mission.* 1975.

BLACK RELIGION AND AMERICAN EVANGELICALISM

*White Protestants, Plantation Missions, and
the Flowering of Negro Christianity, 1787-1865*

by
MILTON C. SERNETT

with a Foreword by
Martin E. Marty

ATLA Monograph Series, No. 7

The Scarecrow Press, Inc., Metuchen, N. J.
and
The American Theological Library Association
1975

Library of Congress Cataloging in Publication Data

Sernett, Milton C   1942-
    Black religion and American evangelicalism.

    (ATLA monograph series ; no. 7)
    A revision of the author's thesis, University of
Delaware.
    Bibliography: p.
    Includes index.
    1. Negroes--Religion. 2. Evangelicalism--Southern
States. I. Title. II. Series: American Theological
Library Association. ATLA monograph series ; no. 7.
BR563.N4S47 1975   280'.4'0975   75-4754
ISBN 0-8108-0803-X

Manufactured in the United States of America

To the Three Women in My Life

EDITOR'S NOTE

Since 1972 the American Theological Library Association has undertaken responsibility for a modest dissertation publishing program in the field of religious studies. Our aim in this monograph series is to publish in serviceable format and at reasonable cost two dissertations of quality each year. Titles are selected from studies in the several religious and theological disciplines nominated by graduate school deans or directors of graduate studies in religion.

Professor Milton Charles Sernett received his undergraduate training at Concordia Senior College, Fort Wayne, Indiana. He studied theology at Concordia Seminary, St. Louis and received the doctorate in history from the University of Delaware. Mr. Sernett has taught in the University of Delaware, Wilmington College, and Brandywine College. Currently he teaches Christian Social Ethics and in the area of American and Modern Church History at Concordia Theological Seminary, Springfield, Illinois. We are pleased to publish his study of black religion as number seven in our series.

A special word of appreciation goes to Professor Martin Marty for his fine Foreword.

Kenneth E. Rowe, Editor

Drew University Library
Madison, New Jersey

ACKNOWLEDGMENTS

Even though research and writing is often a solitary and sometimes a lonely endeavor, as most authors know, I have incurred many debts along the way. The lengthy bibliography at the end of what follows includes the names of scores of scholars who have made my task easier by laying a foundation upon which I could build. Prof. Donald H. Meyer of the University of Delaware oversaw this work while in thesis form, saved me from many a blunder, and proved to be both perceptive mentor and good friend. Prof. Lawrence N. Jones of Union Theological Seminary, New York City, read the dissertation draft, alerted me to possible revisions, and gave a timely word of encouragement. A special word of acknowledgment is extended to Professor Martin E. Marty of the University of Chicago Divinity School. Though I have never had the privilege of studying under him, his personal interest in this work and his gracious agreement to write the Foreword have meant a great deal to me.

Through a rather fortuitous set of circumstances, I have benefited from the supervision of Dr. Kenneth E. Rowe, editor of the American Theological Library Association monograph series, who was first sounded out about the possibility of publishing this study by Prof. Barbara Steege, librarian of Concordia Seminary, Springfield, Illinois, and benefactress of young faculty members. To Dean Lorman Petersen, campus colleagues, and the students in the Black Religion in American History course with whom I have shared much of this material, I also owe a word of gratitude.

Finally, as the dedication indicates, there are three women in my life to whom expressions of formal gratitude are woefully inadequate. To my mother I owe more than I can say; when others may have doubted, she has kept the faith, in spite of my rather circuitous pursuit of an education and a profession. My wife Jan has kept the home fires brightly burning and served as a willing but critical editor without portfolio. Little Rebecca reshuffled the manuscript a number of times and on one occasion nearly shredded an entire chapter. Thus I was made aware of my other responsibilities and of the fact that there are even more important things than writing of the past, irreverent as that may seem in light of historians' perceptions of what they do for a living. Any shortcomings in what is to come, are, of course, due to my own limitations.

Springfield, Illinois   Milton C. Sernett

CONTENTS

ILLUSTRATIONS AND CREDITS

the Era of the American Revolution, 1770-1800.
City of Washington: New York Graphic Society
in assoc. with Smithsonian Institution, 1973.

118   Oil portrait by Raphaelle Peale, 1810. Delaware
             Art Museum, Wilmington, Delaware.

119   Lithograph by W. L. Breton. The Historical So-
             ciety of Pennsylvania. Reproduced by permis-
             sion. Photo used by courtesy of the publisher
             from: Kaplan. Black Presence in the Era of the
             American Revolution. City of Washington: 1973.

121   Mother Bethel African Methodist Episcopal Church,
             Philadelphia (from a postcard).

124 left   Woodson. History of the Negro Church, 2nd ed.
             Washington, D. C.: Associated Publishers, Inc.,
             1945. Reproduced by permission.

124 right   Carter G. Woodson and Charles H. Wesley. The
             Negro in Our History. 11th ed. Washington,
             D. C.: Associated Publishers, Inc., 1966. Re-
             produced by permission.

127   Used by courtesy of Rose Memorial Library,
             Drew University, Madison, N. J.

129   Illustrated London News, April 30, 1853. From:
             the Schomburg Collection, New York Public Li-
             brary at Lincoln Center; Astor, Lenox, Tilden
             Foundations. Reproduced by permission.

130 left   Flood and Hamilton, eds. Lives of Methodist
             Bishops. New York; Cincinnati: 1882.

130 right   Woodson. History of the Negro Church, 2nd ed.
             Washington, D. C.: Associated Publishers, Inc.,
             1945. Reproduced by permission.

132 left   Daniel Alexander Payne. Recollections of Seventy
             Years. Nashville, Tenn.: Publishing House of
             the A. M. E. Sunday School Union, 1888.

132 right   Flood and Hamilton, eds. Lives of Methodist
             Bishops. New York; Cincinnati: 1882.

142 left   Simmons. Men of Mark. Cleveland: 1887.

142 right   Oil portrait by unknown artist, ca. 1815. The
             New-York Historical Society. Reproduced by
             permission. Photo used by courtesy of the
             publisher from: Kaplan. Black Presence in
             the Era of the American Revolution. City of
             Washington: 1973.

144   African Methodist Episcopal Church. The Budget
             for 1883, comp. and ed. by B. W. Arnett.
             Dayton, Ohio: Christian Publishing House, 1883.

160 left   Woodson. History of the Negro Church, 2nd ed.
and right   Washington, D. C.: Associated Publishers, Inc.,
             1945. Reproduced by permission.

FOREWORD

Martin E. Marty
The University of Chicago

The movement stressing black power and identity in America ten years ago led to a field of black studies. History inevitably played its part. While white middle class collegians were contending that history was irrelevant, black contemporaries wanted their story retold as a means of learning who they were, what they had become, and what their prospects were. While the faddish side of black history has passed, serious students of American history and peoplehood have through them learned to rethink their whole past in the light of the episode.

Societies do not have collective memories. They need history and historians for the telling of stories that help them find themselves and determine courses of action. In the chaos of recent America the historian has begun to find his function again. Seldom has this been more clearly demonstrated than in the case of the retelling of black history. Such a retrieval serves not only to inform black minorities but also white majorities. Another illustration: the movement of women's liberation has turned both male and female historians back to their sources. They see the whole past from a different point of view. Their consciousness has been raised.

The retellings are full of hazards. First, the newly self-conscious people, who have the heaviest investment in the fresh visits to the past, also have a tendency to engage in myth-making. Historian Milton Sernett is not reticent about pointing out that some fashioning does go on among black students who need a ready-made ideology. He serves them by doing what he can through a reading of both original and secondary sources to set the record straight, even where it enhances the claims of neither race.

A second hazard appears when the retelling exists for the tellers' purposes, when he or she loses interest in the intrinsic worth of the story being told. Thus many of us who have been writing about the American racial majorities, through our discovery of the role of minorities have often in a sense used their history in order to define the outlines of their oppressors' past. Then, black history has little value for its own sake; its potency lies in its contribution to understanding what white majorities are about. Here again Professor Sernett avoids most of the temptations to use blacks and make them actors in a drama not of their choosing.

In fact what is distinctive about this book is its almost mathematical sense of division into black and white halves; the first part tells how whites saw, treated, served, and used blacks; the second part chronicles the rise of black religious organization. In some cases the halves interlock within chapters and paragraphs. Such an outline is decent and sensible; thus the events occurred. The destinies of southern whites and blacks overlapped and were intertwined. Half stories here would be half truths.

If there is racial balance in this accounting, let it also be noted that here as in almost all revisitations of the American Negro past the role of religion is lifted out of a long-undeserved obscurity and given its rightful place. In the late decades of the nineteenth century and the early decades of the twentieth, American higher education had to be almost steadfastly secular in order to push off the embrace of sectarian religion, the original sponsor and later suffocator of so much higher education.

In the understandable, necessary process of keeping religion at a distance, something of a distorting character occurred both in curricula and in perceptions. Religion came to be either too controversial a subject to touch or was seen to be epiphenomenal, vestigial, marginal, trivial, or boring. In the 1960s there was at last an extensive recovery of the study of religion in the secular higher academies. Just before this recovery became highly visible Carl Bridenbaugh in his presidential address at the American Historical Association complained that it was difficult to teach graduate history in America. Undergraduates had not confronted the highly revelatory and explanatory religious strand in the American past.

What sense can be made of Hawthorne or Lincoln or Wilson without some understanding of their religious matrices and circumstances? If any part of the American past cannot be understood without reference to religion, it is the webbed

drama of blacks and whites.   As Sernett shows, blacks did
little innovating so far as religious structures were concerned,
and had to be content with borrowed religious substances.
But they did improvise personal meanings.   That is, they
had to accept and did accept forms and substances from their
white owners, persecutors, and saviors.   They were free,
however, to invest their borrowings or impositions with private meanings.   In this instance, too, it is easy to turn to
ideology and mythmaking.   Some recent scholars have tried
to make it seem as if blacks used religion almost entirely
as a coding system to keep their own covert and subvert
meaning systems alive.   Not at all; in many cases the symbols meant for them what they meant for whites.   They did
have supernatural, otherworldly, and not always militant and
liberating references.

     This accent in Sernett's work actually helps reveal
more of the character and role of American religion--or,
perhaps, almost anyone's religion--than do the biased accounts of all black religion as liberating radical ideology.
Very few peoples have used their spiritual sustenance only
in order to organize for eventual revolution.   They use religion to situate themselves in a universe which demands interpretation, where they must be as Sartre has called them,
"stalkers of meaning."   Much of what is incorporated with
religion has to do with behavioral nuances that are no less
potent or salutary because they help people keep their sanity,
ward off despair or suicide, or give them day to day places
in the world and ultimate hope.

     An accidental by-product of this account of both white-
derived and black-generated religion is its delineation of
"evangelicalism."   Most casual Americans bless or curse
Puritanism as the source of what is right or wrong with
themselves, their psyches, and their social world.   Fewer
of them know what to make of evangelicalism, a highly transformed successor to Puritanism.   In the nineteenth century
this religion of the heart, based on a faith that took root in
revivals, centered in the love of Jesus Christ, and issued in
organizations and personal endeavors for the world's redemption or human charity, swept Protestant America (when America was almost wholly Protestant).   The later American past
cannot be understood without a comprehension of evangelicalism, yet for years many have tried to make their way past
it or around it.

     These have been great years for the recovery of the

history of evangelicalism.   Try to discern the roots of American voluntary associations, imperialism, manifest destiny, racism, dogoodism, moral conscience, social gospels, images of man, and you will soon find yourself knotted in the story of evangelicalism.   Professor Sernett straightens out the strands in a sane, economical, and generally balanced account of what that kind of religion was and what it meant.   The Marxist historian E. J. Hobsbawm has given Anglo-American evangelicalism its due when he noted that it was the expansive faith in the imperial century.   It will take a generation of Sernetts to redress imbalances in the reckoning with the American religious past; here, at least, is a good beginning.

If anything impresses the reader in the pages that follow it is the adaptability and inventiveness of humans, especially when they are dealing with myth or symbol or ultimate reality.   American Negro slaves were deprived of their native land and memories, imported without permission to carry with them much of any tradition, demeaned and degraded.   Their masters dehumanized themselves while depriving blacks of full humanity and even small measures of freedom.   One would have expected almost nothing essentially humane to have remained.   Yet in the midst of suffering, people found ways to produce joy; in the face of despair, they learned to affirm; despite the chains, they danced and sang; without figurative straw they made the bricks of religious institutions that imparted meaning and hope.

I have implied that the story of black religion has intrinsic validity and need not exist for any larger scheme. But in the case of this book we once again find accidental benefits because of the clues provided here concerning the character of soul, spirit, and substance in the human drama.

Prologue

THE TIE THAT BINDS

There is a church in Philadelphia known as Mother
Bethel. She stands at the corner of Sixth and Lombard
Streets, hemmed in by shabby shops and the usual clutter of
an inner city. Although now an historic landmark, Mother
Bethel was for many years unknown to the general public.
No great fuss was made over this church as was made over
Independence Hall, only a short distance to the North. Because of the upsurge of interest in the history of the American Negro, Mother Bethel is no longer obscure. In the past
several years the church's sexton, a gentleman who also hap-
pens to be a member of her historical committee, has been
so importuned by school children, tourists, and researchers,
that he is rather weary of the whole business. Each week
visitors come asking to see the church that Richard Allen
founded and to visit the undercroft where his burial vault is.

Bethel A. M. E. Church of Philadelphia was the mother church of thousands of Negro Christians before the Civil
War. Within her doors, and those of other independent black
churches, the Negroes in the North found a place of refuge
and their own house of worship. Many of them first heard
the Christian Gospel, as Richard Allen did, while they were
still slaves. In most instances the preacher had been a white
missionary of one of the great Evangelical Protestant denominations. The slaves, however, did not leave the care of
their souls entirely in the hands of white people. They developed a religious life of their own under the "peculiar institution"--a kind of underground church.

Negro religion before the Civil War did not represent
a fourth American faith after Protestantism, Judaism, and
Catholicism. In matters of work and life, it is true, there
were two different worlds in which white Christians and black
Christians lived. But in matters of faith and order the Negro
churches reflected the structure and doctrines of Evangelical
Protestantism. To borrow an image used by Booker T. Washington, black religion and white religion were as distinct

17

socially as the five fingers of the hand, but they were one
like the hand itself in sharing the Evangelical heritage.

This does not mean that blacks simply imitated white
piety in the antebellum era. They brought to American Christianity a unique and powerful folk element. Black folk religion was first hammered out on the anvil of the slaves' experience under the dehumanizing forces of chattel servitude
and then brought by them into their own churches in the North.
They took the Gospel as preached by the plantation missionaries and shaped it to fit their own needs, making a creative
synthesis out of what whites taught them, of what they discovered for themselves, and of what they remembered from
the African past. The great lesson to be learned is that
black Christianity cannot be judged, even among the slaves,
as if the African was simply a passive receptacle for Cau-
casian mysteries.

Historians of American Christianity have been slow in
making amends for having written the drama of this country's
religious heritage without the presence of its black participants. In the late 1950s the sociologist Will Herberg observed that the Negro church, because it had always been a
segregated division within American religion, constituted "an
anomaly of considerable importance in the general sociological scheme of the 'triple melting pot' along lines of religious
community." Vincent Harding has appropriately described
our ignorance of Negro religion in the United States as "a
variety of cultural lag." And Robert T. Handy has pointed
out that despite renewed interest on the part of the general
academic community in American religion within the last
decade, Negro Christianity has continued to be thought of as
a "special topic." It has been left to those with a particular
interest in church history and has been treated "rather inci-
dentally, even casually" in the standard surveys of American
religion. 1†

For the most part, the story of the black church has
been left to representatives of the various Negro connections,
who, in the tradition of denominational historians, have generally written filiopietistic accounts from the point of view
of their own heritage. The general neglect by other historians of Negro Christianity has, of course, been an aspect of
the larger inattention to all things black within the American

---

†See page 175 for notes to this and succeeding chapters.

panorama. Some writers, perhaps unsympathetic to religion
as an important aspect of human culture, have not appre-
ciated the significant role which the church has played in the
story of the American Negro. Yet as far back as 1939,
Carter G. Woodson wrote in The Negro History Bulletin:
"A definitive history of the Negro church ... would leave
practically no phase of the history of the Negro in America
untouched. "2   And Prof. Lawrence N. Jones, appointed to
the chair of Afro-American Church History at Union Theological Seminary in New York City, has pointed out that in
antebellum America "Black history and Black church history
intersected at so many points as to be virtually identical. "3

     Black folk religion touched every aspect of the lives
of the slaves and was brought by them into the independent
church to provide Negro Christianity with a unique and en-
during genius. Few whites before the Civil War recognized
the contributions of Negroes to their own religious life. It
was generally thought that the Christianity of the slave cabin
was shaped by that of the master's house. The South took
great pride in the missionary endeavors on the plantations.
One of the proslavery defenses was that Christianity took the
African and lifted him up from degradation and idolatry in
a fashion that would have been impossible in Africa itself.
Even Robert Baird, an English observer, accepted the argument that the Gospel among the slaves "secured to them
manifold more blessings, hard as the lot of many may have
been, than they could have enjoyed in Africa. "4   The impli-
cation of his thesis is that it was better to be a Christian
slave in America than a free heathen in Africa.

     Baird raised other issues to which a more reasonable
consideration can be given. He suggested that the introduction of Christianity among the slaves moderated the harsher
aspects of life on the plantation by, for example, providing
a day of rest on the Sabbath and causing masters to treat
their slaves more kindly. One of our concerns, therefore,
should be to examine the effects of the plantation missions.
Did the spread of the Gospel in the South put slaveholders
on notice that there was a dimension to their relationship
with blacks which could not be dealt with in terms of the account book and the overseer's rawhide? Did Christianity
bring blessings to the slaves which would not have been available had the South made no effort in behalf of religious instruction?

     To answer these questions we shall have to examine

the anatomy of American Evangelicalism and survey the history of the Evangelical effort to convert the slaves, especially in the vehicle of the organized plantation mission.
Then we shall have to analyze the kind of gospel which was
preached in the plantation chapel. But to stop here would
be to repeat past errors--to write once again of black religion simply on the basis of white perceptions. Instead we
must let black voices from the past tell the story of the
"hush-arbor" church and of the way in which the slaves
discerned truth from fiction in the missionaries' messages.

Solomon Northup, a free black man of the North,
who, like the Biblical Joseph, was kidnapped and sold into
slavery, testified that in Louisiana whites generally remarked
that a master who gave the Bible to his slaves was "not fit
to owne a nigger. "5 Francis Henderson, a fugitive slave in
Canada, told Benjamin Drew that his master had refused him
permission to attend a Methodist church in the South, saying,
"You shan't go to that church--they'll put the devil in you. "6
Why should a society that had the force of arms, the courts,
and public opinion on its side to keep the slaves in submission, balk at placing the Bible in black hands or allowing
slaves to attend Methodist preaching? The traditional view
that the South simply used religion as a tool of oppression
has never asked this question or taken seriously the evidence
provided by Northup and Henderson. Timothy L. Smith iso-
lates the problem: "Abundant evidence that slaveholders
hoped Christian instruction would persuade Black people to
acquiesce in their bondage has been readily taken for proof
that acquiescence was in fact the usual result of their conversion. "7 The fact is that there were two notions of the
true meaning of the Gospel in the South, one belonging to the
slaveholder and the other to the slave. We shall have to
take a look at both of them.

It is difficult to know how much the slaves knew of
the world outside the South. Before the abortive insurrection of Denmark Vesey, the African Methodist Episcopal
Church had a large congregation in Charleston which some
of the slaves in the area attended. Other than this, there
is scant evidence that the masses of the slaves knew that in
the North their free brothers had churches of their own.
Benjamin Quarles has pointed out that Southerners rarely
mentioned the presence of blacks in the Northern antislavery
campaign, for this would have destroyed the myth that the
free Negro was incapable of great deeds. 8 Surely the same
motive which kept many of the slaves in ignorance of the

exploits of Frederick Douglass contributed to the conspiracy of silence about the deeds of Richard Allen and his coadjutors.

Before the Civil War there was no single ecclesiastical entity which can be called "the Black Church." There were, instead, black Baptists, black Methodists, black Presbyterians, and the like. In the case of the Methodist denomination, Negroes did organize into self-governing bodies. Even here there was a distinct lack of unity. The African Methodist Episcopal Church and the African Methodist Episcopal Zion Church, the two largest independent Negro organizations, continually competed for prestige and converts within the Negro community. To this very day the Bethelites and the Zionites have not achieved structural unity. Denominationalism has been both a bane and a blessing to American Christians. Unfortunately for the black churches, it has often been more bane than blessing. Disunity has muted what otherwise might have been a great single voice of protest against injustice and racism in American society.[9]

Despite this lack of organizational cohesion, we shall, in what follows, be referring to "the black church" and "black religion" as metaphors for the shared historical and spiritual experience of Negro Christians in America from 1787 to 1865. Black religion, as we have said, was not a fourth American faith, but it was the result of the peculiar sufferings and trials, hopes and victories of the American Negro. Within the perimeters of Protestant Evangelicalism, the black church sought to meet the needs of an oppressed yet ever resilient people. It had to serve the Negro community as an all-comprehending institution.

Today there are over twelve million black Christians in the United States within the independent Negro denominations. Thousands of others remain within the major white-governed Protestant bodies.[10] Because of the emergence of black religious leaders in the struggle for civil rights, we have all been made aware of the importance of religion to the black experience. Even some of the most outspoken advocates of black liberation are now cautious about dismissing the Negro church as dysfunctional and escapist. In their search for a useable past, as we shall see in the last chapter, some present-day writers have sought to align black Christianity with "Black Power." The current debate over the significance of the historic Negro church is frequently engaged in only by those with a special interest at stake.

This has been the fate of Negro religion ever since whites
first started arguing about the African's capacity for religious instruction.

Because of the grand sweep of the story that follows,
there no doubt are many stones left unturned, debates left
unresolved, characters of no less importance than those
introduced left off-stage, and questions that have gone un-
asked. Sometimes, as in the accounts of the establishment
of the plantation missions and the independent Negro churches,
our approach has been a narrative one.   Elsewhere the angle
of vision is expository and thematic.   Individual chapters
have been designed as integral units that can stand by themselves even though they are part of a larger story.   Although
there is an evident movement from white to black, from
American Evangelicalism to the Negro churches, as the study
unfolds, this is neither a chronological nor conceptual necessity.   One might as well have established a black-to-white
continuum, so that Negro religion is not viewed in a crude
kind of stimulus-response framework.   I have begun with a
portrait of American Evangelicalism because it was, after
all, Christianity rather than traditional African religion
which won out in the fusion of cultures and became the faith
of the Negro church.

The reader is asked to exercise a kind of double consciousness.   Sometimes our spotlight is on whites, sometimes on blacks, yet both groups are on the same stage.
They often interact, but there is reason to believe that their
scripts are not the same.   Or to change the metaphor, imag-
ine a man wearing glasses, each lens of which is of a different refraction.   His outlook on the world depends upon
which lens he concentrates through at a given moment.   The
prism of experience likewise shaped the Negro's perception
of Christianity.   He made of it something more than customary white Protestantism.   When the Gospel was first
preached to the African it had, of course, already been
wedded to Western Civilization for a long time and thus was
hardly in its pristine or primitive character.   According to
Christian doctrine, however, the Gospel has self-authenti-
cating power and breaks through culture embellishments to
address each man in life's course regardless of the banner
under which it is first proclaimed to him.   Black Christians
tended to have an existential understanding of Christianity
rather than a magesterial conception of God and a scholastic
view of the Scriptures.[11] Their faith was both personal and
social, their hope both individual and corporate, their charity
both private and public.

The Christian faith, then, is the tie that binds our story together. Like that portion which overlaps when two intersecting circles are drawn, it was shared by both white and black but was totally absorbed by neither. There was much in the black experience which the white Christian could never know. There was much of nineteenth-century white piety that black people rejected. But both white and black worlds touched common ground in claiming allegiance to the Christian Gospel.

Chapter I

ANATOMY OF AMERICAN EVANGELICALISM

> Religion has been the basis of the most im-
> portant American settlements; religion kept
> their little community together; religion as-
> sisted them in their revolutionary struggle;
> it was religion to which they appealed in de-
> fending their rights; and it was religion, in
> fine, which taught them to prize their liber-
> ties.
>
> --Francis Grund[1]

The nature of American religion after the Revolution
was neither that of the state-church pattern common to the
Old World nor was it that of a secularized nation in which
the religious and political concerns were completely distinct.
It was an experiment in cooperative separatism, a totally
unprecedented arrangement which satisfied neither the es-
tablishmentarian nor the outright secularist. In an essay
entitled "What is America?", G. K. Chesterton once wrote
that America was "a nation with the soul of a church."[2]
In the young Republic, the entire nation, rather than the
"gathered" church of the elect of Puritan days, was thought
of as the instrument of providential purpose.

Religion at Ebb Tide

Christianity in America is said to have been at "the
lowest low-water mark of the lowest ebb tide" in post-Revolutionary America.[3] The Presbyterian General Assembly,
meeting in 1798, bemoaned "the general dereliction of religious principles and practices among our fellow citizens" and
"the visible prevailing impiety and contempt for the laws and
institutions of religion."[4] Conservative clergymen were
alarmed at evidence of widespread religious apathy and neglect

of the Sabbath, which was reflected in a statistical depression in church membership. Perhaps as little as 7 to 10 per cent of the American populace was actually found on church rosters. While this may not indicate the overall strength of Christianity, because of the narrow definition of church membership then prevalent, there certainly seemed to be some basis for the pessimism found in the jeremiads of alarmed religious spokesmen. [5]

The Rev. Benjamin Trumbull, representative of establishment orthodoxy in Connecticut, came to the conclusion that war "hardens and emboldens men in sin; it is productive of profaneness, intemperance, disregard for property, violence, and all licentious living."[6] The War for Independence did indeed leave its mark upon American religious life. Church property was destroyed, congregations scattered, and young men discouraged from entering ministerial training. Tory ministers abandoned their charges in the face of adverse public sentiment. More than seventy thousand Anglicans joined the Tory exodus, and the missionary labors of the Society for the Propagation of the Gospel were severely restricted. Because of John Wesley's Loyalist sympathies, the English representatives of Methodism, with the exception of Francis Asbury, returned home. The Anglicans and Methodists who remained in the rebellious colonies were cut off from their mother country and confronted by serious questions of ecclesiastical self-identity. [7]

Once political independence had been achieved, the former colonies gradually moved toward implementing religious freedom, voluntary church membership, and an acceptance of denominationalism. Disestablishment was in keeping with the unique relationship established between church and state in the young Republic. Now Anglicans and Congregationalists, once having received favored treatment, had to compete with the energetic Baptists and Methodists in a free market. In New England, the old Puritan fortress, disestablishment was slow in coming, but even in the diehard states of Massachusetts, Connecticut, and New Hampshire, church-state forms eventually gave way to religious pluralism. Dissenters, heirs of the left-wing of the Protestant Reformation, and rationalist disciples of the Enlightenment had conducted a two-sided campaign against the privileged status of the established churches, but the relative alacrity with which most American churchmen accepted denominationalism is evidence of an undercurrent of pragmatism and a consensus that now the nation as a whole, rather than any particular church or sect, was the object of Divine pleasure.

The spread of religious rationalism added to the woes of orthodox Christianity during the Revolutionary era. Republican deism, as expounded by such as Ethan Allen, Joel Barlow, and Thomas Jefferson, raised the specter of religion without revelation and morality without threat of divine judgment. As a Francophile and political liberal, Jefferson was bitterly attacked by the Federalist clergy. Anti-clericalism, immorality, infidelity, atheism, and a host of other horrors were said to be the consequences of his flirtation with Enlightenment skepticism. Upon hearing the news of Jefferson's death, a New England cleric wrote in his diary, "It is hoped it is true."[8] Republican Deism flourished but briefly in the afterglow of the Enlightenment, but even when it was no longer a serious threat to religious orthodoxy, American clergymen continued to exploit the image of the infidel as a foil to their own tenets. Not until American Evangelicalism captured the soul of the nation did the infidel give way to the less alarming village atheist as object lesson in the rhetorical arsenal of the American pulpit.[9]

In 1783 the Treaty of Paris extended the young Republic's domain to the Mississippi River. Tentative footholds had already been established in the wilderness by hardy frontiersmen. Thousands of Easteners joined the exodus to the West in the late eighteenth century, abandoning both the amenities of civilization and the sanctuaries of Christianity. Irreligion and barbarism, it was said, prevailed among the backwoodsmen. In New England there had been respect for the Bible and the Sabbath, for ministers and churches. But along the frontier, as a missionary to the Western Reserve tract reported, many who formerly frequented God's house now "in that land of sinful liberty they fight against God without fearing man."[10] Not until the 1830s did the West receive the imprimatur of the Eastern clergy as a place where religion might flourish.[11]

The Evangelical Flowering

Despite the deleterious effects of war, the specter of an infidel takeover, and the threat of irreligion in the West, there were good omens as early as 1787 that a time of refreshing was at hand. A period of revival, sometimes called the Second Great Awakening, was beginning. The revivalistic fires flamed brightly from Connecticut to Virginia and the Carolinas in the 1790s. By 1800 a great conflagration could be witnessed in the Appalachian mountains of Kentucky and

Tennessee. The much-heralded session at Cane Ridge, Kentucky, in 1801 was the model for hundreds of revivals in the following decades. So many revivalistic preachers tramped across western New York State that it became known as the "burned-over district." Out of this area came Charles Grandison Finney, bringing the campaign to the urban areas of the East. By 1835, when Finney's Lectures on Revivals of Religion appeared, the anxious bench and the phenomenon of potential converts undergoing the "jerks" were no longer peculiar to the frontier.[12]

The revivalistic movements of the early nineteenth century contributed to a sense of national unity and helped link the East and the West. Americans felt as if they were sharing in some great endeavor under the controlling hand of God. On the frontier the churches were much more than mere places of worship. They offered an antidote for isolation, served as a means toward maintaining cultural stability, operated as institutions of participatory democracy, and served as moral courts.[13]

The Evangelical churches into which the converts from the revivals came had a high view of membership. Church discipline was no perfunctory matter. Backsliders were given no peace. The apparatus for disciplinary action varied among the different denominations, but the general purposes of the procedure and its unqualified necessity were never questioned. According to the Presbyterian Book of Discipline, church discipline served to remove offenses, vindicate the honor of Christ, promote the general edification of all, and last but not least, benefit the offender himself.[14] In the Methodist and Baptist communions, the two most important Evangelical bodies, the entire fellowship served as an effective espionage system to rid the church of moral impurity. One's peers were one's guardians of the conscience; both public and private behavior were under scrutiny from fellow members.[15]

Having swept and cleansed their own tabernacles, the Evangelicals went forth to make the Nation one vast house of God. Between 1815 and 1860, the forces of Evangelical Protestantism organized in unprecedented fashion in a massive campaign to bring Christ and culture into greater proximity. Once the task was accomplished, they optimistically predicted, nothing would be left to hinder the coming of the Kingdom of God.

The Evangelical campaign began in earnest when in
1816 the American Bible Society and the American Education
Society were organized. Thereafter a host of highly en-
gineered societies addressed themselves to such issues as
education, temperance, prison reform, better treatment for
the mentally ill, poor relief, the promotion of tract and
Bible distribution, domestic and foreign missions, and the
abolition of slavery. Largely lay-sponsored and financed by
voluntary contributions, these societies formed a kind of
benevolent empire. Increasing sectional tensions in the
1830s weakened the network, but it is a mistake to assume
that the Evangelical united front disintegrated. Concerned
Christian laymen continued to labor in behalf of humanitarian
reform until the very onset of the Civil War. As late as
1857 and 1858 the revivalistic and reformist crusade brought,
as Prof. Timothy L. Smith has shown, a "symphony of salvation" to America's largest cities.[16]

Because of the prevalence of revivalism in the growth
of American Evangelicalism, the Evangelicals have been
charged with fostering a spirit of anti-intellectualism. They
are said to have dispensed with traditional theological questions for a simplistic religion of the heart. Enamored of
the exploits of critics of a seminary-educated clergy, such
as Peter Cartwright, the famous Methodist circuit rider,
some historians have accused the Evangelicals of a disre-
spect of all pursuits of the mind.[17] While it is true that
some of the Evangelicals, chiefly those in frontier areas,
fostered the notion that piety and intellect were not readily
compatible, there was more to American Evangelicalism than
is suggested by the stereotype of barely literate backwoods
preachers.[18]

Contrary to the notion that the Evangelicals simply
derived their theology out of the frontier experience and the
campmeeting, there is evidence of the continued influence
of traditional patterns of thought even in the backwoods. The
frontier circuit-riders carried in their saddlebags the Armi-
nian belief of the depravity of man yet "grace for all." John
Wesley's message, while simple and direct, was not without
intellectual content. Baptists in Kentucky based their associations on principles derived from their brethren back in
the East. Presbyterians, Congregationalists, and other seminary-educated clergy were heavily influenced by the school of
common sense realism that flourished in the early nineteenth
century under the tutelage of such moral philosophers as
Francis Wayland and Noah Porter. These academic moralists

derived much of their intellectual orientation from the Scottish school of realism, which served as an antidote for both uncompromising Berkeleyan idealism and freewheeling Humean skepticism. Common sense realism provided the Evangelicals with a firm philosophical foundation upon which to undertake moral reform. The academic moralists wrote confidently of a clear distinction between Right and Wrong, between Good and Evil. The Evangelicals firmly rooted their whole theology on this basic premise.[19]

After 1830 American Evangelicalism came to share the principal tenets of popular romanticism and the democratic credo that is associated with the Jacksonian frame of mind. Like the Romantics, the Evangelicals stressed the value of the individual and the significance of the emotions in man. Nathaniel William Taylor and Horace Bushnell, to cite but two examples, did much to bring American Protestantism out of the gloomy closet of Calvinist theology into the heady atmosphere of freewill Arminianism. The doctrine of original sin, which in its classic formulation mired the individual in pessimistic other worldliness, was modified so as to allow for progressive reform. This change of emphasis provided the benevolence movement with a viable theological foundation. Despite their circumstances, men and women were able, it was felt, to make moral progress in this world. According to the teachings of John Wesley, the Christian who experienced rebirth should strive for "perfect love." Americans in the age of the Jacksonian common-man and Manifest Destiny wanted an optimistic and heart-pulsing kind of faith.[20] Even Lyman Beecher, a defender of traditional Calvinism, was carried away with the possibilities open to mankind. "Men are free agents," he wrote, "in the possession of such faculties, and placed in such circumstances as render it practicable for them to do whatever God requires...."[21]

In 1842 Robert Baird wrote: "I know of no one idea that has been so dominant in the American churches for the last hundred years as that of the importance of the office and work of the Holy Spirit."[22] This emphasis on the immanence of God as Spirit in history gave the Evangelicals an assurance that their endeavors would not be in vain. Good would eventually triumph over Evil. The Kingdom of God was at hand. The adventist teachings of William Miller, while not taken literally by most Evangelicals, were certainly not incongruous with the Evangelical heritage. Like Miller, most Evangelicals believed that history was rapidly

moving toward a grand consummation. The night was far
spent; the Day of Judgment was not far off. But men were
not to sit idly by awaiting that day. They were to be up
and about, assisting the Spirit in the work of the Gospel.[23]

The Evangelical Outreach

        The American churches responded to this sense of
providential imperative to such an extent that Kenneth Scott
Latourette, the most eminent historian of Protestant expansion, has termed the nineteenth century, the "great century."[24] Having assured themselves of divine assistance,
the American Evangelicals carried the banner of Christ to
the multitudes. Foreign missions began in 1812 when the
Rev. Adoniram Judson went to India.[25] In 1826 the American Home Missionary Society was formed to coordinate the
energies of the churches in a great crusade to save the West
from infidelity.[26] Home or domestic missions often suffered the twin handicaps of a lack of an impelling sense of
urgency and the common assumption that the work was not
as glamorous or romantic as that in some far-off exotic
land.

        Mission work among the slaves in the South was con-
sidered an especially unglamorous task. Even among the
best-intentioned churchgoers there was a tendency to think of
the plantation missionary as a practitioner of a "low calling"
and a "caste ministry."[27] Throughout the first half of the
nineteenth century a handful of dedicated clergymen sought to
rid mission work among the slaves of this prejudiced image.

        "I feel as you do," the Rev. Henry Ruffner* wrote to
the Rev. William S. Plumer, * "The moral absurdity of the
zeal that has been manifested for the conversion of Hindoos
and Armenians, while a nation in the midst of us, as miserable as the worst of them, was past [sic] unheeded by,
and suffered to perish in ignorance at our very doors.[28]
Men, like Ruffner and Plumer, seeking to prod the conscience of the American religious community in behalf of

---

*In order not to burden the text with biographical details,
sketches of some of the significant individuals, white and
black, in this study are contained in the Appendix (beginning
on page 291). An asterisk * after the first use of an individual's name indicates such a treatment.

the slaves, claimed that an undue amount of attention was
being given to the unsaved in other lands. The Methodist
leader James O. Andrew,* who figured prominently in the
famous General Conference of 1844, frankly expressed his
annoyance at hearing "incessantly of mighty efforts for civi-
lizing and evangelizing the Hindoos, Burmese, Hottentots and
savages in different parts of the world." Plantation missions
here at home, he argued, "would do ten times the amount of
good."[29]

　　　As late as 1847, the Rev. Charles C. Jones* of
Liberty County, Georgia, sounded the ominous warning that
unless the American churches gave as much of their energies to Negro missions as they did to the heathen overseas,
"multitudes of these poor people are destined to go down,
annually, from the very bosom of a land denominated en-
lightened, and Christian, and benevolent, into everlasting
ruin!"[30] It is significant that it was Jones who made such
a dire prophecy. More than any other single individual in
the antebellum South, this Presbyterian minister attempted
to gain an over-all view of the progress of the spiritual
harvest among American blacks. For him, and for many
other church leaders, Negro missions were in reality a form
of foreign missions, which demanded a program and a meth-
odology distinct from that used for whites. "We believe, "
he wrote of the slaves, "that their moral and religious condition is such as, that they may justly be considered the
Heathen of this Christian country, and will bear comparison
with Heathen in any country of the world."[31]

　　　The black man in America was something like the un-
wanted child. He was part of the total society by the very
fact that the whites had brought him to America from the beginning, and yet, because he was black, he had little claim
to communal life, communal wealth, or communal freedoms.
Still, as the churches soon realized, someone had to be
responsible for him, both physically and spiritually. During
the Colonial era, a few individuals had spoken out for the
missionizing of the slaves. The Puritan divine John Winthrop reported that the first slave to be baptized in New
England was a Negro woman who was "well approved by
divers years experience for sound knowledge and true godliness."[32] This took place in 1641, only three years after
slaves were introduced into Massachusetts. So it is that,
almost from the beginning of American settlement, white
Christians viewed blacks in their midst as potential converts.

The story of Puritan, Anglican, and Quaker efforts
to proselytize slaves in the American colonies has been told
by others. [33] Once the dilemma of baptism and bondage had
been resolved by statutes which declared that conversion did
not free the slave, the colonial churches found that masters
were more receptive to having the Gospel preached to their
slaves. [34] The religious revivals of the 1740s, known as the
First Great Awakening, brought blacks into the churches in
growing numbers. Methodist and Baptist preachers, with
their egalitarian Gospel, reaped a bountiful harvest among
the slaves.

In spite of progressive efforts of individuals like
Cotton Mather and Thomas Bray, the state of religion among
the slaves at the end of the Colonial era was not encouraging.
Strong planter opposition remained in those areas where the
majority of the slaves lived. Even in New England and in
the Middle Colonies, the contemporary opinion was that the
Negro was but little advanced spiritually from the heathen of
Africa. Specialized studies on slavery and conversion in
colonial America have concluded that the practical results
fell far short of good intentions. [35] Only a small fraction of
the blacks, both slave and free, were in formal connection
with American Protestantism, although an unknown number
may have been exposed to the Gospel in a cursory way. It
has been estimated that there were about a half million
slaves in 1775. The Negro constituency of the churches
was certainly less than five per cent of this figure, while
actual membership was no doubt even smaller. [36]

The Evangelicals Seize the South

During the period of general irreligion which followed
the American Revolution, the American churches, as we have
seen, were in a state of internal disorganization and external
turmoil. Little effective mission work was done for Negroes.
But by the early 1790s, the first signs of a spiritual awakening not only in the general American population but also in
the cause of Negro missions can be detected. According to
the first federal census, in 1790 there were 757,208 Negroes
--19.3 per cent of the total population. Nearly nine-tenths
of this number were slaves in the South Atlantic states. [37]

It is clear that during these first four decades of the
nineteenth century a remarkable transformation took place in
the religious configuration of the slave states. Southern white

Protestantism of the Evangelical variety rapidly supplanted
the liberal Anglicanism and rarefied Deism which had per-
vaded the South prior to the Great Revival of 1800. The
Episcopal church in the South too became low church and accepted the Wesleyan theology which emphasized the primacy
of religious experience, the conviction of sin, the need for
repentance and the importance of close fellowship and discipline.[38] However, in spite of the conversion of the Anglicans to America's peculiar style of Christianity, they constantly found themselves at a disadvantage when seeking to
attract the so-called Jacksonian common man.

Subsequent to the demise of the Anglican establishment, the Presbyterians had a grand opportunity to capture
the South. The Methodist Episcopal Church was still in its
infancy, having been formed in 1784 at the famous Christmas
Conference in Baltimore. The Baptists were found mainly
among those without much economic or social status and, as
a denomination, they lacked a formidable organizational machinery. Even so, these two church bodies were aggressive
and soon gave the Presbyterians stiff competition. The Rev.
Benjamin H. Rice, a Presbyterian missionary in North Carolina, reported in 1811: "At this place there are a few red
hot Methodists and a great many red hot sinners.... The
fact is that the Methodists, Baptists, and the Devil have
taken this whole country so that there is no room for a
Presbyterian."[39] Part of Rice's problem was that he represented a church body which was hampered in its expansion
into frontier areas by a strict doctrine of election, an emphasis upon a seminary educated and resident clergy, and a
weighty dogmatic theology.

In 1784 there were 13,381 Methodists, black and
white, below the Mason and Dixon line. By 1811, there
were 20,863 white and 11,063 black Methodists in the South
Carolina Conference alone. If we compare figures from
1790 with those of 1830, it is clear that the Methodists and
Baptists were the leading battalions in the Evangelical army
as it captured the South. Methodists expanded nearly ten-
fold, from 57,631 in 1790 to 511,153 in 1830. Baptist
growth was almost as spectacular. In 1790 the various
Baptist groups numbered about 65,000. By 1830, due, for
the most part, to a great expansion among the Regulars, the
total approximated 320,000, or five times that of 1790.[40]
The total American population had merely trebled in the
same four decades. The other major Protestant denominations -- the Presbyterians, Episcopalians, and Lutherans --

also showed strength by 1830, but they could not match the
statistical achievements of the Methodists and Baptists in the
Nation as a whole or in the slave states.[41]

What was it, then, about the Evangelicals that so
attracted the Southern citizenry? In his Autobiography, the
Rev. William Capers,* the founder of Methodist plantation
missions, contended that it was not the Methodists' social
condition so much as their message which was the source of
their appeal. He described it as follows:

> Nothing but the Bible, and just as the Bible holds
> it, was its testimony of truth. It was all spiritual,
> experimental, practical, not speculative, abstracted,
> or metaphysical. When it exhorted, it was to en-
> force its preaching, as it ever saw sinners sporting
> on the brink of a precipice, and believers in dan-
> ger of being seduced from their safety. And
> preaching or exhorting, its inexhaustible argument
> was eternity--eternity at hand--an eternity of heav-
> en or hell for every soul of men.[42]

It was this "red hot" faith of the common man which characterized the periodic revivals that helped to bring about the
religious transformation of the South. And, more importantly, it was this content and style of faith which the Evangelicals first brought to the cause of Negro missions.

At their annual conferences held at Salisbury, North
Carolina, Petersburg, Virginia, and Abingdon, Maryland,
during 1787, the Methodists were queried: "What directions
shall we give for the promotion of the spiritual welfare of
the colored people?" The answer given was:

> We conjure all our ministers and preachers, by the
> love of God, and the salvation of souls, and do
> require them, by all the authority that is invested
> in us, to leave nothing undone for the spiritual
> benefit and salvation of them, within their respec-
> tive circuits or districts; and for this purpose to
> embrace every opportunity of inquiring into the
> state of their souls, and to unite in society those
> who appear to have a real desire of fleeing from
> the wrath to come; to meet such in class, and to
> exercise the whole Methodist discipline among
> them.[43]

The response to such official directives was no doubt heartening to the early Methodists. Between 1787 and 1803, principally as a result of the first phase of the Second Great Awakening, the black membership of the Methodists increased from 1890 to 22, 453. [44]

The Baptists likewise reached the Negroes of the slave states as a natural consequence of their growth in the South. Unlike the Methodists, they did not proceed so much from conference directive to local action as from a rather haphazard arrangement of simply preaching to blacks wherever they happened to be. When there were no white preachers available, the black Baptists simply carried on on their own. At Allen's Creek, Virginia, for example, "Being left destitute of ministerial instruction, and having a considerable number of black people in their society, of whom there were some preachers of talents, they commenced the administration of the ordinances without ordination. "[45]

No separate figures on Negro members were kept by the Baptist denomination as a whole. Not until the early 1830s did the Dover Association of Virginia report that its member churches contained 9112 blacks and 5755 whites. [46] But the Baptists did not really need statistics to give evidence of their concern for the Negro. The Rev. William S. Plumer, a Presbyterian, testified to what was common knowledge: "From the beginnings of that branch [the Baptists] of Christ's church in the South, the salvation of the Negroes has not been forgotten or slighted in their ministrations. "[47]

Chapter II

SOUTHERN EVANGELICALS AND THE BLACK HARVEST

> It is not necessary that you should banish
> yourself to a distant and unhealthy region,
> as intimated in a recent letter to Eliza-
> beth--those stations, our Richardson justly
> remarked, should belong to such as have
> no mothers--You have no doubt read the
> Bishop's Pastoral Letter on the Religious
> Instruction of Servants--Now here is a
> broad field for missionary enterprize in
> our very midst--and the more to be
> coveted because it is so lowly.
> --Mrs. M. J. Davis, writing to her
> son, Richard, a theological student in
> Virginia, January 26, 1854.[1]

The first quarter of the nineteenth century was, as
Carter G. Woodson discovered, a time of "better beginnings"
in the general education of the Negro.[2] It was also a period
in which the churches began to express more interest in the
spiritual welfare of the Negro.   But as far as the slaves in
the South were concerned, it is extremely difficult to ascertain the exact extent of the mission work done among them.
No agency or religious organization was devoted exclusively
to Negro evangelization.   The period was marked by the efforts of individual Southern clerics who preached to the
blacks as an adjunct to their regular charges.

The success of these individual efforts depended on
how much time and energy the minister was willing to devote
to the Negroes near his church.   The work was not easy.
Usually the whites were reluctant to share their preacher's
talents with the Negro population, but with persistence and
patience black candidates were persuaded to attend worship
and catechetical classes.   In Charlotte County, Virginia, for

example, the Rev. David H. Rice devoted one-fourth of his
time to the slaves, instructing them in the fundamental doctrines of the Gospel. He also hoped to counteract the bane-
ful influence of unregulated preaching by self-appointed Negroes. Here and there throughout the South, concerned
ministers of the Gospel carried on mission work among the
Negroes where public opinion and the white membership allowed, but the conscience of the South was as yet unchal-
lenged. [3]

In some urban areas of the South, the clergy were
showing concern for the religious instruction of the Negro.
As the Rev. Charles C. Jones reported, they made "it a
part of their pastoral care to devote frequent and stated
seasons for the religious instruction of catechumen from
amongst the black population."[4] Such was the success of
this work that in 1819 the Board of Managers of the Bible
Society of Charleston was able to report that "upwards of
one fourth of the communicants are slaves or free persons
of color." It was also estimated that of the some forty
thousand communicants in all of South Carolina, Negro
Christians accounted for one-eighth of the total. [5]

The first special effort to reach the great numbers
of slaves in the rural areas is said to have been in 1809,
when the South Carolina Conference of the Methodist Episcopal Church sent James H. Mallard to convert the blacks
from the Ashley to the Savannah River and James E. Glenn
into the territory from the Santee River to the Cooper. But
Mallard and Glenn soon resigned their commissions, perhaps
because of strong planter opposition. [6] "We are defrauded of
great numbers by the pains that are taken to keep the blacks
from us," wrote Bishop Francis Asbury in 1809; "their masters are afraid of the influence of our principles." Who
would take the pains to lead the slaves into the way of salvation and watch over them, Asbury wondered, if it were not
for the Methodists. Having traveled extensively throughout
the slave states, this "Prophet of the Long Road," as Asbury
came to be known, realized that little could be accomplished,
even by the stout-hearted Methodist preachers, in the face of
public indifference and planter animosity. [7]

Compromise with Slavery

In the late eighteenth century the Methodists were
handicapped in their efforts to reach the slaves because of

their antislavery reputation. A highly disciplined denomination, the Methodist church presented a military-like posture and conducted their missionary work as if it were a battle campaign. The Baptists, on the other hand, did not seem so pretentious or threatening, as they had no regular conferences at which constant declarations against slavery could be made. [8]

Although the planters continued to view the Methodists with suspicion well into the nineteenth century, the church began to soften her hardline stance against the "peculiar institution" in the early 1800s. In 1804 the General Conference acceded to the removal of the restrictions against the buying and selling of slaves from the rules of societies in the Carolinas, Georgia, and Tennessee. In 1808 all that related to slaveholding by non-office holding members was struck out. The Southern conferences were allowed to write up their own rules. Then in 1816 the general statement on slavery in the Discipline was amended so as to read that a slaveholder was to be ineligible only if "the laws of the state in which he lives will admit of emancipation and permit the liberated slave to enjoy freedom."[9] Few of the slave states, of course, had such laws.

This compromise with slavery by the spiritual sons of Wesley, Coke, and Asbury was rationalized on the grounds that it would enable the Methodists to gain greater access to the plantations. However, the Methodist preachers still found that they were not always welcome. The Rev. William Capers, for instance, was puzzled by the fact that he, a "white man, a citizen, born and bred on the soil, and even owning slaves, for being a Methodist preacher was excluded, as if by some sentence of outlawry."[10] (Yet at this time, about 1820, Negro preachers were still permitted to conduct meetings.) In the thickly populated slave regions, such as on the rice and sea island cotton plantations, thousands of blacks were excluded from the Gospel because, as a Methodist journal stated, there was "an inveterate prejudice against having religious instruction imparted to the blacks by Methodist preachers."[11]

The trial of Denmark Vesey and his fellow conspirators in 1822 revealed a kinship between Methodism and slave revolt that further heightened planter animosity. The official court report frequently referred to the membership of some of the conspirators in the African Methodist Episcopal Church, which had a local branch in Charleston. Much of the plotting was said to have been done at the class meetings of the African Methodists. [12]   Vesey had instructed his followers to kill all Charleston's whites.   But in the mutiny led by Gabriel Prosser (Henrico County, Virginia, 1800), the insurgents were expressly instructed not to harm the white Methodists, presumably because of their egalitarian and emancipationist reputation. [13]

In the wake of the Vesey episode, the Southern clergy were forced by public opinion to swear allegience to the racial status quo.   They were charged with having gone to the slaves with the Bible in one hand while, as Edwin C. Holland, a Charleston editor, wrote, "with the other [having sown] the firebrands of discord and destruction; and secretly dispensed among our Negro Population, the seeds of discontent and sedition. "[14]   Immediately the spokesmen for the Baptists and Episcopalians in the Charleston area disclaimed any intention of interfering with slavery.   Dr. Richard Furman, a leading Baptist, published a position paper which has been called "probably the most significant pro-slavery statement of the twenties. "[15]   Were the slaves to receive instruction from "right sources, " Furman declared, they would not be "in danger of having their minds corrupted by sentiments unfriendly to the domestic and civil peace of the community. "[16] The Episcopalians took refuge in the claim that in their order of worship and method of teaching there was nothing "to inflame the passions of the ignorant enthusiast; nothing left to the crude undigested ideas of illiterate black classleaders. "[17]

As the Southern clergy moved gradually into the pro-slavery camp, they became more and more enamored of the "positive good" defense of slavery.   Christianity, they claimed, was not incompatible with the institution of human bondage.   "No class of Negroes well instructed in Christianity, and connected with churches under the care of white pastors, " they pointed out, "have ever been engaged in any insurrectionary disturbances. "[18]   Henceforth only preachers who were deemed "safe" in the planters' eyes would be given credentials by the Southern churches.   For this reason, representatives of the great national mission boards, such as the American Home Missionary Society and the American Baptist Home Mission Society, were seldom if ever numbered among the missionaries to the plantations. [19]

The first quarter of the nineteenth century was more significant for setting the stage for plantation missions than

Left: the Rev. William Capers (1790-1855), "Founder of Methodist Plantation Missions"; right: the Rev. Charles C. Jones (1804-1863), "the Apostle to the Negro Slaves."

for concrete results. The War of 1812, like the American
Revolution, dampened religious fervor and slowed the growth
of the Evangelicals. Bishop Francis Asbury estimated that
the Methodists lost one thousand members "by wastage, expulsion, and death" each year the war continued.[20] The
presence of the African Methodists in Charleston and the
formation of the African Methodist Episcopal Church in 1816
drew many Negro Christians away from the white-controlled
churches.[21] But the principal cause for slow progress in
Negro missions was the lack of any special ministry designed
for the peculiar circumstances of the masses of the slaves
who were on the plantations.

The Churches Go to the Plantations

        The year 1829 marks a new era in the history of the
Southern Evangelicals and the black harvest. In that year
two planters in South Carolina requested that a Methodist
preacher be appointed to a full time mission station among
their slaves. Five years earlier the South Carolina Conference had called for a separate agency exclusively for the
evangelization of the slaves. Nothing was done until 1829
when the Rev. William Capers received an appeal from,
strangely enough, two Episcopalian masters in the Charleston District who wished to have preaching among their slaves
on a regular basis.[22]

        At about this same time, Charles Cotesworth Pinckney
put his prestige and influence behind the cause. In an address to the South Carolina Agricultural Society, he declared
on August 18, 1829:

>   Every denomination of Christian teachers are
>   willing and ready to send white Southern Mission-
>   aries to the plantations (whose owners permit it),
>   to instruct the people orally in the duties and
>   principles of Christianity.[23]

Pinckney set an example by requesting Capers to send a
missionary to his plantation on the Santee River. Pinckney
was convinced that the Gospel, if properly taught, would not
be a threat to the discipline or efficiency of his plantation.
Yet he felt compelled to warn the Agricultural Society that
it would have to proceed with caution. Many Southern
planters still believed that the Gospel was simply used by
the slaves to hide "the nefarious designs of insurrection."[24]

The South Carolina Conference soon appointed Capers
as superintendent of a special department for plantation missions. Only men deemed "competent and safe in the judgment of Mr. Capers" were allowed to preach to the slaves.
The first two individuals sent into the field were the Rev.
John Honour and the Rev. J. H. Massey. After nine months
of service, Honour died of a fever contracted in the low-
country region of rice fields and swamps. The Rev. George
W. Moore, who had earlier preached to the slaves without
the benefit of a regular appointment, took up the station
which Honour's death left vacant. At the end of the first
full year of activity, 417 Negro conversions were recorded
as having taken place under the plantation preaching. [25]

Methodist plantation missions soon spread into the
Georgia Conference and eventually into other states. In
1840 Capers became Secretary of the Southern Department
of Missionary Work. From this vantage point he stimulated
enthusiasm for Negro missions throughout the South. In
1844 the Missionary Society reported that there were 68
stations, 22,063 black adults, and 80 missionaries under its
auspices. Yet most of the activity was still centered in the
South Carolina Conference. This is reflected in the fact that
in 1845 this region alone accounted for 17 stations, 22 missionaries, and 8314 adult black members. In addition, some
4000 black children were being taught the fundamentals of the
Christian faith. [26]

Four years after the Methodists began plantation missions, a 28-year-old Presbyterian clergyman resigned his
charge in Savannah and returned to the malarial regions of
Liberty County, Georgia, to minister to the slaves on his
father's plantation. This young cleric, a recent graduate of
Princeton Seminary, was the Rev. Charles Colcock Jones.
On December 2, 1832, he became the first functioning missionary of the Association for the Religious Instruction of
Negroes, which had been organized by local planters. [27] He
has justly been called "the Apostle to the Negro Slaves. "[28]
Of a distinguished Georgia family, the eventual owner of
three plantations totaling about 3600 acres, and (by 1860)
129 slaves, Jones was a man of noble Christian character
who possessed a conscience sensitive to the religious plight
of Negroes throughout the South. His catechism, annual reports, sermons, essays, and especially The Religious Instruction of the Negroes in the United States, published in
1842, manifest an unrivaled knowledge of and concern for
missions among the slaves. No thorough biography of Jones

Old Midway Church, built A.D.1778, Liberty County, Georgia.

exists, but a marvelous collection of family correspondence
gathered by Robert Manson Myers, under the title The Children of Pride, has been preserved. [29]

Jones began labors among the slaves in the vicinity
of historic Old Midway Church of Liberty County.   Blacks
outnumbered whites nearly four to one.   In the Fifteenth
Company District, which included Arcadia, the largest of
Jones' plantations, 4540 slaves sweated from sunup to sundown in the production of rice and cotton. [30] At the conclusion of the first year's labors, Jones reported that six
mission stations had been established.   During the Summer
and Fall months he was forced to suspend the plantation
meetings "from motives of prudence in regard to health."
Attendance had been good.   He observed that there was "no
defect of interest" on the slaves' part toward the Gospel
message.   The planters seemed willing to give him a hearing.   Nearly fifty of them indicated that he would be allowed
to conduct services among their slaves.   The first year was
designed as one of "experiment and discovery," but Jones
was optimistic that mission work would become a permanent
feature of plantation life. [31]

Perhaps the optimism evidenced in Jones' first annual

report was merely reflective of the high spirits with which
any new enterprise is begun. In his next report he was
more cautious, warning that no one should "anticipate any
thing like a general and radical reformation of this people
[the slaves] in a short space of time." The year 1834 had
been one of "great spiritual declension" in the white churches.
This, Jones felt, had extended to the Negro members, with
the result that conversions among the slaves were less frequent. Nearly the same situation prevailed in 1835.[32]

The following year, Jones moved his family to Columbia, South Carolina, home of the Presbyterian Theological
Seminary. In addition to teaching ecclesiastical history and
church polity, he conducted a flourishing Sunday school for
blacks and encouraged young seminarians to become zealous
in the cause of Negro missions.[33] In early 1839 the family
returned to Liberty County, where for the next nine years
Jones worked tirelessly at the task he loved the most. En-
ticed back to Columbia in 1848, he made his last official
report in behalf of the Association for the Religious Instruction of Negroes. In addition to Georgia, the Presbyterians
now had a missionary or two in eight of the slave states.
According to the records of the General Assembly of 1848,
Negro membership (2793 communicants) was about one-
sixtieth of the white membership. This figure was, admit-
tedly, significantly less than the 124, 961 Negro Methodists
and Baptists which Jones reported for the same year. He
felt, however, that "the aggregate would be greatly increased,
perhaps doubled or trebled by full reports."[34]

By 1850 the sectional crisis was at hand. In recognition of his "experience in missionary life" and "sound
judgment and conciliatory manner," Jones was elected cor-
responding secretary of the Presbyterian Board of Domestic
Missions. For the next three years he resided in Philadelphia, where he, a Southerner and a slaveholder, effectively and efficiently promoted the mission work of the
national body. The enfeebling effects of "inaction" or "pa-
ralysis affection" caused him to return to his beloved Liberty
County in 1853. In the following decade, worn in body but
undaunted in spirit, he supervised his extensive holdings,
kept pen to paper, and preached as often as he could. The
"Apostle to the Blacks" died on March 16, 1863, a victim of
the mysterious "wasting palsy."[35] His death was hastened,
a contemporary said, by "a period of unusual mortality
among his servants, and solicitude on their account, and his
anxiety about the war."[36]

Burial site of Dr. Jones with its "faithful guardians."

Early in his career, Jones had said about the slaves that if "only one soul is saved from amongst them, the Gospel meets with great success." The truth, and the tragedy, of this man's life was that much else was involved, factors which were beyond his control. In June of 1834, Jones wrote to his friend the Rev. William S. Plumer:

> The Religious Instruction of our Servants is a duty. Any man with a conscience may be made to feel it. It can be discharged. It must be discharged, whatever becomes of us or them in a civil point of view. It must be discharged as speedily as possible. Our salvation from sore evils, from divine judgment depends upon it. The Religious Instruction of the Negroes is the Foundation of all permanent improvement in intelligence and morals in the slave-holding states. (The only entering wedge to the great and appalling subject of slavery.) The only sun, that appearing through the dark clouds, will show down pure holy light, and if the institution of slavery is to be abandoned, will cause the nation to relax its hold, and gradually and peacefully lay it off, and then sit down in delightful repose. [37]

It was not just the souls of the blacks which were at stake.
Jones, and men like him, were contending for the salvation
of the entire South.

    In view of the emotional, social, political, and eco-
nomic complexities of the sectional conflict, Jones' belief in
religious education as the "entering wedge" in the dilemma of
slavery seems ingenuous. Yet, as a man of God burdened
with the public pastoral office, he was most of all sensitive
to the criticisms of fellow Christians in the North who condemned slavery because it allegedly denied the slave free
access to the Gospel. Jones deplored the incendiary rhetoric
of the abolitionists, but he could not ignore the misgivings of
conservative and moderate religious leaders in the nation.
Thus he urged his Southern brethren to "look at home" and
discharge their "Duty" to the slaves. Thereby Christians in
the South would merit not only the approbation of God and
their own consciences, but they would also win the commen-
dations of the North. 38 Charles C. Pinckney had put forward the same argument at the beginning of the Methodist
plantation missions. He, like Jones, believed that a properly
instructed Negro population"... would give us the advantage
in argument over our Northern Brethren, whose members and
principles are respectable; and whose objection to our system
is partly grounded on the deficiency of religious instruction. "39

    The radical abolitionists abhorred such sentiments and
did not buy the pious aim of substituting religious instruction
for personal freedom. But conservative Northern churchmen
came to support the work of men like Jones and Capers.
They saw it as the only alternative for Christians who lived
in a society where civil law and public opinion allowed for
nothing else. 40

    The Nat Turner insurrection of 1831 had made the
subject of Negro missions one of great tenderness. It was
widely reported that Turner, like Denmark Vesey, claimed
religious sanction for his actions. This association of slave
rebellion and slave religion brought about a wave of pros-
criptive laws throughout the South. Most of the laws had to
do with the banning of religious services conducted by black
preachers. The entire spiritual welfare of the slaves was
legally confined to the white clergy, who now found that oral
instruction was the only means deemed "safe" by the political
leaders of the South. 41 For the most part, the plantation
missionaries readily adapted to the new restrictions. Jones
promised that only verbal instruction would be used. He

pledged that his missionaries would not "intermeddle with the
concerns of the plantation in any manner, nor repeat abroad
what their ears hear, or their eyes see on them." "Our
plan," he told anxious planters in Georgia but one year after
Turner's rebellion, "carries our security in it."[42]

The early 1830s, despite the fears raised by the
Southampton insurrection, witnessed a revival of interest in
Negro missions.[43] Then came the "gag resolution" of 1836,
proposed by Henry L. Pinckney of South Carolina to stifle
the antislavery petition campaign. The abolitionists organized
to repeal the rule, retard the spread of slavery, and abolish
it in the District of Columbia.

Angered and upset by abolitionist rhetoric, the Southern public temporarily lost interest in plantation missions.
Jones declared that the effect of the excitement was to divert
attention from the religious conditions to political questions.
"The very foundations of society were assailed," he recalled,
"and men went forth to the defense." Every effort to improve the lives of the slaves was regarded with suspicion.
Jones was himself able to continue preaching each Sabbath to
congregations of blacks varying from 150 to 500 persons.
But others were forced to quit the field and "it was considered best to disband schools and discontinue meetings at
least for a season."[44]

Institutional Disunion and the Mission Cause

The slavery controversy could not be kept out of the
church assemblies. Beginning with the Presbyterians in the
middle 1830s, the great Evangelical communions were split
along sectional and idealogical lines. Critics of the American pattern of voluntaryism and denominationalism, such as
Stanley M. Elkins, have pointed to the breakup of the national denominations as evidence of the failure of American
institutions in the hour of greatest need.[45] The division of
the Evangelicals into Northern and Southern wings did not,
however, adversely affect plantation missions.

When the Old School faction of the Presbyterians
captured the Assembly of 1837, it was apparent that any
schism which might result would be both doctrinal-discipli-
nary and sectional in character. The controversial issues
were Hopkinsian theology, the Plan of Union, the powers of
church courts, and the orthodoxy of the benevolent agencies.

Ever present, however, was another controversy, one which
was not strictly between Old School and New School.[46] The
Southern delegates realized that a separation from the New
School wing, which was largely concentrated outside the
slave states, on theological grounds might also rid the church
of the abolitionists.[47] With the exception of those in Tennessee, the majority of the Southern presbyteries eventually
aligned with the Old School. As a consequence it was able
to take a more sympathetic attitude toward slavery and in-
tensify its efforts in behalf of Negro missions without
arousing Southern animosity.[48]

    Among the Methodists, too, a schism resulted in re-
doubled efforts on the part of the Southern contingent to increase mission statistics among blacks. But unlike that of
the Presbyterians, the Methodist division was a clear out-
come of the sectional controversy about what position an
ecclesiastical body should take on the slavery question. The
central debate at the General Conference of 1844 centered
on the right of James O. Andrew of Georgia to retain his
episcopal title. Andrew described himself as "a slaveholder
for conscience's sake" because he refused to "resort to
trickery" in order to get rid of slaves which he had, through
the death of his first wife and a subsequent marriage, in-
herited.[49] It was indeed a delicate situation. In order to
defuse the powder keg, Andrew attempted to resign from the
pro-Southern caucus. The Southerners, not wanting to give
the abolitionists so easy a victory, refused his offer.

    Andrew's critics pressed for an indictment that would
not only expel him from the Methodist episcopacy but also
atone for past compromises with slavery. In 1844 the
General Conference had upheld the suspension of Francis A.
Harding from the Baltimore Conference for refusing to manu-
mit his slaves, which, like those of Andrew, had come into
his possession by marriage. A year later the antislavery
faction achieved its greatest victory. By a vote of 110 to
69 the general body declared that Andrew must "desist from
the exercise of his office so long as this impediment re-
mains."[50]

    Bishop Andrew, taking the Southern position that the
General Conference had only derivative rather than inherent
powers, argued that to disbar him would be a violation of
the laws of the Discipline, an invasion of the rights secured
to me by that book."[51] The Southern delegates also contended that if Andrew were censured the Methodists would no

longer be allowed to preach to the slaves. Andrew was an
ardent supporter of plantation missions and often preached
to Negroes. Early in his ministerial career he had thought
seriously about taking a post in Africa. During the Great
Debate of 1844, Andrew addressed the assembly as follows:

> To whom am I unacceptable? Not to the people
> of the South--neither masters nor slaves. Has
> my connection with slaves rendered me less ac-
> ceptable to the colored people of the South--the
> very people for whom all this professed sympathy
> is felt? Let those who have labored long among
> them answer the question. Sir, I venture to say
> that in Carolina or Georgia I could today get more
> votes for the office of Bishop from the colored
> people, than any supporter of this resolution, let
> him avow himself an emancipator as openly as he
> pleases. [52]

The Northern delegates contended that a slaveholding bishop
could not be a bishop of all the people, as he could not fulfill his duties in the free states. The Southern Methodists
took the position that a bishop was responsible to a local
rather than national constituency.

After the suspension of Andrew, William Capers
brought forward a plan to form two equal general conferences. As Missionary Secretary for the slave states, he
voiced the fear that hard times would befall plantation missions if the Southern delegates did not come home with their
honor intact. With passionate voice, he proclaimed:

> Never, never, have I suffered, as in view of the
> evil which this measure threatens against the
> South. The agitation has begun there; and I tell
> you that though our hearts were to be torn from
> our bodies, it could avail nothing when once you
> have awakened the feeling that we cannot be trusted
> among the slaves. Once you have done this, you
> have effectually destroyed us. I could wish to die
> sooner than live to see such a day. As sure as
> you live, there are tens of thousands, nay, hun-
> dreds of thousands, whose destiny may be periled
> by your decision on this case.... O close not
> this door! Shut us not out from this great work,
> to which we have been so signally called of God. [53]

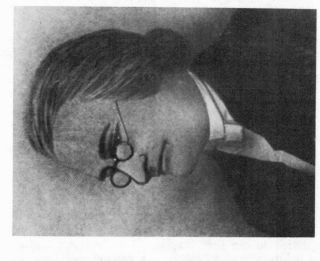

Left: Bishop James Osgood Andrew (1794-1871), "a slaveholder for conscience's sake"; right: Bishop William Meade (1789-1862), Episcopalian advocate of plantation missions.

After many years of experience, some of it bitter, Capers
knew full well that public opinion in the South was not a matter to be trifled with. In an effort to show his deep loyalty
to his heritage he had even declared at one time that slavery
"TENDS TO THE SALVATION OF THE NEGROES."[54] Now
he feared all would be lost and so he laid the souls of hundreds of thousands of slaves upon the conscience of the
General Conference of 1844. Upon reading Capers' oration,
a Georgia minister stated, "I could be willing to risk the
whole cause upon that speech alone...."[55] In May, 1845,
the Southern Methodists met in Louisville, Kentucky, and
formed the Methodist Episcopal Church, South.

Despite their loose organization, the Baptists were
not immune to the sectional tensions which had so troubled
the Presbyterians and the Methodists. The issue which
brought the Southern Baptists to Augusta, Georgia, in May
of 1845 was similar to that which had triggered the Methodist schism. The Board of Foreign Missions had forced
the resignation of John Busheyhead, an evangelist among the
Cherokee Indians, because he was a slaveholder. It subsequently announced that it would not again appoint a slaveholder as a missionary nor "be a party to any arrangement
which would imply approbation of slavery."[56] Like their
counterparts in the Methodist and Presbyterian denominations,
the Baptists in the South were particularly sensitive to any
interference in the affairs of the slave states. The formation of the Southern Baptist Convention in 1845 was yet another manifestation of the victory of sectionalism over the
Evangelical conscience.

At the time of division, over 22,000 slaves were being
cared for by the Methodists on the plantations and thousands
more were being preached to. Altogether, some 121,000
black Methodists were reported for the South in 1844. This
represented a large majority of the 145,000 Negro Methodists
throughout the nation. The Baptists claimed some 200,000
Negro members in the South. The Presbyterians, Episcopalians, and Lutherans had small Negro memberships. Perhaps as many as 370,000 Southern Negroes were on the rolls
of the Protestant churches in 1844. But the presence of
over two and a half million blacks in the slave states at the
same time indicates that hundreds of thousands still remained
to be missionized.[57] The Southern Evangelicals were confi-
dent that they would be. As William Capers asserted in his
address before the Methodist General Assembly, "... we
only announce the beginnings of our work."[58]

The "Crowning Glory" of the South

Institutional fragmentation on the national level should
not be confused with institutional impotence at the local level.
After separation from their respective national bodies, the
Southern churches contradicted even Capers' most pessimistic
prophecies and made religious instruction of the slaves their
supreme glory and greatest institutional success. They found
that the Southern public was ready to aid them.

Even as the walls of the united ecclesiastical assemblages were crumbling and falling, Southern churchmen proclaimed that mission work among the slaves was "THE
GREAT DUTY, and in the truest and best sense, THE FIXED,
THE SETTLED POLICY OF THE SOUTH."[59] This mandate
was issued in 1845 by representatives of the Southern
churches at a meeting in Charleston, South Carolina. Charles
C. Jones, as might be expected, helped to organize the convention and busied himself in gathering testimony from throughout the South as to the moral and spiritual welfare of the
slaves. The published Proceedings was the South's manifesto
to the North that it intended to win, at least, a moral victory.

The chief significance of the Charleston meeting was
that it brought the various Southern denominations together
behind one great cause. Before the sectional division of the
churches there had been several attempts to consolidate the
work in behalf of Negro missions. In 1834, for example,
Kentucky Presbyterians proposed such a joint endeavor.
Nothing came of this nor of similar plans. In the same
year Charles C. Jones wrote to the Rev. William S. Plumer
deploring the inefficiency of multiple associations. But he
did not think that a unified effort was yet advisable, citing
"the opposition which may be awakened, the supposition being
that it will lead to Emancipation, and nobody knows what besides...."[60] Public opinion had become less antagonistic by
1845.

The intentions of the organizers of the Charleston
meeting were to measure the extent of the missionary work
currently being done, compare notes on difficulties and
methods, and, most of all, to promote the cause of missions
as a boon to the slaves and a blessing to the entire South.
Much of the testimony emphasized how converting the slaves
would benefit both labor and discipline on the plantations.
Spiritual and temporal matters were the subjects of the questions contained in the original circular letters which had been

sent throughout the South. The committee wanted information on how religious instruction had affected slave morals,
chastity, truth, parental and marital duties, and the observance of the Sabbath. It also asked for evidence of the
effect of the Gospel on plantation discipline and the slaves'
observance of property rights. [61]

The report of the Charleston meeting tells of many
others besides Jones and Capers who were instrumental in
fostering plantation missions. There were the Episcopalians,
Bishop William Meade* and the Rev. Alexander Glennie.
There were the Presbyterians, Dr. John B. Adger and the
Rev. Thomas Clay, and the Methodists, John Blair and
James H. Cadson. No specific Baptist missionaries were
mentioned, but the denomination was reported as having
numerous black members, 45,000 in Georgia alone. [62] After
evaluating all of the reports, the coordinating committee concluded:

> In looking back for fifteen years, we rejoice with
> gratitude at the progress which the work has made.
> The truth is not to be disguised. The leaven hid
> in three measures of meal has been silently and
> powerfully pervading the mass. From Maryland
> to Texas, and from the Atlantic to the Ohio, the
> subject is spoken of; the great duty is urged and
> acknowledged; and feeling lives in action. What is
> peculiarly a subject of gratitude is, that all de-
> nominations of Christians are entering the field. [63]

The Charleston meeting gave a new impetus to Negro missions in the South. After 1845 Southern churchmen proclaimed with strident rhetoric that, as James O. Andrew
had said, the slave mission "is the crowning glory of our
church."[64]

Outsiders now learned that charges about the spiritual
neglect of the slaves no longer drew a sympathetic audience
in the South. In fact, all such criticisms were vociferously
and self-righteously denied. William Wilberforce of the
English antislavery party assailed the South on the grounds
that it had not treated the slaves as having souls. Using
the region of the Methodist Charleston Synod as an example,
he charged that at least one hundred thousand slaves had
never heard of the Gospel. The Missionary Society of the
South Carolina Conference was quick to respond. They accused the Archdeacon of being a bumbler when it came to

statistical matters.   Then they called him a liar, asserting:

> There is no truth in the statement; it is false, out
> and out; --a mere figure of speech, one of the gay
> flowers of abolition rhetoric. This Charleston
> Synod, referred to by Wilberforce, is covered,
> length and breadth, by Methodist missions, not to
> refer to efforts now made by other denominations
> of Christians for the religious instruction of the
> blacks. The best-digested, longest-tried, most
> efficient missionary organization to be found in the
> world for the salvation of the coloured population,
> is found in active operation, in the very district of
> the Southern States, which this English writer se-
> lects as the experimentum crucis against American
> slavery. [65]

Wilberforce had made a tactical mistake in leveling his criticisms at the very region in which the plantation missions had
begun.   The Charleston Synod was properly incensed.   It is
doubtful whether any area in the South after 1845 would have
countenanced the charge of spiritual neglect toward the slaves
by an outsider.   Negro missions had become a great moral
cause.   The evangelization of the Negro was the balm applied
to the Southern conscience.

A small segment of the Northern clergy and laity refused to leave the religious instruction of the Negroes entirely to the South.   On September 2, 1846, the American
Missionary Association was formed in Albany, New York, for
the purpose of laboring among the slaves.   Unlike the older
American Home Missionary Society, this organization expressly denounced fellowship with slaveholders.   In view of
the South's hostility to outside interference, it is remarkable
that the American Missionary Society was able to function at
all.   Yet in the upper South and in the border states, missionaries sponsored by this group established several congregations, effected slave conversions, and established an integrated school at Berea, Kentucky.   In 1859 the raid upon
Harper's Ferry so incensed the slave states that even these
limited activities were curtailed and several missionaries of
the society were arrested. [66]

The Southern Aid Society, being more conservative,
was more welcome.   This organization, established in New
York on September 28, 1853, filled the breach which had developed between the American Home Missionary Society and

the American Missionary Society. It restricted its activities
to the promotion of the Gospel and pledged to treat "our
Southern fellow-citizens and fellow-Christians with generous
confidence ... with paternal appreciation." Composed of
representatives of both sections, the Southern Aid Society
served primarily to give financial and organizational support
to churches which desired to evangelize the slaves. It was
hailed by a Southerner "as a welcome and efficient auxiliary. "[67]

        In the North, however, the compromising stance ex-
emplified by the Southern Aid Society increasingly became
abhorrent to the Evangelicals. After the denominational
divisions, especially those of the Methodists and the Baptists,
Northern religious leaders began to speak out more forcefully for emancipation. [68] Increasing radicalization was also
evident among the Presbyterians which had remained with the
New School in 1837. In 1858 the Southern Presbyterians
finally felt that the slavery position of their Northern counterparts compelled them, in spite of doctrinal agreements, to
form a distinct communion. Instead of joining up with the
Old School, they formed the United Synod of the Presbyterian
Church in the U.S.A. The Old School attempted to squash
all discussion of slavery and emancipation within its circles,
but it too was plagued by antislavery memorials and the loss
of members to the theologically conservative but abolitionist-
minded Free Presbyterians. Little wonder, therefore, that
the Northern religious community became less and less sympathetic to missionary work that involved cooperation with
slaveholders. [69] The editor of the Boston Congregationalist
put the matter bluntly when he told his readers to let the
Southerners finance their own missionaries so that "we can
find out whether they have any religion or not. "[70]

        In the 15 years prior to the firing upon Fort Sumter,
Negro missions did receive a good deal of both moral and
financial support from the citizenry of the South. Money
came from the slaveholders, non-slaveholders, and the Negroes themselves. Southern women sold their jewelry to
benefit the plantation Sunday Schools and preaching stations.[71]
From 1845 to 1861 the plantation missions of the Methodist
Episcopal Church, South, alone received about one and a half
million dollars. Statistically, too, the missions evidenced
vitality. In 1845 there were 83 stations, 25,380 black members, and 95 missionaries. The figures given for 1861 were
329 missions, 66,559 slave members, and 327 workers. [72]

During this period, the Southern Baptists suddenly awoke to the necessity of organized support for domestic missions. Even though they had numerous black members, they decided to establish missions for the express purpose of instructing the slaves. In 1850, James Tupper, the chairman of the Baptist Home Mission Board of the Charleston Association, declared:

> Other denominations have done and are still doing much for this neglected class. We almost alone are standing idle. Our coloured membership is perhaps equal to that of any other denomination. They need peculiar instruction; they want knowledge, not excitement. What they want is careful and solid instruction. They need to be taught as little children the rudiments of the Gospel, and then led on step by step. Yet, out of Charleston, we know not a single school in our Association for their oral instruction. The advantage of employing missionaries is obvious to all. [73]

Throughout the South the Baptists responded to such appeals. In the first 13 years after the division of 1845, the Southern Baptists gave seven times as much for home missions as the united body had expended in the seven preceding years. [74]

The other Southern denominations also increased their efforts in behalf of the slaves. In 1849 the Episcopalians of the Diocese of Mississippi dedicated a special society "for the diffusing of Christian Knowledge" which had as its purpose the giving of aid to plantation owners who desired to instruct their slaves. Fifteen thousand dollars were expended prior to 1861. [75] The Episcopalians established near Macon, Georgia, a rather unique arrangement for controlling the spiritual welfare of blacks. At the Montpeliar Springs Academy, white youths were taught farm management and rural economy. They were also trained in "the best mode of performing their duties as the owners of slaves and masters of human beings for whose souls they must give an account." [76] The slaves obtained by the school to run the accompanying stock farm provided the students with a convenient field for practical experience. More significant and successful than this novel arrangement was the regular mission work done by the Rev. Alexander Glennie in the Waccamaw region of South Carolina. For many years this Episcopalian minister worked among the slaves in the most inhospitable of climates. By 1858 he had 236 Negro members and 698 Negro children

in catechetical instruction and was serving nineteen plantations. [77]

When the Rev. Charles C. Jones was forced by ill
health to gradually lessen his activities in behalf of the
slaves, others stepped forward among the Presbyterians to
follow his lead and eventually claim his mantle. An out-
standing missionary was the Rev. John B. Adger, who for
12 years had been an apostle to the Armenians. He returned to his homeland in 1846 to devote his energies to the
black population in and around Charleston. The congregation
which he established later came under the pastoral charge of
Dr. John L. Girardeau, a firm supporter of Negro missions.
In 1860 the Second Presbyterian Church of Charleston had
600 Negro members. [78]

At the outbreak of the Civil War the religious situation
of the slaves in the South had improved considerably over
what it had been in 1790 and 1830. Daniel Robinson Hundley
published his Social Relations in Our Southern States in 1860
as a rebuttal to what he derisively called "the Uncle Tom
School." He wanted to prove that the slaves' moral and
spiritual needs had not been neglected by the South. He
claimed that there were 468,000 black Christians in the slave
states, or one-seventh of the total Negro population. [79] The
overall figure of 468,000 does not seem to be an exaggerated
count. Other estimates run as high as a half million. [80] In
at least one slave state the percentage of black Christians to
the general black population exceeded the one-seventh figure.
Luther P. Jackson estimated that the four major denominations contained 85,000 blacks in South Carolina on the eve of
Civil War. This was 20 per cent of the total Negro population. For the state of Virginia, Jackson determined that the
ratio of black church membership to the total black population was one to nine. In 1830 it had been one out of 17 and
in 1790 only one out of every 23. [81]

According to the 1860 United States census, there
were 4,097,111 blacks in the Southern states. [82] A half
million Christian blacks would suggest that about one out of
every eight Negroes was claimed by the Southern churches.
Was this the moral victory Jones had longed for? Back in
1847 Jones had predicted that if the slaves continued to increase at a rate of 25 per cent every ten years there would
be over 3,800,000 in 1860, over 4,800,000 in 1870 and over
6,000,000 in 1880. [83] Unless the Southern churches responded immediately, he had urged, the cause of plantation

missions would be overwhelmed by sheer numbers. Jones'
estimate for 1860 was not far wrong.   But what he could not
foresee, and did not live to see, was that in 1870 and in
1880 there would be no more slaves.   Jones died two years
before the passage of the Thirteenth Amendment. After
1865 the Southern churches had to work out a new relationship with those whom they had once considered their God-
given special mission and their nation of heathen at home.

Chapter III

THE GOSPEL FOR THE SLAVES

> The Gospel should be communicated to the
> entire Negro population, statedly, frequently,
> intelligibly, and in its fullness.
>   --Charles C. Jones[1]

Evangelical Protestantism was based upon the tenet
that the baptized individual was a free inner-directed man,
responsible to himself, to others, and, most importantly,
to God. Such was the status which Baptism theoretically
conferred upon the Negro. If the baptized Negro was a
slave, however, there was one great stumbling block. He
was the chattel property of another, having no personal
rights nor freedom of conscience. Since the churches had
pledged not to disturb the social relationship between bondsman and master, the dilemma of how to preach a Gospel
premised on individual autonomy within the framework of
slavery was thrust upon them from the very beginning. This
dilemma was intensified by the general belief that even a
baptized Negro belonged to an inferior race.

There were two distinct difficulties which confronted
the missionaries. First, there was the problem of adapting
the Gospel to fit the capabilities of an allegedly inferior
race. Second, there was the need to make the Gospel apply
to the Negroes as slaves. Even the best minds of the South,
however, refused to acknowledge this distinction. They persisted in identifying the Negro as a representative of a supposedly inferior race with the slave or servant of Biblical
days. In the process of instructing the Negro slaves in the
ethical implications of the Christian Gospel, this comfortable
analogy often broke down. Then the paradox inherent in the
baptism-bondage compromise revealed itself.

On the Souls of Black Folk

"It is a public testimony to our faith, " James Henry
Thornwell wrote in 1850, "that the Negro is one blood with
ourselves--that he has sinned as we have, and that he has
an equal interest with us in the great redemption. " This
seems a strange notion to have come from the pen of a man
who was known as the "Calhoun of the Church. " Yet this
spokesman for Southern Presbyterians self-righteously waged
battle with those who linked the Negro with the brute. False
science, Thornwell contended, might exclude the Negro from
the brotherhood of humanity, but natural instinct and the
Word of God plainly directed otherwise. [2]

The abolitionists pointed out the hypocrisy of the idea
that by declaring the slaves to be humans you could, in
reality, make them human. That could only be done when
you destroyed that which destroyed their humanity--slavery. [3]
Proponents of the plantation missions did not wish to debate
such a concept. Their first task was to convince the slaveholder that Negroes were, like all humans, capable of religious instruction. On the question of mental aptitude, the
Rev. Charles C. Jones wrote, "We must believe that their
general ignorance on Divine subjects is wholly owing to their
want of proper instruction, and not at all to any natural defect of mental constitution. "[4] If the premise was granted
that the Negro was a human and that all humankind had a
common origin, Jones maintained, then it must be plain that
Negroes "all are capable of exercising proper affections
towards God; and this necessarily implies a capability of
understanding the divine law. "[5]

The Christian character, however, is measured not
only by understanding but also by ethical behavior. Some
slaveholders sought to excuse themselves from spiritual
responsibility for the slaves by arguing that the Negro's
moral character was so degraded that little could be done.
The light of the Gospel simply would not be able to penetrate
the darkness of the heathen soul. Defenders of plantation
missions did not deny that the slaves had a poor standard of
moral conduct and were practitioners of all the prevailing
vices, but they refused to accept the notion that the Negro's
soul was beyond redemption. The Rev. William Capers
pointed out that a distinction was to be made between the
slaves' behavior and their essential character. Of the alleged
immorality of the Negro, he wrote:

> This degradation by no means strips the slave of
> his ethical character; it does not destroy the great
> and fundamental peculiarities of his nature as
> man--his reason, his responsibility, and his im-
> mortality. Low as he is, divine law has to deal
> with him. He is gifted with conscience, however
> darkened; with will, however perverse; with affec-
> tions, however earthly and sensual. [6]

Capers and Jones gave a spiritual personhood to the slaves.
Like all men the slaves were hastening onward to a tribunal
from which reward and punishment would be meeted out for
eternity according to the deeds done in the body. The task
of the plantation missionary was to prepare the slaves for
that eventuality.

In the writings of Southern religious leaders there
was a recognition of the slaves' religiosity. "They are a
people of religious dispositions, " wrote the Rev. Andrew
Flinn Dickson, "beyond any other race in the whole world."
The Negro character, he felt, had an "undertone of plain-
tiveness" which found "vent in devotion. "[7] A professor of
moral and intellectual philosophy at Randolph-Macon College
wrote, "The religious sentiment is strong in the African.
Both his mind and his heart respond readily to the fear of
God, the love of virtue, and the hope of heaven. But they
are religious beings in a low state of civilization. "[8] This
statement, by William Andrew Smith, * makes clear that
even though some in the South granted the slave a religious
nature, it was thought to be of a very inferior kind. Still
it could not be neglected. To suppress the religious principle among the slaves, Dr. John Holt Rice* said, would be as
difficult as "to exclude the light of the sun by a leaf of the
statute book."[9]

Thus it appeared that the choice was not whether the
slave was to have religion or no religion but whether his
religious temperament could be controlled and channeled into
acceptable patterns. The plantation missionaries were well
aware of the threat posed by survivals of African religion.
The American counterparts of the African priests were also
seeking to win the slaves. These "chimeras of a diseased
fancy, " Henry Ruffner warned the Rev. William S. Plumer,
would disdain proper instruction and set up for themselves.
"They will be your rivals, " he warned, "and have the advantage of you too, when once the flame of blind enthusiasm
is kindled in the congregation. "[10] The first task of the

plantation missionaries was to convince the slaveholders that
it was better that their slaves be in the chapels and the
churches rather than in praise meetings listening to their
own folk preachers.

Saving the souls of the slaves was the principal aim
of plantation missionaries. In order to win public approval,
however, evangelization often took a backseat to other goals.
Charles C. Pinckney, at the time of the first Methodist missions, made sweeping claims as to what might be expected:

> Were true religion propagated among this numerous
> and important class, a sense of duty would counter-
> act their reluctance to labour, and, diminishing the
> cases of feigned sickness so harassing to the Plant-
> er, would augment their numerical force and con-
> sequent production. The social relations of life
> being better observed, a greater proportion of do-
> mestic happiness would prevail and render them
> more contented with their situation, and more
> anxious to promote their owner's welfare. The
> absence, or diminution of theft, falsehood, and
> many other vices, would render the home of the
> Agriculturist far more agreeable than it can be,
> where guilt, which escapes human detection, knows
> not, and fears not, another tribunal. [11]

This was an undisguised appeal to the planters' self-interest.
Even Charles C. Jones was not above dangling the account
book before the planters' eyes. Assuming the truth of the
commonplace that virtue is more profitable than vice, he
claimed that the plantation which enjoyed religious instruction would do better for the interests of its owner. [12]

In addition to appealing to the pecuniary bias of the
planters, the missionaries disclaimed any intention of interfering with the social status quo. But they did hope that
within the prescribed relationship of master and slave the
Gospel would be of some benefit. Bishop William Meade,
in a pastoral letter to the Episcopalians of Virginia, claimed
that if masters would attempt to substitute religion in the
place of fear as the governing factor between masters and
slaves it would "increase our affection for them, cause us
to feel more deeply that they are our brethren, and thus
render more easy and delightful every other duty." Surely,
he felt, none could seek the salvation of the slave's soul one
day and be unjust and cruel the next day. [13]

The Plantation Ministry--Methods and Means

In theory Southern Christians, lay and clerical, were all to assume the duty of instructing the slaves. But as in many religious activities, there was in reality a gap between the pew and the pulpit. Some masters and mistresses did regularly gather their slaves together, perhaps in the big house after the day's work was done, for a simple service of worship and instruction in the Lord's Prayer and the Ten Commandments.[14] For the most part, however, the Southern clergy assumed major responsibility for bringing the Gospel to the slaves.

Jones hoped that "the settled pastors and stated supplies of our churches" would be sufficient for meeting the spiritual needs of the slaves.[15] This was clearly not to be. The great masses of the slaves were either prohibited from attending the mixed churches, which ordinarily were in towns and cities, or they were in regions where little organized religious activity took place. The slave's world was circumscribed by the boundaries of the plantation; the Gospel had to come to him. The plantation missionary conducted a peripatetic ministry among the slaves, preaching, teaching, exercising church discipline, visiting the sick, performing marriage ceremonies, and conducting funerals. For the slaves on isolated plantations, the missionary was the personal embodiment of the entire Christian church, with power to bless and power to damn.

After the missionary obtained permission from the planter to preach among the slaves, the first task was to secure some kind of worship facility. Jones envisioned each plantation as having "a neat little chapel, with its tower or steeple and bell." Such an "ornament," he felt, would give an air of stability to the plantation, awaken the religious feelings of the slaves, and produce the best of influences all around.[16] Most planters, either because of the cost involved or because they lacked Jones' taste for steeples and bells, failed to furnish the missionaries with special accommodations. The Rev. Holland M' Tyeire* was disappointed in what some masters pointed out as "the prayer house." He desired a real chapel, not a barn, cotton-shed, or sugarhouse. "These have a work-day association," he wrote, "and, especially when attendance is compulsory, the servant comes to look upon religious services as part of the plantation police, and the preacher in the light of the overseer."[17]

Some of the wealthy planters did construct a special building for the missionary to conduct his services in. In rare instances they even employed a full-time chaplain. Such was the case with William Mercer, the owner of the Laurel Hill plantation in Mississippi. He had a chapel built for his several hundred slaves and brought in two Episcopalian preachers to serve it. This enabled him to exercise an unusual degree of lay control over what went on there. [18]

Jones did not think it advisable to have the slaves worship in the houses of their owners, "where they are not sufficiently at home to be at ease." He also rejected the cotton-house, being neither convenient nor safe, and the slave cabins, for being too small. At first he tried preaching in the open air, but he soon found this to be uncomfortable both for him and his hearers. Therefore he had "a neat plaster building, with belfry and bell" erected for his own slaves. [19]

Most missionaries, like the frontier Methodist circuit riders, travelled about from preaching station to preaching station, meeting with the slaves on conditions laid down by the planters. Sometimes the white clergy would simply post a public notice for the convening of Negroes in a certain neighborhood. Then they would preach to whoever showed up. The standard procedure, however, was to go directly to the larger plantations and, after gaining the master's approval, gather the slaves from the quarters, being careful not to interfere with the plantation routine. [20]

The Rev. Ralph Q. Mallard became a Methodist missionary to the slaves in the middle 1850s. As a lad he had frequently witnessed the labors of Jones among the slaves of his father's plantation. According to Mallard's recollections, Jones came early in the morning and as soon as possible held a prayer meeting, at which faithful Negro watchmen led in prayer. The service was composed both of sermon and song. In the afternoon Jones taught a Sunday school and drilled both adults and children orally in his catechism. Next came the "inquiry-meeting" and then a meeting of the watchmen during which Jones was given a report on the state of religion and conduct of the slaves. "And all this was interspersed," Mallard reported, "with wise counsels given to these humble under-shepherds appointed by church and pastor as his helpers." Finally, when the sun was low in the sky, "the servant of God, weary yet rejoicing, turns his steps homeward. "[21]

There are a number of significant omissions in Mallard's account of a day's missionary labors among the slaves. Nothing is said of the hazards of travel, the risk of contracting fever in the lowlands, or the danger of bodily harm from irate whites and unsympathetic masters. Nor is there mention of the "inertness, incapacity, untractableness, untrustiness, wastefulness and supiness" of the slaves of which the Rev. John B. Adger, a Presbyterian missionary, complained. [22] In addition, the missionaries to the slaves had to contend with a popular sentiment which regarded their work as less glorious or heroic than that of the foreign missionary, who when he fell at his post was as honored as the most renowned warrior. "The humble teacher of the poor slaves," Mrs. M. J. Davis wrote to her son, a seminary student, "is never heard beyond the scene of his labors...."[23]

The greatest handicap which confronted the missionaries was the ban on the use of written materials in the instruction of the slaves. In 1853 Mrs. Margaret Douglass was imprisoned in Norfolk, Virginia, for teaching Negro children to pray and read the Bible. She commented that it seemed rather ludicrous that the State should feel threatened "that a few little negro boys and girls had learned that famous sentence 'In Adam's fall we sinned all.'"[24] The South's real fear, of course, was not simply the distribution of the Holy Scriptures but the instruction in reading and writing that was necessary for their use. "Teaching me the alphabet," Frederick Douglass said of his boyhood, "had been the "inch' given, I was now waiting only to 'take the ell.'"[25] The defenders of slavery knew full well that knowledge unfitted a man to be a slave.

The law under which Mrs. Douglass was prosecuted had been first passed in 1831 in the wake of the insurrection led by Nat Turner. Eventually all the slave states, with the exception of Tennessee, restricted the instruction of Negroes to oral means. By 1855 nine of the 15 slave states had made it illegal to distribute Bibles among the slaves.[26] Only by stealth or with the assistance of a sympathetic white were the slaves able to learn to read and write. According to William Heard, who had been a slave in Georgia, "any slave caught writing suffered the penalty of having his forefinger cut from his right hand, yet there were some who could read and write." Heard himself had been instructed from Noah Webster's blueback speller by a poor white boy for ten cents a lesson.[27]

Although Northern critics were certain that religious instruction without letters would fail, the Southern missionaries quickly resigned themselves to conformity to the slave code. Jones felt that instruction by oral means would work because of the remarkable memories of the slave children whom he catechized. "Their memory," he wrote, "is their book." Once the Biblical story had been told them, it was "stamped on the tablet of memory forever." A fellow missionary, the Rev. Henry Ruffner, rationalized the use of mere oral instruction by pointing out that in the primitive Church the spread of the Gospel had been principally by word of mouth and that in Africa principles and character were formed mainly by oral means. The Rev. Holland M'Tyeire actually felt religion without letters was better than religion with letters, for it would force the slave to "partake more and more of the life-giving civilization of the master."[28]

To meet the requirements of oral instruction the Southern clergy had to devise special materials designed for learning by rote. Yet what was called the "precept by precept" method of religious instruction actually antedated the reactionary legislation of the 1830s. In 1821, for example, the Rev. John Mines published a catechism for those who could not read. Although it was principally intended for use among children in Sabbath schools and within the family circle, it was also especially fitted for use among illiterate Negroes. Mines' Evangelical Catechism set the pattern for those that would follow by presenting the fundamental doctrines of Christianity in question and answer form.[29]

A number of catechisms were written with the oral instruction of the slaves especially in mind. Two of those which were most frequently used came, respectively, from the pens of William Capers and Charles C. Jones. Capers' catechism, first published in 1833, was only 16 pages long and was used principally by the Methodist missionaries. The one by Jones went through nine or ten editions from 1834 to 1852 and was considerably more complex. Yet we are told that even young white children used it to instruct slave children. It was also translated into the Armenian, Armeno-Turkish, and the Chinese languages for use in foreign mission fields.[30]

The fact that these catechisms were used also for the instruction of non-slaves indicates that they were not designed to pervert the Christian faith for plantation use. Jones' own children and grandchildren used his Catechism of Scripture

Doctrine and Practice.[31] Before the passage of laws barring instruction in letters, the Southern churches had used the catechisms common to their particular religious heritage. Among the Methodists that of Isaac Watts was especially popular because it was designed for use among children of a very young age and, therefore, was adaptable for use among illiterate slaves. Back in the seventeenth century, Cotton Mather saw the need for fashioning a special program of religious instruction for the Negro, who needed a simple and unadorned Gospel. This same realization stood behind the special catechisms for the oral instruction of the slaves.[32]

When sermonizing among the slaves the plantation missionaries were supposed to employ pictorial and expository rather than didactic or doctrinal language. They were urged to employ familiar narratives, illustrations from every day life, parables, accounts of the striking works of God, and the like.[33] The Rev. Henry Ruffner advised:

> The whole carcass of modern technical theology-- its metaphysics--its subtle distinctions--its mystical dogmas--its sectarian polemics--its technical phrases, etc., etc.,--should be all cast away from him who goes to this simple and ignorant people as a Christian teacher.[34]

Yet the missionary was not to overcompensate for the ignorance of his hearers by using their corrupt expressions and broken English. Jones felt that the slaves were capable of understanding "pure simple Saxon as well as most people."[35]

The truly effective missionary attempted to maintain the dignity of his office and yet get to know the slaves personally. Jones customarily mingled with the slaves both before and after the services and tried to remain on the plantation until they had gone to their respective homes or returned to their duties. He talked to the slaves privately, all the while preserving "a mild dignity" without condemning their "ignorance and degradation." He advised the plantation missionaries to endeavor to know personally all those to whom they preached and to inquire after their families, health, and prosperity. While the missionary ought to attempt to win the slaves' respect, he should not, Jones warned, seek to impress them with the fact, "should he unfortunately believe it himself," that there was an impassible gulf between his intelligence and theirs and "that he has

humbled himself amazingly to take their instruction into his
hands. "[36]

Lessons on Salvation

Malcolm X once made the accusation that in the days
of slavery white Christians brainwashed the Negro "to look
for his pie in the sky, and for his heaven in the hereafter,
while right here on earth the slavemaster white man enjoyed his heaven."[37] Similar charges were made by nineteenth-century critics of Southern religion. William Ellery
Channing, for example, accused the Southern clergy of in-
doctrinating the slaves with a gospel emphasizing those virtues which would benefit their owners, such as obedience,
respect for property, and fidelity to their master's interests.[38] In The Suppressed Book about Slavery, George
Washington Carleton, a Northern abolitionist, made much of
the testimony of "a conscience-stricken Slaveholder" who
reported that in 40 years in the South he had never heard a
sermon to the slaves "but what made obedience to Masters
by the Slaves the fundamental and supreme law of Religion."[39]
In light of this evidence, we must examine whether or not the
slaves were given the heart of the Gospel message.

Despite what the Southern clergy may have thought of
the alleged degradation of the slave, they began with the assumption that he was "one for whom God the Son died; one
whom the Spirit can re-fashion."[40] Evangelical Protestants
did not believe that any man, be he black or white, could
experience regeneration unless he acknowledged his utter
dependence upon the mercies of God. The first step was to
make manifest how man was in revolt against the Creator.
All of the slaves, especially the small children, were expected to learn the Ten Commandments so they might have
a mirror in which to see how far they had strayed from
God's ordinances.[41]

Having been "convicted of sin," the slaves were then
to be assured of God's forgiveness. The soteriological doctrine of Evangelical Protestantism comes through clearly in
the following excerpt from the catechism written by the Rev.
John F. Hoff, a Presbyterian clergyman in Virginia:

Q.   And what must you do to be saved from the anger of
     God, which your sins have desired?

A. I must be sorry for my sins: I must pray to God to forgive me what is past, and serve him better for the time to come.

Q. Will God forgive you if you pray for it?

A. I hope he will forgive me if I trust his mercy, for the sake of what Jesus Christ has done, and what he has suffered.

Q. Do you know who Jesus Christ is?

A. He is God's own son, who came down from heaven to save us from our sins, and from God's anger.[42]

The all-sufficiency of Christ's merit was also stressed by the Rev. William Meade, assistant Bishop of Virginia. "God is very merciful," Meade preached, "but it is only through the righteousness of Him who stood in the sinner's place, who in his own person bore our sins upon the accursed tree." Meade made the twisted argument that since the slaves did not have much in this world upon which to fasten their hearts, they ought to find it easier not to presume upon earthly merit. "After all your strivings for it," he told the slaves, "you cannot get much in this life, as some people can who choose to lose their souls for some poor treasures they are laying up here."[43]

Arminianism was rife in Evangelical piety. It is little wonder that the slaves were often given the notion that in order to be saved they had to conform to a certain standard of behavior. Bishop William Meade penned a series of sermons, dialogues, and narratives especially for use in the instruction of slaves. Among them we find the following exchange between two slaves. Sambo, a pious Negro is trying to convince Toney, an unconverted slave, that he should attend religious services:

Sambo: "Do you never go to meeting, Toney, to hear the minister preach?"

Toney: "Yes, I go sometimes, but the minister never preach to us."

Sambo: "Why, Toney, the minister preach to every body. May-be you think he don't preach to you, because he don't say, now, coloured people, I speak to you. The Word of the Lord, speaks to everybody alike, white people, black people, rich man, poor man, old man and young man--it says, repent every one of

> you. I thank God, this word has done great things
> for me since you and I lived together. Then I thought
> just as you do now; I loved frolic and dance, and a
> great many bad things, but I am a great deal happier
> now, than I was then. "[44]

This fictional dialogue illustrates how easily the notion could
be conveyed that becoming a Christian simply meant giving
up certain bad habits and conforming to white patterns of
piety. Good servants went to Heaven. Bad servants went
to Hell. Good and Evil were defined according to prevailing
ideas of honesty, chastity, temperance, and the like.

The plantation slaves, especially the younger children,
were taught that cleanliness was next to godliness. They
must surely have associated Christianity with the freshly
scrubbed face and clean clothes. Every Sunday morning Mrs.
Victoria Clayton had the mothers of the slave children bring
them to her so she could satisfy herself as to "the care they
gave them, whether they had received a bath and suitable
clothing for the holy day. "[45] William Andrew Smith believed
that the Sabbath would be the great civilizer of the slave. In
Lectures on the Philosophy and Practice of Slavery, he wrote:

> The clean skin, the Sunday suit, the companionship
> of friends, all unite with the sound instruction of
> the pulpit, and the warm-hearted reception of the
> truth, to raise men in the scale of being, to make
> him a better servant, and a better citizen--an heir,
> together with the master, of the inheritance of the
> saints in light. [46]

Here again we detect a confusion of temporal and spiritual
goals. Not only was the Sabbath to make good saints; it
was also to make good servants.

The plantation missionaries found difficulty in asses-
sing the validity of the conversion experiences which the
slaves recounted and in measuring their spiritual progress.
In an attempt to resolve this predicament, the missionaries
began to admit the slaves to the church on probation for a
period of six months or longer. Jones complained that often
this did not bear fruit. After an entire year the slaves gave
no more satisfactory evidence of conversion than when they
had first come, "save that their seriousness and perserver-
ance indicated an abiding interest in religion. " Finally Jones
was compelled to compromise. "We seem almost obliged,

after long waiting, " he reported, "when nothing offensive to good morals can be alleged against them, to receive them into the church upon the hope that they may be converted."[47] In effect, the plantation missionaries established for the persevering slaves a kind of half-way covenant, such as was allowed the non-professing Puritans in New England in the seventeenth century.

Jones' Suggestions on the Religious Instruction of the Negroes in the Southern States provides a sample of the kind of church register which was used for Negro members. It includes the following categories--plantation residence, names, number of slaves, and dates that the individual slave was admitted, dismissed, suspended, excommunicated and restored. There was a special column for indicating whether or not the slave had been "removed, " which was a euphemism for being sold elsewhere. The slaves were expelled for a variety of reasons, such as immorality, intemperance, uncleanliness, theft, abuse of the Sabbath, lying, and in some cases, for deserting the church. Because excommunication was frequent among the adult slaves, one missionary participant in the Charleston meeting despairingly said, "Our main hope of success is with the young."[48]

The institution of the family and the sanctity of marriage ranked supreme in the pantheon of virtues among American Protestants in the nineteenth century. Nothing plagued the missionaries more than offenses of the slaves in these two areas. The extent to which adultery, fornication, licentiousness, and similar sexual offenses among the slaves troubled the Rev. Holland M'Tyeire and his colleagues is evident from the following statement:

> From the uniform testimony of clergymen of different denominations who have endeavored to embrace this part of our population in church communion, it appears that this is the chief stumbling block to their Christianity. At least two-thirds of all the irregularities and scandalous offenses calling for the exercise of the church discipline originate here, directly or remotely.[49]

M'Tyeire speculated that the high incidence of irregularities in matters of sex among the slaves could be caused by "that predominance of passion always pertaining to inferior races." This was, he felt, aggravated by the close association of the slaves during labor and leisure, which was conducive to an undesirable intimacy.[50]

M'Tyeire was not, however, insensitive to the problems caused by the informality of the marriage relationship between slaves. It is well-known that the laws of the dominant society did not recognize the marriage alliances of the slaves. Those stable relationships which might be developed between two slaves could at anytime be dissolved at the whim of their master. The sexual demands of white males upon black females made the sanctity of the slave family a difficult virtue to maintain.

Under these pressures, conformity to the ideal of Christian marriage was not often found among the slaves. The missionaries sought to instill in the slaves a higher regard for "the sacredness and perpetuity of their marriage relations" than the laws of the South did. Jones urged the plantation missionaries to solemnize slave marriages whenever possible--"at their own homes and at such times as may best suit their convenience." This would, he hoped, rebuke their polygamy and licentiousness, and cause their masters to make greater efforts to protect slave families from separation. [51]

Problems dealing with slave marriages point out vividly the conflict between religious and civil law. According to church law, the only justifiable cause for the dissolution of the marriage contract was infidelity. But the Southern clergy recognized that often slave marriages were broken up by causes beyond the slaves' control. The English Baptists in the West Indies attempted to resolve the dilemma by declaring that a female slave who was forcibly separated from her husband was "to all intents and purposes reduced to a state of widowhood." She was allowed to marry again, lest she fall into sin. The same approach was taken in 1827 in the case of a male slave by the Presbyterian Synod of North Carolina. [52]

The ultimate resolution of the difficulty was to gain civil recognition of slave marriages. Under abolitionist pressure, the Southern clergy intensified their efforts to reform the "peculiar institution" by seeking its legal recognition. Several clergymen in Kentucky actually began to issue marriage licenses to Negroes. [53] The Christian duty of keeping slave families together was emphasized. Jones spoke out in 1847 in behalf of reform. He admonished:

> The owner should frown upon, and restrain, and
> punish immorality. He should encourage marriages,

and defend families from the invasions of unprin-
cipled men and women and conscientiously keep
them together. We know that it has been said,
'The owner can do no good here;' i.e. in checking
lewd immoralities. But we beg leave to say, that
our experience and observation teach the opposite
doctrine. [54]

During the Civil War numerous religious spokesmen echoed
the words of Jones, appealing to the Christians of the South
to eliminate those aspects of slavery which did not conform
to Biblical standards or which compromised the Christianity
of the slaves. In 1863 Bishop George F. Pierce of the
Methodist Episcopal Church, South, told the Georgia legislature: "All laws which authorize or allow arbitrary interference with the connubial relations of the slaves ought to
be rescinded. "[55]

Frank Tannenbaum, in Slave and Citizen, argued that
American Protestantism, unlike Roman Catholicism in Latin
America, was ineffective in protecting the sanctity of the
slave family because Protestant theology did not recognize
marriage as a sacrament of the Church. [56] It is true that
the American Evangelicals thought of marriage as a civil
rather than an ecclesiastical institution. Nevertheless, marriage was an ordinance of God and worthy of all respect and
protection. The real difficulty was that the Southern churches
had pledged not to interfere in the social or political aspects
of the institution of slavery. [57] Thus it took them some time
to realize that only by urging the reform of affairs in the
State could they bring about reform in matters that concerned
the Church.

Lessons on Duty

Frederick Douglass first came to the attention of
Northern audiences with what was described as "a very funny
imitation of the way in which slaveholding clergymen would
exhort their servants to obey their masters." The citizens
of Boston, for example, were entertained one evening in
Faneuil Hall by Douglass mimicking a sermon on the text
"Do unto others as you would have others do unto you." The
slaves were told: "Oh! if you wish to be happy in time,
happy in eternity, you must be obedient to your masters;
their interest is yours. "[58]

Douglass' parody on a sermon to the slaves was not
pure fiction. The subject of obedience was a common theme
in the religious instruction of the plantation missionaries. In
order to win a sympathetic hearing in the South, the Evangelicals began to stress more and more the duties of servants.
After Thomas Coke had preached to a hostile crowd in Virginia he wrote in his Journal:

> Here I bore a public testimony against slavery,
> and have found out a method of delivering it without
> causing a tumult, and that is by first addressing
> the Negroes in a very pathetic manner on the Duties
> of Servants to Masters, and then the Whites will re-
> ceive quietly what I have to say to them. [59]

To gain access to the plantations, the missionaries used the
same technique, first telling the planters that the Gospel
would make their slaves "the most virtuous, respectable, and
orderly and faithful servants in the Country. "[60] The Rev.
Nicholas Ware, an Episcopalian, frankly stated "that when
every good motive may be wanting, a regard to self-interest
should lead every planter to give his people religious instruction. "[61]

In The Evangelical Catechism by John Mines we find
the question, "What is the first duty of Servants?" In response the slaves were to recite:

> The first duty of servants is, to be contented with
> their condition, for the Scripture says, 'Art Thou
> called, being a servant, care not for it; let every
> man wherein he is called therein abide with God. '
> I Cor. VIII: 21, 24. [62]

The Southern clergy, not wishing to be accused of perverting
the Gospel, sought justification for preaching on the duties
of slaves by pointing to those portions of the Bible which
dealt with the Christian obligations of servants. Portions of
the Pauline letters which give attention to the station of servants in life were found to be highly useful. Paul's admonition to Onesimus in the Epistle to Philemon with respect to
the duty of a Christian slave to return to his master was
frequently used. One wonders if the slaves in the South did
not get the notion that this man Paul, of whom they heard so
frequently, must not have been a great plantation owner himself.

The South took the position that chattel slavery, as
the nineteenth century knew it, was equivalent to the servant-
hood spoken of in the Bible. It was, therefore, simply one
of the many God-approved stations in life which had Christian duties attached to them. In a sermon based on Ephe-
sians VI: 7, the Rev. Alexander Glennie said:

> What a blessed book the Bible is, my brethren!
> It speaks comfort to all people in every station of
> life: it shows how every one must live here, so
> as to please our heavenly Father. The rich are
> taught in the Bible, how they must do good with
> their riches; and the poor, how they must be con-
> tented with the portion that God has given them:
> and both poor and rich are taught how to lay up
> treasure in heaven. Parents are told in the Bible,
> how they must bring up their children in the nur-
> ture and admonition of the Lord; and children,
> how they must obey their parents. Masters are
> taught in the Bible, how they must rule their ser-
> vants and servants how they must obey their
> masters. [63]

Northern critics refused to accept the South's contention that
chattel slavery was a contemporary manifestation of the kind
of slavery that was common in the days of the early Church.
But the Southern clergy did not relent in identifying the
Greek doulos and the Latin servus with the status of the
blacks on the plantations. [64]

"The duty of obedience, " Jones told the planters,
"will never be felt and performed to the extent that we desire it, unless we can bottom it on religious principles."
Jones argued that the slaves were frequently "guilty of
notorious sins and know not that they sin at all."[65] Many
masters complained that their slaves commonly lied and
stole without evidencing the slightest degree of guilt. On
the matter of theft, for example, the Rev. Holland M'Tyeire
reported:

> There is among the servants a sophistry before
> which their scruples stand a poor chance, and
> from an early age they are expert in it! They
> have worked for what is their master's and made
> it, and have a right to share in it; if he does not
> help them, they may justifiably help themselves:
> they are not stealing, only taking of their own. [66]

Deception as a technique of survival was common among the
slaves. The missionaries, having established to their satisfaction that much improvement in the master-slave relationship would come if the fear of God could be substituted for
the fear of the lash, clearly used the Scriptures to instill in
the slaves a sense of moral guilt.

In Colossians III: 22, the Apostle Paul urges servants
to obey their masters not with "eyeservice, as men-pleasers;
but in singleness of heart fearing God." The Southern clergy
freely applied this Scriptural injunction to the problem of
mere "eye-service" among the slaves. Holland M'Tyeire,
recognizing that "deception, among inferior animals, supplies
the place of strength, " hoped that the Gospel would put an
end to "powerful temptations to prevarication" among the
slaves. Alexander Glennie was simply paraphrasing the
Pauline injunction when he told the slaves "not to be double-
minded, professing to be one thing but really being another."
Bishop Meade portrayed God as a kind of omniscient overseer, who looked down upon the slaves, accusing them of
sin, and who would punish them even though they might escape detection by their earthly master. "Bring to bear upon
the negro's head, " M'Tyeire advised, "the great truth that
God sees him, and that wherever he goes and wherever he
turns, by day or by night, the eye of the Eternal, the Omniscient One, is upon him. "[67]

The missionaries frankly tried to substitute for the
fear of corporal punishment, or the love of reward, a
Christian conscience of duty as an incentive to promote
docility, honesty, and fidelity among the slaves. "Take
away the fear of God from your Negroes, " M'Tyeire asked
the planters, "and what security have you for the safety of
your property, to say nothing of your person?"[68] Ordinarily
the Southern clergy avoided making public fools of themselves.
But when Bishop Meade told the slaves that they ought to be
content with indiscriminant punishment from their masters in
instances where they were completely innocent, so as to
atone for those times that they violated plantation law but
went undetected, he clearly overstepped the boundaries of
common sense. And when Meade told the slaves that they
ought to do their business faithfully and honestly because if
the roles of masters and servants were reversed they would
expect the same from those who were now their servants,
he clearly deserved public ridicule. In A Key to Uncle Tom's
Cabin, Harriet Beecher Stowe wrote:

> The reverend teachers of such expositions of
> scripture do great injustice to the natural sense
> of their sable catechumens, if they suppose them
> incapable of detecting such very shallow sophistry,
> and of proving conclusively that 'it is a poor rule
> that won't work both ways. '69

In their more reflective moments, the plantation missionaries did realize that the slaves could detect a flagrant
abuse of the true Gospel. From personal experience the
Rev. William S. Plumer had learned that the slaves often
felt "that all scriptural passages which bear upon their peculiar situation have been interpolated by white men. " This
was to Plumer the "one obstacle to success" in preaching
to the slaves. A fellow Presbyterian clergyman advised
Plumer that he ought not to press the duties of the slaves
to their masters too strongly and frequently. Such an excess would "beget the fatal suspicion that you are but execut-
ing a selfish scheme of white men to make them better
slaves rather than to make them Christian freemen. " If that
happened, the Rev. Henry Ruffner told Plumer, "Your labor's
in vain. "70

Jones, when offering several suggestions to other missionaries, once wrote that the slaves were "wise enough ...
and proud enough not to be put off with any sort of sermon,
and have therefore stayed at home or gone where they have
thought they could do better."71   Jones had had some firsthand experience in this area. On one occasion, early in his
missionary career, he was preaching to a congregation of
slaves when some of them staged a walkout. As he recounted
the incident,

> ... while enforcing a certain duty from the Scrip-
> tures, which servants owe to their Masters, more
> than one half of my large congregation rose up and
> went away every man to his own house, and the
> part that remained, seemed to remain more from
> personal respect to the Preacher, than from any
> liking to his doctrine. 72

A decade later the same thing happened when Jones attempted
to use the story of Onesimus to make a case against running
away. After the service those blacks who had remained
came forward and told Jones that they did not believe that
the story, as he interpreted it, was actually in the Bible,
and that he preached to please the masters. 73

Some missionaries, it is apparent, had some second thoughts about making the Gospel into a new law to underwrite plantation discipline. The planters had been told that the fear of God among their slaves would be beneficial in protecting not only their property but also their own persons. Apparently some took this to mean that once the slaves had been converted to Christianity there would no longer be any need for "police control" in the South. In Liberty County, Georgia, there were few regular patrols. Jones thought that this circumstance spoke well of the general good effects of the Gospel. Yet he felt constrained to warn:

> Let no one suppose that religious instruction will do away with the necessity of Patrols, and other regulations touching their [the slaves'] civil condition. Does the preaching among the whites do away with the necessity of Law? Are all white men converted and respect the persons and property of their neighbors as they ought?[74]

The answer Jones wanted was clearly a negative one. He did not feel that it was just to lay the charge of bad conduct among the slaves at the door of the plantation chapel. It belonged, he argued, "to a looseness of discipline on Plantations, and to the inefficient Police in the community."[75]

As they became more secure in their work, the plantation missionaries spoke out more strongly on the duties of masters to servants. Like the pious brother in the Melville Letters,[76] they admonished the recalcitrant planters to fulfill their obligations toward the slaves. They were no longer willing to accept the excuse of the planter who felt that his duties were finished when he called in the missionary, saying, "Pray, preach to my people this evening." They wanted "the actual and active cooperation of the owners themselves."[77] There would be an anomaly in God's government, the Rev. Holland M'Tyeire argued, if kings had duties to their subjects, parents to children, and husbands to wives, but masters had none to their servants. "When you call them to fulfill their duties," Jones told the planters, "they will expect you to set the example, by a fulfillment of your own." Jones knew full well that the slaves could discern inconsistency of conduct as well as other men. He was sure this was true in cases which involved their own interest and happiness. Therefore, the first duty of the masters was to give their full support, financially and by their own participation, to the religious instruction of the slaves. "Corn and bacon and woolen are not all that immortal beings need," M'Tyeire asserted.[78]

Although the spiritual and moral improvement of the
slaves was the principal goal of the plantation missionary,
he also became concerned about more mundane matters. The
planters were told that they were to be good stewards by providing the slaves with comfortable houses, adequate clothing,
wholesome and abundant food, and care for the sick and the
aged. They ought not expect their slaves to make bricks
without straw; neither ought they to administer punishment
without justice and mercy. Jones used the analogy of the
stern yet loving father who must at times chastise his children, yet does so fairly. [79]

The Southern clergy had not wished to do more than
save souls when the plantation missions began. Jones ex-
plicitly denied that he labored to effect changes in the temporal conditions of the slaves. "My grand, exclusive object," he wrote as late as 1842, "has ever been to put them
in possession of that which confers peace with God in time
and blessedness with him in eternity." Despite this claim,
Jones began making some very practical suggestions for the
improvement of the temporal circumstances of the slaves.
For example, he urged that the planters give each of their
slaves "a small lot for a garden, poultry yard, or apiary."
And he urged them to allow the slaves to raise chickens
and hogs so that their diet could be improved. [80] William
Andrew Smith condemned "the miserable smokey hovels in
low damp situations" that masters sometimes passed off as
the slave quarters. To the planters, Smith declared:

> A gang of half-starved, meanly clad, overworked
> slaves, with no heart to laugh or sing, and even
> without that attachment to their owners which the
> ox and the ass have for theirs, is a disgusting
> spectacle, and as revolting to every feeling of
> humanity as it is in violation of every principle
> of economy. [81]

On the doctrinal and theoretical level, nothing would have upset the Southern clergy more than to accuse them of con-
fusing the spiritual and temporal realms. But they did come
to realize that there were social implications of the Christian
message which could not be avoided--even on the plantation.

There is conflicting testimony as to the overall effect
of plantation preaching upon the slaves. Frederick Law Olmsted, the Northern journalist, was told of "a very religious
lady" in Texas who required all of her slaves to be at worship

services three times on the Sabbath. Yet this woman's
slaves were reported to be "the dullest, and laziest, and
most sorrowful looking Negroes he [Olmsted's informant]
ever saw. "[82] At the great Charleston meeting of 1845,
evidence was given that "some of our very worst Negroes"
were the ones with whom the greatest pains had been taken
in religious instruction. One clergyman complained that although the slaves readily joined the church, especially during
periods of revival, they just as readily declined in religious
zeal after the first excitement was over. [83]

Other sources, however, gave considerable credit to
the plantation missions for effecting beneficial changes
among the slaves. The Rev. M. D. Banks, who worked
among the slaves of the Sea Islands, reported that some complained that slave piety was sadly deficient in the three car-
dinal virtues of veracity, chastity, and honesty. Yet he
noticed that under the Gospel, as preached by the Methodists,
the slaves began to affirm the sacredness of the marriage
relationship and fewer cases of lying and theft came to his
attention. [84] Advocates of the plantation missions, as one
might expect, gave extensive reports of the beneficial results of having the Gospel preached to the slaves. Because
of the Gospel, one such individual testified in the 1840s,
there was an "acknowledged change of things for the better,
both religiously and morally, " among the slaves. He explained:

> Now they are seen clean and neat in their persons
> --choice in their company--proud of their owners--
> regular attendants of Church, and the Sabbath
> school, and as apologizing as any of our white
> tiplers when caught taking a drink, by far more
> cautious of uttering oaths before religious people
> than are some of us. Youths and children are
> seen in the Sabbath schools intelligently answering
> the questions of their teachers, and readily re-
> peating their hymns. They sing wonderfully well.
> The prayer of the Black man is heard in the prayer
> meeting, with envy for his gift; and, in short, every
> thing in regard to him goes on better. [85]

A planter from the Santee River region of Virginia reported
that since the introduction of the Gospel among his slaves
his neighbors had remarked that he had "a well-ordered
people. "[86] According to his brother-in-law, Jones' labors
resulted "in the increased intelligence, good order, neatness,

and general morality of the colored people, their elevated
regard for marriage vows, and attention to the morals and
manners of their children. "[87]

It is obvious that each Southerner judged the effectiveness of the Gospel on the plantation on the basis of his or
her stereotype of what a Christian slave ought to be. A pious
slave was thought to be one who conformed to his master's
or the missionary's expectations. An antebellum Southerner
would have bristled at the accusation that he did not "know"
the Negro. The Rev. John B. Adger of Charleston, South
Carolina, maintained that there was an unusual intimacy between the white and the black races in the South because
from birth to death they mingled in a thousand ways, "eating
from the same storehouses, drinking from the same fountains,
dwelling the same enclosures, forming parts of the same
families. "[88] According to Adger, this intimacy of the races
was advantageous to the cause of plantation missions.

More perceptive minds were not so sure. Jones felt
that one of the obstacles which the plantation missionary encountered was the difficulty of obtaining an insight into the
Negro character. Jones recognized that the blacks were often
a distinct class in the community and kept to themselves.
"They are one thing before the whites, " he wrote, "and another before their own color. "[89] The Rev. S. L. Graham
warned the William S. Plumer that it was very difficult for
whites to judge the Christian character of the slaves. He
wrote:

> Besides, say what you will, they are an imperiam
> in imperio, a separate class, with prejudices,
> opinions, and modes of thinking of their own, be-
> tween whom the whites have little of that free
> social intercourse which throws open the door of
> the soul. [90]

In order to open that door, we shall have to look at the
Gospel on the plantation from the slaves' point of view. The
Gospel of the slaves was not a mirror reflection of the Gos-
pel among the slaves as preached by the Southern clergy.
Nor was the religious life of the slaves cut from the same
pattern as that of their masters and mistresses.

Chapter IV

STEAL AWAY TO JESUS

The letting out of water, or the letting in
of light, in infinitesimal quantities, is not
always easy.
                    --Frances Anne Kemble[1]

The plantation missionaries recognized that the antebellum slave was no black Adam in the Southern garden.
"The superstitions brought from Africa," Jones complained
as late as 1842, "have not been wholly laid aside." Witchcraft, alleged superstitions and fetishist practices were
often cited as evidence that the plantation Negroes refused
to abandon African paganism for American Christianity.
White Christians damned the religious heritage of the slaves
twice over. It was "heathen" and "pagan" because Africans
did not worship the God of the Judaeo-Christian tradition and
because the beliefs, ceremonies, and rituals of Africal religion were regarded as inferior, uncivilized, and unen-
lightened. [2]

Because of these white attitudes toward traditional
African culture, the plantation missionary really had two
tasks. He was dedicated to rescuing the souls of the slaves
from benighted paganism. He was also an agent in the ac-
culturation process, bent upon transforming the "savage"
African into an acceptable expression of white American civilization. The task of proselytization, Southerners felt, was
made easier by the institution of slavery. How wise of God,
David Christy exulted, "that the barbarian was brought to the
Christian instead of the Christian going to the barbarian."
Slavery would be justified, Edward Pollard claimed, "if nothing else was accomplished in taking the African from the
gloom and tangles of his forests, and from savage suffering
and savage despair" than his conversion to Christ. [3]

Acculturation and Conversion

By nineteenth-century standards, the Africans were "a wretched stock of heathen, in utter darkness of a loathsome pagan idolatry."[4] Yet there is a folk saying among the Ashanti that "No one shows a child the Supreme Being." Although the African's world was populated by a plurality of powers, including the forces of nature, lesser magical spirits, and the tribal ancestors, most tribes believed in a Supreme Being who was viewed as creator, giver of rain and sunshine, the all-seeing, the one who exists by himself, and the like. In traditional Africa there was no distinction between the sacred and the secular. The Africans were already a religious people long before their contact with white civilization.[5]

The African beliefs in one Supreme Being, in a realistic distinction between good and evil, in lesser spiritual powers, and in creation as the handiwork of God, paralleled much in the Hebraic background of Christianity. These similarities lessened the cultural shock as the African came into contact with the tenets of white Evangelicalism.[6] On occasion there was conflict. A Methodist missionary reported that an aged Negro, to whom he had been trying to explain the dogma of the Trinity, once asked which of the three "was the head man to which he should go when asking for anything."[7]

The debate over the extent and persistence of Africanisms in the religious life of the American Negro has been a lively one.[8] Linguists, folklorists, cultural anthropologists, and specialists in the history of music, art, and dance have been interested in the question. There seems to be a consensus that African cultural forms were not as overwhelmed by the slavery experience as was formerly believed. But the evidence is mixed and the conclusions tentative.[9] There is, therefore, little to be gained by trying to determine whether a particular religious phenomenon is an Africanism, a direct borrowing from white religion, or a free creation of the slaves themselves. Many of the slaves' beliefs were the result of a free exchange between African and Anglo-Saxon cultures.[10] Religious institutions among the slaves, as George Rawick suggests, were not "specifically African." But African religious behavior was not totally effaced, as is clear from an examination of Negro music, dance, and folk practices.[11] And, as will become evident, the religion of the slaves was something more than conventional white Evangelicalism.

Those slaves who were born and reared within the
tribal culture, such as Gustavus Vassa, no doubt remembered
well their native religion.[12] But the second and third generation of slaves, who were born on the plantation, had no
memories of Africa, except through stories told by the native-
born Africans. For those slaves, Christianity was not grafted
onto the living tree of African religion. They were not
Christians in name only. Instead, the American-born slaves
incorporated into their Christianity certain beliefs and practices which paralleled those of the traditional tribal cults.

The slaves' love of Baptism by immersion is a good
example of the interaction between their African heritage and
Christianity. When Frederick Olmsted toured the slave
states he was told that most of the Negroes "ain't content
to be just titch'd with water; they must be ducked in all
over." Even the Negroes who joined the Methodists wanted
to be "ducked."[13] Perhaps the slaves liked being immersed
because they understood the symbolism of drowning the Old
Adam and rising again to a new Christian life. But it may
also be, as Melville J. Herskovitts has suggested, that the
slaves were attracted to the immersion ceremonies of the
Baptists because of the importance of flowing waters to the
river cults of Africa.[14]

Antebellum Christians felt that to be properly converted they must have a dramatic conviction of sin and be
"born again." The slaves, too, told how they were seized
by the Spirit, struck dead, as it were, and then raised to
a new life. Conversion could take place in a field, in the
woods, at a camp meeting, in the slave quarters, or at a
service conducted by the blacks themselves. John Jasper, *
a famous Negro preacher in Richmond, was converted while
at work as a stemmer in a tobacco factory. He recalled
that when "de light broke; I was light as a feather; my feet
was on de mount'n; salvation rol'd like a flood thru my soul,
an' I felt as if I could 'nock off de fact'ry roof wid my
shouts."[15]

Before this event Jasper had felt as if he were in the
pit of despair and his sins were as large as mountains. This
seems to have been a common feeling of the slaves before
conversion. But after their confrontation with the Spirit, the
slaves testified that they felt like new men and women. A
Negro revivalist preacher, by the name of Pompey, is said
to have been so amazed at the change that came over him
that he doubted that he was the same person. Then "he looked

at his hands and felt of his wool, and found that it was Pompey's skin and Pompey's wool but it was Pompey with a new heart."[16]

Conversion to Christianity gave the slaves a fixed point in a world filled with uncertainty, contradiction, and crisis. Conversion involved the discovery by the slaves that God was not remote and unconcerned but at their side in all the sufferings of daily life. Josiah Henson recalled how he was "transported with delicious joy" upon hearing a sermon on a text from Hebrews which told of Christ having tasted death "for every man." "O the blessedness and sweetness of feeling that I was LOVED," he exclaimed. This was in sharp contrast to the brutality that he daily experienced from his earthly master. For John Thompson, too, the conversion experience was God's "spiritual answer of approval." He recalled how while seeking divine protection before attempting to escape, "a voice like thunder" entered his soul, telling him "though wicked men hunt you, trust in me, for I am the Rock of your Defense."[17]

Whites were often critical of the slaves' professions of conversions. Charles T. Raymond, a Northern reporter, was amused by the account of a Negro youth who related how he "went to hebben, and dere I see de Lord Jesus, a sittin' behind de door an' a reading his Bible." And he was thoroughly mystified by the actions of an aged female slave who achieved religious ecstasy by throwing water on herself.[18] The plantation missionaries were also suspicious of the dreams and visions which the slaves related. Jones felt that the Negro converts were simply following a pattern of behavior which had been handed down for generations, or which had begun in the wild fancy of some religious teacher among them.[19] To be sure, excited states of feeling with visions and voices were often found in the white campmeetings and revivals. However, certain features of the conversion stories related by the slaves may have reflected their African background. Frequent references to a "little man" as the emissary of God have an African flavor.[20]

The life of a slave was sometimes made more miserable because he or she professed to be a Christian or sought to practice religion. An ex-slave from Virginia recalled how some Southerners would rather have the Negro fiddling and dancing than praying and preaching. A slave who wished to be baptized needed his master's permission and might be whipped if he failed to obtain it. Irony of ironies, a group of Methodist rowdies once stole Henry Bibb's church ticket, watch, knife, Bible, and 14 dollars while he was on his way to worship services. [21]

The planters violated the Christian principles of pious slaves by forcing them to work on the Sabbath and by encouraging them in the old vices. John Thompson's owner purchased a slave who could fiddle with the express purpose of enticing the others away from the Methodists by "worldly pleasures." During the Christmas holidays or at harvest time, when it was the custom of some masters to give their slaves liquor, the slave who wished to abstain because of religious scruples might be forced to sin against his conscience. In an atmosphere of fear and licentiousness, the pious female slave had great pressures put upon her to violate her Christian principles. All in all, chattel slavery was an extremely hostile environment in which to conform to the Evangelical standard of piety. For as a fugitive slave in Canada told the journalist Benjamin Drew, "a slave cannot pray right when, while on his knees, he hears his master, 'here John'--and he must leave his God and go to his master." [22]

Slave Piety vs. Slaveholding Piety

On the Georgia plantation where Frances Anne Kemble resided in the late 1830s, a slave was accused of stealing a ham. Mrs. Kemble pleaded "that the ignorance of these poor people ought to screen them from punishment." The master replied that as his slaves had had religious instruction, "they knew well enough what was right and wrong." He, according to Mrs. Kemble, was not a supporter of the plantation missions. [23] Christian morality seems to have been viewed by certain masters as good for their slaves but not for themselves. Harriet [Brent] Jacobs told the story of a slaveholder by the name of Litch who had a very peculiar notion of what "Thou shalt not steal" meant:

> On his own plantation, he required very strict obedience to the eighth commandment. But depredations on the neighbors were allowable, provided the culprit managed to evade detection or suspicion. If a neighbor brought a charge of theft against any of his slaves, he was browbeaten by the master, who assured him that his slaves had enough of everything at home, and had no inducement to steal. No

sooner was the neighbor's back turned, than the
accused was sought out, and whipped for his lack
of discretion. [24]

Sometimes the slaves were made to kill the pigs and chickens
or run off the cattle of a neighboring plantation and then,
after the sheriff had departed, stay up all night preparing the
stolen goods for their own master's larder. [25]

The Rev. John Dixon Long honestly admitted his frustration in preaching to the slaves. They could not but be
suspicious of the Christian Gospel, he felt, when they daily
observed whites who were assumably Christian violating its
basic tenets. Long was not surprised that many of the slaves
became "secret infidels." He wrote:

They hear ministers denouncing them for stealing
the white man's grain; but as they never hear the
white man denounced for holding them in bondage,
pocketing their wages, or for selling their wives
and children to the brutal traders of the far South,
they naturally suspect the Gospel to be a cheat,
and believe the preachers and the slaveholder in a
conspiracy against them. [26]

Black criticism of the hyprocrisy of Southern white religion
is a prominent theme in the slave narratives. [27] The slaves
were able to judge inconsistency of conduct by holding up the
performance of their masters and mistresses against the
mirror of common humanity and the Christian Gospel. They
especially condemned the whites who prayed with them on
Sunday but beat them on Monday. Jermain W. Loguen* went
so far as to contrast the hyprocrisy of white religion with
the religion of the Indians, whose deeds, he felt, did not
belie their creeds. [28]

The slaves were also critical of the kind of preaching
which was obviously motivated by a desire to keep them in
their place rather than offer them the freedom of the Gospel.
Daniel Alexander Payne* told a convention of abolitionist-
minded Lutherans in 1839 that he had often seen Negroes in
the South scoff at the slave-holding white clergy while they
were preaching, saying "you had better go home, and set
your slaves free." And he had often witnessed house servants
sneering and laughing among themselves when summoned to
family prayers by their mistress. For they knew that she
would only read, "Servants obey your masters," but she would

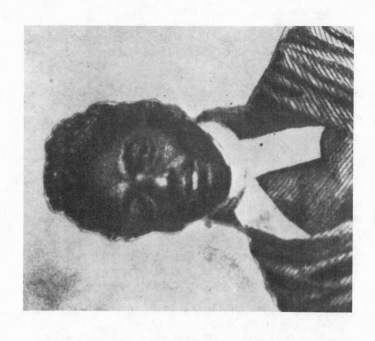

Left: John Jasper (1812–1901), "the sun do move" preacher; right: the Rev. James W. C. Pennington (1809–1870), "the fugitive blacksmith."

not read, "break every yoke and let the oppressed go free."[29]
The aversion to family prayers, the Rev. J. D. Paxton reported after having spent forty years in the South and having
been a slaveholder himself, was "so common as to be the
subject of frequent remark."[30]

Frederick Douglass testified that although "many good,
religious colored people" in the South believed that God required them to submit humbly to slavery, they seldom had
confidence in the piety of their masters. Of the slaveholder
whose actions were inconsistent with his Christian profession,
the slaves said: "He can't go to heaven with blood on his
skirts."[31] As Louis Hughes wrote, the slaves were able to
distinguish between "the truths of the 'Word' and the professed practice of those truths by their masters."[32] There
is even a self-congratulatory note in some of the slave narratives, a feeling that the slaves practiced true religion and
were closer to God than most whites.

It was slaveholding piety and not Christianity itself
which was offensive to Frederick Douglass and other dis-
cerning blacks. They knew full well the meaning of the
spiritual which says "Old Satan's church is here below; Up
to God's free church I hope to go." Douglass described
slaveholding piety as "a cold and flinty-hearted thing, having
neither principles of right action nor bowels of compassion."
But Christianity, rightly understood, was to his mind "pure,
peaceable, gentle, easy to be entreated, full of good fruits,
and without hyprocrisy."[33] When William Craft's supposedly
Christian master sold his aged parents because they were no
longer an economic asset to him, Craft felt "a thorough
hatred, not for Christianity, but for slaveholding piety."[34]
Without the ability to make this distinction, many slaves
would certainly have abandoned Christianity altogether.

The slaves, it must be said, were not blind to the
existence of pious white Christians who did the best they
could to live up to the demands of their faith. William
Wells Brown said of his master: "For his Christian zeal,
I had the greatest respect, for I always regarded him as a
truly pious and conscientious man...." Solomon Northup
had a master of whom he wrote: "It is but simple justice
to him when I say, in my opinion, there never was a more
kind, noble, candid, Christian man than William Ford."
Ford's moral blindness to the inherent wickedness of slavery
was, Northup felt, due to "the influences and associations
that had always surrounded him." Several of the slaves of

the Rev. Charles C. Jones defended the "honor of their
master and his labors for the good of the colored people"
against Yankee marauders who swore that he had preached
"damned lies" and was a "damned infernal villain."[35]

The slaves seemed to have developed a deep feeling
of gratitude toward those plantation missionaries who, like
Jones, braved the rigors of climate and travel to minister
to them. A Methodist missionary, taken ill by what was
described as a "hemorrhage of the lungs," was deeply moved
by the kindnesses shown to him by the slaves who visited his
bedside after their labors were completed. Henry C. Bruce,
the older brother of the famous Senator Blanche K. Bruce,
recalled how the Negro congregation of one Methodist preacher collected 45 dollars for a new suit for him to wear to a
conference meeting and signed a petition that he be reas-
signed to them. Perhaps the best example of the kind of
bond which occasionally developed between the slaves and a
missionary is a phenomenon reported by the Rev. J. F. W.
Toland, who was active in Mississippi just before the Civil
War. The first year of mission work, he wrote, the blacks
would say in seeing him coming, "'Yonder comes the
preacher;' the second year, 'our preacher;' and the third,
'my preacher'."[36]

Christian Slaves and Situation Ethics

In order to survive, in order to keep body and soul
together, the slaves often had to resort to behavior which
was, by a strict accounting, in violation of the customary
standard of Christian morality. Theft and deception, for
example, were violations of not only the police law of the
South but also, in the eyes of the planters, of the ethics
of Christianity. Some slave-traders actually asked more for
Christian slaves because it was assumed that they would be
more faithful and trustworthy.[37] The truth of the matter
was that many slaves were able to justify theft and deception
by an appeal to a higher morality than that prescribed for
them by slaveholding piety.

William Wells Brown readily admitted that slavery
"had the effect of brightening the mental powers of the negro."
He reported that when the slaves could get advantage of their
owners through deception or trickery they felt that they had
a perfect right in doing so.[38] At times deception was a
means of avoiding punishment or of keeping the slave's true

feelings hidden when to express them would be to invite
trouble. At other times deception was a technique to win
certain favors from the slave's master.

When James W. C. Pennington* was captured during
an escape attempt, he manufactured a story about having
been with a slave coffle, bound for Georgia, which contracted
smallpox. Upon hearing this, Pennington's captors dispersed,
leaving him the the hands of a white youth. By tricking the
boy into getting him a glass of water, Pennington was able
to run off. The portion in Pennington's autobiography which
recounts this incident is entitled, "Great Moral Dilemma."
Pennington's parents had taught him that "truth may be
blamed but cannot be ashamed." Yet in this instance telling
the truth would have brought about physical punishment and
perhaps eventual sale to the deep South. Pennington finally
decided that the facts in this case were his private property
and that his captors had no more right to them than a high-
way robber had to his purse. His freedom was worth infinitely more to him than telling the truth in this instance. [39]

The slaves often resorted to petty theft as a means of
supplementing their meager diet, obtaining a certain small
luxury, or, simply to harass their masters. Lewis Clarke
reported that the slaves considered it a crime to steal from
a non-slaveholder but felt justified in appropriating the
property of those who claimed property in men. Such was
the case with an old slave whom Charles Raymond suspected
of rifling the corncrib "to supply his own exhausted exche-
quer." Although this Negro was as "punctilious as a Phari-
see" in his Sabbath observance he felt no qualms about taking
the corn. He told Raymond: "Nigger take wat nigger
raises."[40]

Both Frederick Douglass and Booker T. Washington
justified theft by the slaves on the grounds that slavery had
its own code of ethics. Douglass' reasoning was that in
order to satisfy "the pitiless pinchings of hunger" he was
simply taking what was rightfully due him to enable him to
labor for his master. It was simply a matter of removing
his master's meat "out of one tub and putting it in another;
the ownership of the meat was not affected by the trans-
action. At first he owned it in the tub, and last he owned
it in me." Washington's pious mother was compelled to
steal eggs at night to feed her family. "Perhaps, by some
code of ethics," Washington wrote, "this would be classed
as stealing, but deep down in my heart I can never decide

that my mother, under such circumstances, was guilty of theft."[41]

These examples make one point clear--the slaves worked out a contextual ethic in the demands of day-to-day living. They were not willing to be duped by a sham Christian piety which was mandatory for slaves but not for masters. "When a man has his wages stolen from him year after year," Harriet [Brent] Jacobs wrote, "and the laws sanction and enforce the theft, how can he be expected to have more regard to honesty than has the man who robs him?"[42] We would be in error, however, if we assumed that when the Christian slave had to resort to theft or deception, he did so without a sense of the moral issues involved.

Slavery was brutalizing in its effect on black men and women but it could not destroy the Christian slave's basic sense of right and wrong. Even though Pennington felt he had been justified in tricking his captors, he could not, in later life, think back on that incident except with "intense horror at a system which can put a man not only in peril of liberty, limb, and life itself, but which may even send him in haste to the bar of God with a lie upon his lips." Lewis Clarke claimed that slaves did not think it right for one to steal from another. A slave who stole from a fellow slave was called "mean as master" or "just as mean as white folks." Josiah Henson discovered that there were situations to which a situational ethic could not be applied. He once shrank back from murdering his sleeping master. He recognized that,

> ... it was better to die a Christian death, and to
> have a quiet conscience, than to live with the in-
> cessant recollection of a crime that would destroy
> the value of life, and under the weight of a secret
> that would crush out the satisfaction that might be
> expected from freedom and every other blessing.[43]

The complaint made by whites that the slaves had no understanding of the Christian ethic clearly cannot be sustained. Southerners were judging the slaves according to a standard of piety which protected the interests of the master but denied justice and mercy for the slave. The slaves acted according to a standard of piety which was based on principles of the true Gospel as they understood it. When the two standards came into conflict, the slave appealed to the higher law. The situational ethic enabled the slave to act in his own best interests when the necessity to survive so warranted it.

Black Preachers and the South

At camp meetings, an ex-slave recalled, "mostly we had white preachers, but when we had a black preacher that was heaven."[44] There were many kinds of black preachers in the South. Some were directly under the supervision of the white churches and were known as exhorters, deacons, or watchmen. As early as 1800 the Methodists licensed certain Negroes as local preachers and gave them "all the privileges which are usual to others in the district and quarterly conferences, where the usages of the country do not forbid it." Southern Baptists freely ordained blacks as clergymen until about 1830, when the slaveholding states began to restrict all preaching by Negroes.[45] Most of the slave preachers, however, were self-ordained, the only prerequisite being a kind of self-authenticated "call" from God. Black preachers, regardless of their status with the dominant society, were easily the most important figures in the religious life of the slaves.

Contemporary evidence indicates that the black preacher was often both despised and feared by white Southerners. Olmsted discovered that the bad character of slave preachers was a frequent subject of general conversation. The manager of a large plantation in Mississippi told him such preachers merely used "their religion as a cloak for habits of special depravity" and that they were "the most deceitful and dishonest slaves on the plantation." An Episcopalian bishop from Minnesota was informed by a Florida planter that "many times these black preachers are great rascals." Slave preachers were sometimes beaten and imprisoned. Dr. C. G. Parsons reported that one slave was gagged with a piece of iron because he had stolen off into the woods at night to preach.[46]

Proponents of plantation missions had stressed at the beginning of their work that proper religious education of the slaves would do much towards lessening the influence of "ignorant spiritual guides" among them. Dr. John Holt Rice complained:

> The preachers among them, although extremely ignorant, (often unable to read a verse in the Bible or a line in their Hymn book) are frequently shrewd, cunning men. They see what influence religious feeling gives them over their brethren and they take advantage of it. This thing is growing in the Southern country.[47]

Charles C. Pinckney urged planters to support the missions
among the slaves because they would offset the influence of
those black preachers over whom the owners had little control and who possessed powers of which "they have been
known to make an improper use."[48] Some church leaders
took the position that the system of Negro preaching was "a
mischievous burlesque upon Christianity" and should be
abolished altogether.[49]

In direct contrast to these disparaging and antagonistic
remarks, we find other evidence that blacks were definitely
encouraged to become preachers among the slaves. After
relating his conversion experience to his master, a slave by
the name of Morte was told: "Morte, I believe you are a
preacher. From now on you can preach to the people here
on my place in the old shed by the creek." Another ex-slave
recalled that on one occasion the white missionary was unable
to come to the plantation. Three of the slaves were called
to fill in for him.[50] The Rev. Holland M'Tyeire urged
planters to make good use of those slaves who could read
and write as religious leaders and preachers. And Jones
stated that even if it were possible for the South to exclude
blacks "called of God" from the ministry of the Gospel, he
doubted whether it had the right. He realized that black
preachers would "become leaders in fact, whether they are
made leaders by an official act of the societies in which they
move or not."[51]

Disagreement over the significance of the black preacher on the plantation has continued down to the present. One
party argues that the slave preacher was so entirely under
the domination of whites that he was a traitor to his own
race. He preached obedience to the master and resignation
to perpetual bondage.[52] Others have suggested that the slave
preacher was more like a Denmark Vesey or a Nat Turner
than the Uncle Tom stereotype.[53] Miles Mark Fisher and
W. E. B. Du Bois placed the slave preacher in the role of
the African priest, as leader of a traditional religious cult.[54]

The confusion concerning antebellum black preachers
has been due to a failure to distinguish between the several
kinds of roles which they filled. It is an error to assume,
as some writers have, that the Negro Christian minister
simply "evolved" from the African priest.[55] There was no
straight line evolution from priest to minister, but rather a
development of at least four kinds of religious leaders among
Southern Negroes. We can perhaps best distinguish them as

(1) ministers, (2) exhorters, (3) self-appointed preachers, and (4) cult leaders.

Harry Hosier, Henry Evans and Lott Carey are good examples of Negro ministers. They were principally active in the period when Evangelical Protestantism was still seeking to win the South. Harry Hosier, known to his contemporaries as Black Harry, labored alongside some of the greatest names in early Methodism--Coke, Asbury, Garretson, and Whatcoat. An effective speaker, he was once mistaken for Bishop Francis Asbury by an auditor who could hear Hosier's preaching but could not see him due to a large crowd. The Rev. William Capers knew Henry Evans personally. He described him as the "father of the Methodist Church, white and black" in Fayetteville, North Carolina, and "the best preacher of his time in that quarter ... the greatest curiosity of the town." Lott Carey, a slave born in Virginia, was a famous Baptist preacher who eventually went to Liberia and helped develop a Christian missionary field. [56]

These three individuals, representative of our first group of black preachers, were officially recognized as capable and productive sowers of the Gospel by their respective denominations. They accompanied white clergy and also preached to mixed audiences. Whites so crowded around the pulpit of Henry Evans, for example, that his slave auditors were forced to move to two sheds which were built to hold the overflow. We are told that Caesar Blackwell "traveled alone, and though he was black as a crow, was listened to with the utmost respect by the whites, to whom he frequently preached." In 1828 the Alabama Association of Baptists paid for his freedom so that he could preach where he liked and it would not be "deprived of the labors of our much esteemed brother."[57]

On the whole, it seems, the first class of black preachers was well received by Southern Christians. David Benedict, the pioneer Baptist historian, once visited a fellow clergyman in Virginia who had among his slaves a preacher. This individual, Benedict discovered, was "a sensible man and a very acceptable preacher." He had a wife and family, "all comfortable and happy," a good horse, money at interest, and was invited to preach abroad more often than his master. Of Jesse Peter, another black preacher, Benedict said that he was "no novice in mysteries of the kingdom."[58] In 1835 Gertrude Thomas of Georgia had

the opportunity to hear Sam Johnson preach. She said of
him: "He is one of the most intellectual Negroes I have
ever met with and has a decidedly fine command of language."[59]

Circumstances changed with the insurrection of Nat
Turner and the outbreak of the abolitionist controversy. Although no uniform code existed throughout the South, most
slave states passed laws which prohibited blacks, both slave
and free, from preaching or controlled the manner in which
they were licensed. In Georgia, for example, a Negro who
wanted to be able to preach had to obtain a license from a
local court and be certified by three ordained white clergymen. An Alabama law of 1832 required that five "respectable slaveholders" attend any services at which blacks
preached.[60] These laws had the effect of thinning the ranks
of the first class of black preachers. They also caused the
Southern churches and, in particular, the plantation missionaries, to resort to exhorters, deacons, and watchmen.

The second kind of black preacher was usually not
ordained nor able to exercise all the privileges of the ministerial office. These preachers could not, for example, exercise the franchise in associational meetings nor, if they were
exhorters, choose a text to preach on. On the plantations
the white missionary was considered the "boss preacher."
The black exhorter was his assistant. Jones wrote that the
black deacon or exhorter was to

> assist members in their Christian walk, by warn-
> ings, reproofs, and exhortations of a private na-
> ture; heal breaches; report cases of delinquency to
> the church; see that the children are taught their
> prayers, and that people attend worship; visit the
> sick and bury the dead.[61]

The Rev. J. F. W. Toland was highly pleased with the
assistance that two slave exhorters, named Billy and Emmanuel, gave him. The former was a natural orator and
seems to have been effective in helping Toland maintain enthusiasm at protracted meetings. The latter "always concluded his exhortations to his people by urging them to pay
attention to and profit by the teachings of the missionary."[62]

Supervision by the white clergy was sometimes quite
nominal. A Methodist circuit rider in Mississippi reported
that when the slaves gathered to transact religious business,

The black exhorter at plantation worship, Port Royal, South Carolina

the white clergyman served as chairman of the meeting, but the real power was in the hands of the Negro who had been chosen as "secretary." This individual sat "as the presiding judge of their church trials" and was "the umpire to whom is referred not only the minor difficulties of the church members, but of the colored people at large."[63]

Henry Clay Bruce stated that, as a class, the black exhorters had no education at all "but had a fair amount of brain, good memories, were fluent talkers, and considered pious and truthful."[64] Masters were wary of having any slave chosen as an exhorter who could not be trusted. In some cases it seems that the planters exploited the vanity of the black exhorter by giving him special privileges. An ex-slave from Florida recalled:

> The Pamell slaves had a Negro minister who could hold services any time he chose, so long as he did not interfere with the work of the other slaves. He was not obliged to do hard menial labors and went

about the plantation "all dressed up" in a frock
coat and store-bought shoes. He was more than
a little conscious of this and was held in awe by
the others. [65]

James Lindsay Smith, another black exhorter, said of himself: "I was very proud and loved to dress well, and all
the young people used to make a great time over me...."
He was allowed to possess a fine suit, a watch and chain,
and even his own seal. [66] These special privileges, of
course, lasted only so long as the black exhorter behaved
himself.

Some of these black exhorters seem to have been
traitors to their own people. During the Civil War one by
the name of Bob Cooper was put up to enticing the slaves
into the woods, ostensibly for preaching, so that the slaves
could be captured and forced to serve in the Confererate
Army. An ex-slave told Ophelia Settle Egypt: "We had
some nigger preachers but they would say, 'Obey your mistress and master.' They didn't know nothing else to say."
On the plantation where Louis Hughes lived, there was a
black exhorter whose essential message to the slaves was
that of a patient submission as good soldiers of the cross.[67]

The black exhorter was confronted by a very ticklish
dilemma. If he preached the whole truth of the Gospel, as
he understood it, he would be silenced. His license would
be revoked and he faced the possibility of physical violence.
The Rev. John Dixon Long wrote:

If a colored preacher or intelligent free Negro
gains the ill-will of a malicious slave, all the
latter has to do is to report that said preacher
had attempted to persuade him to 'rise,' or to
run away; and the poor fellow's life may pay the
forfeit. [68]

Yet if the exhorter was honest with himself, he knew that
there was another gospel than the one the masters liked to
hear. That was the gospel of freedom. One ex-slave told
the interviewer from the Federal Writers' Project that when
he first began preaching he had to say what his master
wanted him to, that is, to "tell them niggers iffen they obeys
the master they goes to Heaven." But he knew that there
was something better for the slaves, which he preached to
them on the sly. He recalled: "I tells 'em iffen they keeps

praying, the Lord will set 'em free."[69] Occasionally the truth slipped out even when white observers were present. At the close of his sermon, one black exhorter got carried away and exclaimed: "Free indeed, free from hell, free from work, from the white folks, free from everything."[70]

The most radical black preachers were unconcerned about conforming to the expectations of white society. God, they felt, had called them and no one but God himself could revoke that call. These self-appointed preachers were a continual threat to the police order of the South. An Episcopalian rector complained in 1834 that these preachers had an influence on the slaves that was "almost incredible" and were a threat "to the order and happiness of the community."[71] A Presbyterian missionary warned that once these preachers, with their "chimeras of diseased fancy," had fanned the flame of blind enthusiasm among the slaves it would be difficult to put out. They were formidable rivals for even the most dedicated missionary.[72]

The best example of this third kind of preacher is the famous Nat Turner. No church authorized him to preach. He felt that his call to deliver his people from slavery had come directly from God. He put together a message of religion and resistance that struck a responsive chord in his fellow slaves.[73] The insurrection of 1831 caused the South to blame all Negro preachers for discontent among the slaves. Governor Floyd told the Virginia State Legislature that "the most active incendiaries among us, in stirring up the spirit of revolt, have been the negro preachers."[74] He complained that the South had been too indulgent in allowing slaves to gather together for religious worship when their real purpose, he felt, was to incite rebellion.

The last classification of religious leader among the slaves is the cult leader. The voodoo cult was practiced especially in those areas where the slaves were most concentrated or most influenced by recent arrivals from the West Indies. The slave who knew the secrets of voodooism was called a Hoodoo man or a conjure man.[75] The missionaries and Christian churches frowned upon these individuals. "Jack, a black man belonging to James Nettles" was expelled from the Hephzibah Baptist Church in Louisiana for "pretenting to witchcraft." Jones contended that only through a plain and faithful presentation of the Gospel could the superstitions of the slaves be weakened. He had discovered that a conjurer often had such a strong hold over the slaves "that they have not dared to disobey him in the least particular; nor to disclose their own intended or perpetrated crimes, in view of inevitable death itself. "[76]

Conjuration and voodooism were not indigenous to the slaves in the South but can be traced back to certain African practices.[77] A black sorcerer who conspired with Denmark Vesey in 1822 was a native-born Angolan. Gullah Jack brought to America practices which he had known in Africa. We cannot know how many Gullah Jacks there were, but surely the testimony of many slaves that voodooism and conjuration were widespread indicates that even for those not born in Africa the old ways had considerable attraction. It is difficult to distinguish between what was mere folk superstition among the slaves and what belonged to the secret rites of the voodoo cult. There seems to have been a free exchange of the superstitions common to a folk society with those that belonged to the traditional voodoo cult.[78]

William Wells Brown knew a Hoodoo man by the name of Dinkie. This slave was a full-blooded African of whom the other slaves were in mortal fear. He wore a snake skin around his neck and carried a petrified frog in one pocket and a dried lizard in the other. Dinkie did not work but told fortunes and practiced voodooism and something Brown called "goopherism." Whites "throughout the neighborhood," we are told, "tipped their hats to the old one-eyed negro, while the policemen, or patrollers, permitted him to pass without challenge." Surely Brown was correct in concluding that "this man was his own master." An ex-slave said of another conjure man: "Old Bab Russ was coal black, and he could talk African or some other unknown tongue, and all the young bucks and wenches was mortal 'fraid of him."[79]

The downfall of the conjure or Hoodoo men came when the slaves followed their directions and discovered that their magic had no power. Frederick Douglass, Henry Bibb, and Louis Hughes found out the hard way that herbs, roots, and mysterious potions were no match for the slavebreaker's rawhide. All learned that the whippings came just the same, whether they followed the advice of the practitioners of voodooism or not.[80] One ex-slave summarized this skepticism born of experience: "They had in those days a Hoodoo nigger who could hoodoo niggers but couldn't hoodoo masters. He couldn't make ole master stop whipping him with the hoodooism."[81]

Christian conversion gave some slaves an additional reason for being suspicious of folk superstitions. Louis Hughes condemned the use of voodoo bags as "one of the superstitions of our barbarous ancestry."[82] An ex-slave from North Carolina recalled: "We all knowed about the Word and the unseen Son of God and we didn't put no stock in conjure." Martha Colquitt's pious grandmother and mother had told her that "voodoo was a no 'count doin' of de devil, and Christians was never to pay it no attention." "Us was to be happy in de Lord," she was taught, "and let voodoo and de devil alone."[83]

Group religious activity, not conjuration, seems to have provided many slaves with a more effective means of relief from the day-to-day oppression of plantation life. They often stole off and gathered for "a real meetin' with some real preachin'." Ex-slaves reported that some of the best times they had were when they could shout and sing without the intimidating presence of whites. The slaves looked forward to those times when at a camp meeting or in the "hush-arbor" they could worship God as they pleased and encourage one another to keep a stout heart.[84]

"Hush-arbor" Religion

Religious assemblies composed exclusively of slaves were in flagrant violation of the police regulations of the "peculiar institution." Some masters would sneak among the quarters late at night to spy on the slaves as they were engaged in praying or in corporate worship. Anthony Burns reported that despite all precautions at secrecy, black worshippers were often forced to disperse in pandemonium when the door burst open and in came the patrol, "a throng of profane officials, each with cord in hand, bent on securing as many victims as possible."[85] Whites complained that Negroes met for religious purposes at ungodly hours so that their noise disrupted the night's peace and quiet. Missionaries generally discouraged midnight meetings among the slaves. Masters distrusted any unusual assemblages of the slaves because they were a threat to discipline and plantation efficiency.[86]

Still the slaves persisted. Richard Carruthers, an aged ex-slave who was interviewed during the Federal Writers' Project, told of how between 11 and 12 o'clock the slaves would come in from the fields, "scorchin' and burnin'

up with nothing to eat, " and still want to go down into a
hollow, where they had "a prayin' ground, " in order to ask
the Lord for mercy. [87] Sometimes a song would be sung
which was a signal that all should sneak away. Many ex-
slaves reported that it was a common practice to take a
large kettle or pot and turn it upside down to keep the sounds
of the meeting from reaching white ears. [88] Light was given
by igniting pine torches or grease put into a pan or a bottle.

Peter Randolph reported that in order to mark the
way to the place of worship the leaders would break branches
as signs for others to follow. After reaching the selected
spot, the slaves, according to Randolph,

> first ask each other how they feel, the state of
> their minds, etc. The male members then select
> a certain space, in separate groups, of their di-
> vision of the meeting. Preaching in order, by the
> brethern; then praying and singing all round, until
> they generally feel quite happy. The speaker usu-
> ally commences by calling himself unworthy, and
> talks very slowly, until, feeling the spirit, he
> grows excited, and in a short time, there fall to
> the ground twenty or thirty men and women under
> its influence. [89]

Another description of worship among the slaves was given
by James Lindsay Smith, a shoemaker in Virginia. An exhorter, he was allowed to conduct services on Saturday
nights and Sunday mornings. He recalled:

> The way in which we worshipped is almost indes-
> cribable. The singing was accompanied by a cer-
> tain ecstasy of motion, clapping of hands, tossing
> of heads, which would continue without cessation
> about half an hour; one would lead off in a kind of
> recitative style, others joining in the chorus. The
> ole house partook of the ecstasy; it rang with their
> jubilant shouts, and shook in all its joints. [90]

In these two passages we have the essential features of worship as conducted by the slaves--religious ecstasy and group
interaction.

Louis Hughes reported that many of those who preached
at the Negro prayer-meetings did not know a letter of the
Bible or even how to spell the name of Christ. "But, " he

claimed, "when they opened their mouths they were filled, and the plan of Salvation was explained in a way that all could receive it. " If nothing else, the exhorter could tell about his own conversion experience, about how in times of trouble and stress God had comforted him. The preaching was vivid and literal, with frequent references made to the fires of hell and what the sinner had to do to avoid them. As the speaker's enthusiasm spread to the other slaves, they too forgot their sufferings and trials and sought to catch hold of the Spirit. When the preacher was exhausted, Louis Hughes tells us, "their very countenances showed that their souls had been refreshed and that it had been 'good for them to be there. '"91

Some whites were highly critical of the emotional shouting, clapping, and singing which were typical of the slaves' manner of worship. The owner of a large rice plantation complained to Frederick Olmsted that his slaves had petitioned him to remove the back-rails of the seats in the small chapel which was provided for them. The slaves had said that the rails did not leave them enough "room to pray. " The planter explained to Olmsted that it was the custom of the slaves "to work themselves up to a great pitch of excitement, in which they yell and cry aloud, and finally, shriek and leap up, clapping their hands and dancing, as is done at heathen festivals. "92 Another Southerner who had witnessed a religious meeting of Negroes said that it resembled the worship of "the howling Dervishes" because of its "barbaric frenzy. "93

White revivalistic services were themselves hardly more restrained and dignified. Protracted meetings, either at a local church or at a campground in the woods, were essential to the Evangelical impulse. The slaves were, with the proper passes, allowed to attend these affairs and seem to have eagerly welcomed them as a relief from the usual routine of the plantation. The Rev. John Dixon Long reported:

> But by no class is a camp-meeting hailed with
> more unmixed delight than by the poor slaves.
> It comes at a season of the year when they most
> need rest. It gives them all the advantages of an
> ordinary holiday, without its accompaniments of
> drunkenness and profanity. Here they get to see
> their mothers, their brothers, and their sisters
> from neighboring plantations; here they can sing
> and jump to their hearts' content. 94

We are told that preachers who had the task of "getting up"
a revival actually liked to have the slaves present, for it
was a common belief that they were more easily excited
than whites. [95]

The revivals were usually mixed affairs. The blacks
were often assigned a special section to set up their own
camp, often behind the speakers' rostrum, where they could
carry on their own revival. [96] As the excitement rose the
white and black meetings might merge as one. About 1828
Frances Trollope, with her courage "screwed to the proper
pitch," ventured to a camp meeting in the backwoods of
Indiana. She found that there was one tent exclusively occupied by blacks, all colorfully dressed and having a good time.
One youth "of coal-black comeliness," she noticed, "was
preaching with the most violent gesticulations, frequently
springing high from the ground, and clapping his hands over
his head." Later, at the sound of a horn, both races assembled in front of the speakers' rostrum upon which a white
Methodist preacher was giving a vivid dramatization of how
he wrestled with his Maker. All cried, "Amen! Amen!"
"Jesus! Jesus!" "Glory! Glory!," and the like. Mrs.
Trollope's English sensibilities were much offended. She
could not endure the hysterical sobbings, convulsive groans,
screams, and Dantean-like spectre of hundreds of people
lying about the grounds, their bodies convulsed with the
"jerks."[97]

The riddle as to the origin of religious hysteria and
the other revivalistic phenomena which Mrs. Trollope observed has not been resolved. Melville J. Herskovitts made
a case for the African origin of much of what was common
to both black religion and white revivalism, chiefly in respect
to the forms of motor behavior in which the participants engaged. [98] Antebellum churchmen who, on general principles,
were suspicious of the enthusiastic form of worship chided
blacks for their love of a boisterous sort of meeting. Yet
thousands of whites engaged in similar behavior when the
"times of refreshing" came round. We lack sufficient evidence to indicate whether revivalism is purely a product of
the African heritage or of the American experience. It
should be clear that not all phenomena of a similar nature
necessarily have a common origin. My supposition is that
African modes of worship and American revivalistic patterns
were simply cultural parallelisms. When the slaves came
to the United States and encountered Americans shouting and
jumping much in the fashion of African worship, they were

drawn to those churches which sanctioned and encouraged revivalistic styles. Where else but at the camp meeting could
the slave feel free to release his pent-up emotions without
fear of recrimination at the hands of his master?

Songs of Hope and Sorrow

In his famous poem, "O Black and Unknown Bards, "
James Weldon Johnson asked, "Heart of what slave poured
out such melody as 'Steal away to Jesus'?"[99] Ever since
collectors first began to write down the hundreds of spirituals
which the slaves brought with them into freedom, there has
been a concern to answer the question posed in Johnson's
poem. In 1867 William Francis Allen, Charles Pickard Ware
and Lucy McKim Garrison published Slave Songs of the United
States. Lucy McKim (she was then unmarried) went with her
father and scores of other Northern missionaries and teachers
to work among the slaves who had been liberated by the
Union forces active in the Sea Islands region. Here she was
exposed for the first time to the slave spirituals, now freely
sung in the presence of whites. Miss McKim took down those
which she considered to be the best specimens and had them
published in the North. Eventually others became interested
in the work and before long music publishers and collectors
throughout the country were introducing the spirituals to an
eager public.[100]

Thomas Wentworth Higginson, the famous Unitarian
abolitionist, had only heard of the Negro spirituals from
white singers. Thus when the opportunity came to command
black troops during the Civil War, he was especially interested in collecting the songs which the men of the First
South Carolina Volunteers sang. On starlit evenings Colonel
Higginson would eavesdrop on his troops' "shouts, " writing
down by the light of the campfire the words to their songs.
He listened to such songs as "Hail Mary, " "My Army Cross
Over, " and "We'll Soon be Free. " But the black soldiers'
great favorite was 'Hold Your Light, " which would be sung
for half an hour at a time, each person being named in turn.
The first stanza went as follows: "Hold your light, Brudder
Robert--Hold your light, Hold your light on Canaan's shore."[101]

Higginson found the spirituals to be quaint in expression, frequently in minor key, and thoroughly religious in
tone, with an abiding theme of pathos about this world but
hope for triumph in the next. But he was puzzled as to their

origin. Some of the songs were strikingly similar to old
campmeeting melodies and European ballads; others betrayed
no influence of the Methodist or Baptist hymnbook. Hoping
to discover the source of the latter, Higginson once asked a
black oarsman how the spirituals came about. This man
replied: "Some good spirituals are start jest out o' curiosity.
I been a-raise a sing, myself, once."[102] Harriet [Brent]
Jacobs wrote: "The slaves generally compose their own
songs and hymns; and they do not trouble their heads much
about the measure." And an ex-slave told interviewers from
the Federal Writers' Project: "Us makes up songs, 'cause
us couldn't read or write."[103] The Rev. Charles C. Jones
urged that the slaves be instructed in "good psalms and
hymns" so as to induce them "to lay aside extravagant and
nonsensical chants and catches and hallelujah songs of their
own composing" [emphasis is added].[104]

Specialists in American folklore and music have not
been satisfied with the explanation that the slaves simply
"made up" the spirituals. Newman I. White and George Pullen Jackson argued that the origin of the slave songs is to be
found in the gospel hymns sung by white Methodists and Baptists at their revivals and campmeetings.[105] But Carter G.
Woodson, who was always on the lookout for Africal survivals, declared that this white-to-Negro interpretation of the
spirituals was just another example of the white American
"custom of making history to order in fiat fashion." He and
W. E. Burghardt Du Bois traced the musical expression of
the spirituals back to the shores of Africa.[106] Miles Mark
Fisher went so far as to deny that the slave songs had any
Christian content at all. He contended that they were elabo-
rately devised codes for communicating secular information
which the slaves hoped to keep from white ears.[107]

There is evidence that the slaves did indeed veil their
longing for temporal freedom behind the imagery in the spirituals. A Negro lad told Colonel Higginson that when the
blacks sang "We'll soon be free, When de Lord will call us
home," the expression "de Lord" also meant "de Yankees."
Frederick Douglass reported that when the slaves sang "O
Canaan, sweet Canaan, I am bound for the land of Canaan,"
they meant something more than reaching heaven. The North
was their Canaan.[108]

Even though I acknowledge the probability that the
spirituals often bore coded messages, I do not deny their
essential religious content. Sometimes this content was clearly

derived from the Methodist or Baptist hymnbook, with the slaves making their own adaption. In other cases the songs were simply "made up" by the slaves out of their own experience. The images and symbols were clearly Christian in nature, with a heavy emphasis on events from the Jewish experience as portrayed in the Old Testament.

The themes expressed in the spirituals, according to Benjamin E. Mays, were of a compensatory nature. The slaves sang of the hope that if they only could "keep on keeping on" a righteous Father in Heaven would deliver them from their troubles and reward them with a better life in the hereafter.[109] This emphasis, of course, was not peculiar to the spirituals. Evangelical Christianity had a strong other-worldly strain to it. White Christians too sang of trouble and sorrow as being the lot of the pilgrim here on earth and of their desire to make Heaven their home.[110]

Those who categorically state that the religion of the slaves was dysfunctional because it was escapist or other-worldly fail to account for the psychic needs of black men and women in circumstances where there was little chance for temporal change. The slaves often testified that it was the Christian Gospel which gave them the courage to stand up under the dehumanization of slavery. Francis Henderson told Benjamin Drew:

> I had recently joined the Methodist Church, and
> from the sermons I heard, I felt that God had
> made all men free and equal, and that I ought not
> be a slave, --but even then, that I ought not to be
> abused. From this time I was not punished. I
> think my master became afraid of me....[111]

Another fugitive slave said: "It was through the fear of the Lord, that I endured the persecution put upon me."[112] In the test of wills between master and slave, as John Blassin-game has written, the slave's faith in God was no abstrac-tion. The Christian bondsman took courage in the knowledge that the master might beat the body but could not destroy the soul.[113]

The Negro, as Arnold J. Toynbee has written, redis-covered during slavery the original meaning of Christianity--"that Jesus was a prophet who came into the world not to confirm the mighty in their seats but to exalt the humble and the meek."[114] The chosen people or suffering servant theme

cannot be considered either escapist or compensatory. The
Christian slaves believed that they, as Israel of old, were
called upon to bear an extra burden, to be, as Joseph R.
Washington, Jr. has suggested, "God's humanizing agents."[115]
This special mission gave the slaves a sense of superiority
over the often hypocritical piety of the slaveholder. Jacob
Stroyer felt that "God would somehow do more for the oppressed Negroes than he would ordinarily for any other
people." Because masters did not read the Scriptures the
right way, one ex-slave said, "... they don't know their
danger." The slaves believed that there would be a day of
judgment when those who had oppressed them would receive
due recompense for their evil deeds. Moses Grandy remembered how during violent thunderstorms whites hid between
their feather beds, but the slaves would go outside and,
lifting up their hands, thank God that judgment day was
coming at last.[116] At 90 years of age, Jane Simpson, an
ex-slave, recalled, "I used to hear old slaves pray and ask
God when would de bottom rail be de top rail, and I wondered what on earth dey talkin' about. Dey was talkin' about
when dey goin' to get from under bondage. 'Course I know
now."[117]

     When freedom did come, according to Mrs. A. M.
French, who accompanied her husband on the Port Royal
mission, the Freedmen were found to "have a religious experience deep in the heart, learned in the school of toil and
sorrow, which possessed great value to them." She discovered that "any lack of appreciation, or especially any
contempt manifested toward their religious opinions or feelings, will wound them very deeply."[118] Once the year of
Jubilee came, the slaves were thankful that they could put
behind them the old life of dancing, hunting, and tending the
master's pigs on Sunday. Instead, as Jacob Stroyer said,
they could "become observers of the Sabbath, of good moral
habits and men of equal rights before the law."[119]

     All in all, we must conclude, the attempt to keep the
full Gospel from the slaves was a failure. Christianity,
with its message that God is no respecter of persons, could
not, like the master's corn and hogs, be kept under lock and
key. The English actress and abolitionist, Anne Frances
Kemble, was extremely perceptive and prophetic when she
wrote (in the late 1830s) about the slaveholders' attempt to
dole out the Gospel:

          The process is a very ticklish one ... they are

putting their own throats and their own souls in jeopardy by their very endeavor to serve God and Mammon. The light that they are letting in between their fingers will presently strike them blind, and the mighty flood of truth which they are straining through a sieve to the thirsty lips of their slaves shall sweep them away like straws from their cautious moorings, and overwhelm them in its great deeps, to the waters of which man may in no wise say, thus far shall ye come and no farther![120]

Chapter V

THE NEGRO CHURCHES COME FORTH

> When the Lord shall raise up colored his-
> torians in succeeding generations, to pre-
> sent the crimes of this nation to the then
> gazing world, the Holy Ghost will make
> them do justice to the name of Bishop Allen,
> of Philadelphia.
>
> --David Walker[1]

The slaves' response to American Evangelicalism provided the impetus for the independent Negro church. When
Richard Allen* and Absalom Jones* first began the campaign
for a church of their own in Philadelphia they did so within
the context of the Evangelical movement. While still slaves,
both had been converted through Evangelical preaching.[2] In
the South, too, the story of the movement toward independence by Negro Christians must be told within the framework of the kind of Gospel which the Methodists and Baptists
were preaching. Perhaps, by strict definition, no Negro
church, some of whose members were claimed as chattel
property, can be called truly independent. But in the period
from the end of the American Revolution to around the time
of Nat Turner's insurrection, a small number of Southern
blacks did possess a surprising degree of religious freedom.
By the 1830s, however, the South had closed the door on
religious freedom and the only hope for the black church
existed with the Negro Christians north of slavery.

Negro Baptists in the South

The landmark Negro church in America was born of
the freedom and local democracy which was granted to black
Christians by the Baptists. Heirs of the early Negro Baptist
churches in the South have long disputed the honor of being

110

the first independent black church on American soil. The
best evidence points to the Silver Bluff Church located near
Augusta, Georgia.[3] Here a small group of Negroes, both
free and slave, worshipped under their own vine and fig
tree as early as the time of the American Revolution. White
Baptists extended to them the same kind of religious freedom
which they themselves were struggling for.

In the annals of heroes of Negro church history, the
name of George Liele* must rank with that of Richard Allen.
For he was the dynamic force behind the early Negro
churches in Georgia and South Carolina. Licensed as an
exhorter, Liele travelled up and down the Savannah River
by bateau preaching and interpreting the Scriptures to other
slaves. One of the places he visited was the Galpin plantation near Silver Bluff, South Carolina, a frontier settlement
12 miles from Augusta. Here he and a white itinerant
preacher by the name of Elder Palmer ministered to a
group of some thirty slaves.[4]

During the hostilities between the Colonials and the
British, the Silver Bluff Church broke up. Many of the
slaves came to Savannah seeking freedom at the hands of
the English troops. George Liele, manumitted by his Loyalist master, began to preach to the refugee slaves in and
about Savannah. Upon the death of his former master,
"killed in the king's service, by a ball which shot off his
hand," as Liele reported, there was an attempt to enslave
him once again. Liele escaped to Jamaica in 1782 with a
British colonel. At Kingston he began a small congregation
with four brethren from America.[5]

After the British had been driven out of Savannah,
Jesse Peter, one of the original members of the Silver Bluff
Church, returned to his master's plantation and revived the
ministry there. Sometime about 1793 the First African
Church of Augusta, Georgia, was constituted with Jesse
Peter as its pastor. As nothing further is known of the
Silver Bluff Church, it is probable that in the Augusta con-
gregation we have, under a new name and 12 miles distant
from its original location, the most direct tie to the oldest
independent Negro church on American soil.[6]

In Savannah the mantle of George Liele was picked
up by Andrew Bryan, * a slave who, like Liele, had first
begun preaching on his master's plantation. On the out-
skirts of Savannah, Bryan was allowed to erect a small barn

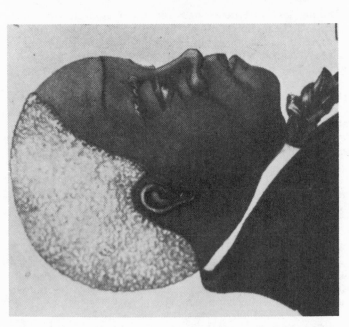

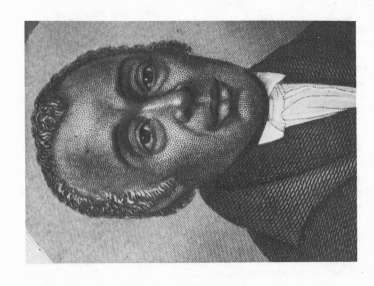

Left: the Rev. Andrew Bryan (1737-1812), organizer of Negro Baptists in Savannah; right: Bishop Richard Allen (1760-1831), founder of the A.M.E. Church.

in which to preach. The white community was hostile to
this venture because the Negroes had sought protection from
the British during the occupation. Andrew and his brother
were whipped and imprisoned. Their sympathetic master
rescued them and allowed them to resume preaching in a
barn on his plantation, but only between sunrise and sunset.
In 1788 the Rev. Abraham Marshall, a white Baptist divine,
ordained Bryan with the assistance of the Rev. Jesse Peter.
In 1794 Bryan erected a church on his own property, having
bought his freedom four years earlier. [7]

Under Bryan's capable leadership the First African
Church of Savannah grew rapidly, having nearly 700 members
by 1800. Bryan reported that members of this church enjoyed the rights of conscience, worshipped freely, witnessed
the baptism of ten to thirty new members at a time, and celebrated the Lord's Supper "not only without molestation, but
in the presence, and with the approbation and encouragement
of many of the white people." Bryan was the owner of valuable real estate and "eight slaves, for whose education and
happiness," he reported, "I am enabled thro' mercy to provide."[8]

The First African Church soon began to sponsor
daughter congregations in the Savannah region. The Ogee-
chee Church was especially designed for the plantation slaves.
Upon Bryan's death in 1812, at the age of 75, the leadership
of the First African Church passed to his nephew Andrew
Marshall. The Savannah River Association expressed its
sorrow at Bryan's passing and described his life as an "extensively useful and amazingly luminous course."[9] But we
are left to wonder about the day-to-day relationship which
the white members of the Association had with Bryan. They
refused to address him as "Brother Bryan" in public as they
had agreed to do in the Association's meetings.[10]

In addition to the Negro churches in and about Savannah in this period, there were congregations at such places
as Williamsburg and Petersburg, Virginia. For the most
part, these churches were in urban areas, with free blacks
in leadership roles.[11] Slaves could attend only if they had
the proper passes which allowed them to come in from the
plantations. This requirement, of course, restricted the
churches' independence. But if a particular congregation
was composed primarily of free Negroes, had title to its
place of worship, a black pastor, and could conduct its business affairs without harassment, it can be called "independent."

The involvement of whites increasingly reduced the freedom of the Negro churches. The Negro congregation with a white pastor was not as free as one with a black pastor. Such was the case with the First African Baptist Church of Richmond, with Dr. Robert Ryland, President of Richmond College, as its pastor. A Superintending Committee, composed of ten whites, elected the pastor, "with the concurrence of the colored Deacons." All meetings of the Negroes had to be conducted in the daytime, with at least one white supervisor and the pastor present. However, these Negro Christians had more independence than those belonging to a "colored branch" of an all-white church, where no decisions were left to blacks. And they certainly had more religious freedom than those who worshipped in an organizationally unified but socially segregated church.[12]

The Negro churches did not have an association of their own but sought admission to whatever local Baptist group would have them. Sometimes this was a long and humiliating procedure, as with a black congregation of Williamsburg and the Dover Association in Virginia.[13] Negro delegates to the associational meetings had the same privileges as their white brethren. In rare instances a black delegate might even represent a mixed congregation.[14] It was in the West, however, where frontier conditions offered Negroes more freedom, that the first all-black Baptist associations were formed.[15]

As tensions over slavery heightened, the South became alarmed at the presence of Negroes with any kind of religious independence. Even the Baptists began to revoke the special privileges which had been extended to the all-black congregations. The powers of the white-controlled Baptist associations were strengthened by the police laws which were passed in the 1820s and 1830s. Negro preachers had to be licensed by white religious authorities, and Negro churches were closely supervised. In some instances, as with the Gillfield Baptist Church of Petersburg, the Negro churches were asked to consolidate with neighboring white congregations. The church founded by Gowan Pamphlet in Williamsburg was abruptly closed down in 1831.[16] That led by Abraham Marshall in Savannah, now 2795 members strong, was divided as a result of a controversy between Marshall and the Sunbury Baptist Association.[17]

From the 1830s until the Civil War, therefore, the existence of Negro churches in the South was at the whim of

The First African Baptist Church of Savannah, established by
Andrew Bryan; photographed ca. 1880.

---

local white authorities. Any independence was strictly nominal. In order to forestall closure, the First African Baptist
Church of New Orleans invited a white minister to take
charge, included whites on its committee of supervision, and
deeded its property over to the white Baptists.[18] The nadir
of religious despotism which was reached in this period is
exemplified in the actions taken toward the Calvary Protestant
Episcopal Church for Negroes in Charleston. In order to
defuse public animosity, the Episcopalians promised that the
church would have a wide aisle separating the races, different colored benches, separate entrances for black and
white members, and 50 special seats reserved for white
supervisors. These seats were set apart and raised so that
the Negroes would keep "a sensible image of the subordina-
tion that is due those to whom, by the course of Providence,
they are to look up to as their rulers."[19]

　　　Unlike the Baptists, the Southern Methodists did not
foster the establishment of independent Negro congregations.
The only autonomous black Methodist church in the South in
the early nineteenth century was that of Morris Brown* in
Charleston, Virginia. Although he had originally joined the

Pulpit constructed and used by Richard Allen, Mother Bethel
A. M. E. Church, Philadelphia.

---

white Methodists, Brown was admitted into full connection
with the African Methodist Episcopal Church after a visit to
Bishop Richard Allen in 1818.   In 1822 Brown was forced
to flee to Charleston as a result of retaliation taken against
Negro Methodists in the wake of the abortive insurrection
led by Denmark Vesey. [20]

Bethelite and Zionite Beginnings

The African Methodists whom Morris Brown joined
were fully liberated from white control in 1816 by a decision
of the Supreme Court of the State of Pennsylvania.   Their
roots go back to the late eighteenth century when Richard
Allen and Absalom Jones were still members of St. George's
Methodist Episcopal Church in Philadelphia.   Allen had come
to Philadelphia in 1786, after having earned his freedom and
after having traveled hundreds of miles as a Methodist itinerant.   "I soon saw a large field open in seeking and instructing my African brethren, " he recalled many years
later, "who had been a long forgotten people and few of them
attended public worship. "[21]

According to Benjamin Rush, Philadelphia's free Ne-

groes were mostly cooks, washerwomen, waiters, day laborers, and "traders in a small way. "22 In April and May,
1787, a number of them, including Allen and Jones, proposed and organized the Free African Society in order to
provide members with decent burials and care for their
widows and orphans. The Free African Society was formed
"without regard to religious tenets, provided the persons
lived an orderly and sober life. "23

        The need for a distinctly religious organization was
not forgotten. It has been traditionally assumed that the
catalyst was provided one Sabbath morning at St. George's
when the white trustees demanded that Allen, Jones, and a
number of other Negro worshippers move to the rear of the
gallery. The date usually given to the gallery incident is
November, 1787, about six months after the founding of the
Free African Society. 24 However, the construction of the
galleries at St. George's was not begun until 1791, during
the pastorate of Henry Willis, and not completed until May
of 1792. 25 In his memoirs Allen stated that the blacks had
contributed toward building the gallery and laying new floors
and "were turned out just as the house was made comfortable. " Bishop Allen, writing in his old age, telescoped the
events from 1787 to 1791. A close reading of his autobiography and examination of the dates of tenure for those
Methodist authorities he cites also makes it clear that the
gallery incident cannot have occurred in 1787. 26 Thus
Allen's memoirs leave the false impression that it was the
rebuff at St. George's which caused the Negro Methodists
to seek their own church.

        It may very well have been that about the middle of
1792 Allen and Jones, who as yet had no building of their
own, were still attending St. George's and on the particular
Sunday in question were asked to move to the rear of the
newly constructed gallery. But by this time they had already
gone to Benjamin Rush and other prominent Philadelphians
seeking subscriptions for an African Church. Recalling his
meeting of July, 1791, with representatives of the proposed
African Church, Rush wrote to his wife: "Never did my
heart expand or triumph more upon any subject. " The principal contributions, Rush remarked, would probably come
from "the Deists, swearing captains of vessels, and brokers
of our city. " "The clergy and their faithful followers of
every denomination, " he sarcastically added, "are too good
to do good. " But Tench Cox, Robert Ralston, who became
the African Church's treasurer, Benjamin Franklin, and,

The Rev. Absalom Jones (1746-1818), first Negro Episcopalian priest in America.

according to Dr. Rush, both President Washington and Thomas Jefferson, all promised moral and material assistance. [27]

By August, 1791, Rush was able to report: "The African Church goes on swimmingly."[28] After some initial disagreement as to location, a foundation for a preaching-house was dug in February of 1792. Except for Allen and Jones, the company of Negroes wished to follow the Episcopalian order of worship and government. The assistant rector of St. Paul's Episcopal Church had promised to

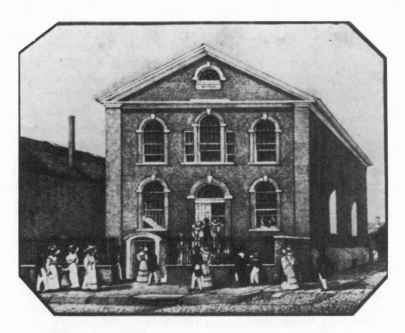

The African Episcopal Church of St. Thomas, Philadelphia, ca. 1829.

officiate for them on occasion, but the white Methodist elder threatened to expel them from the Methodist connection if the idea of an African church wasn't abandoned. Even though Absalom Jones favored the Methodist form of government, he went with the majority into the Episcopalian fold to form the African Episcopalian Church of St. Thomas, which was dedicated on July 17, 1794. A year later, Jones, born a slave in Delaware, was ordained as the first Negro Episcopalian priest on American soil.[29]

Richard Allen had rejected an offer to be the pastor of the African church. For he remembered with gratitude the way in which the Methodists had sought out the slaves, how they preached a plain and simple gospel, and how, while still a slave near Dover, Delaware, he had been converted because of the Methodist witness. While supportive of the African Episcopalians, Allen still hoped for a church for Negro Methodists erected on a lot he had purchased. This was realized when, with an old frame blacksmith shop as its

building, Bethel Church was dedicated on July 29, 1794, by
Bishop Francis Asbury. Thus Allen had a church for separate worship, but it was still under the control of the elders
of the Methodist Episcopal Church. [30]

Philadelphia was not the only place where free Negroes
were moving toward religious independence. In Baltimore
black Methodists had been ordered to the galleries and forbidden from communing before the whites at the Lovely Lane
and Strawberry Alley churches. About 1787 they left to worship in private in a boot-blacking cellar. Ten years later
the Baltimore group purchased a building and also named
their mother church "Bethel." By 1812 there were over 600
Negro Methodists attending Baltimore Bethel under the leadership of Daniel Coker,* an ex-slave who, like Richard Allen,
had been ordained as a deacon. [31]

In the early days of Methodism in New York City a
number of Negroes had joined Wesley Chapel on John Street.
In the late 1790s they received permission from Bishop
Asbury to worship by themselves at Zion Chapel, located in
a cabinet maker's shop. At first these blacks had no intention of forming a separate congregation but only "to hold
meetings by themselves in the intervals of the regular preaching houses of our white brethren."[32] A few years later they
decided to build their own church. The increase of Negro
members in the mixed congregation at St. John's was causing
friction between the races. In addition the black preachers
felt hampered because they could not perform all rites of the
church nor join the Methodist conference. The articles of
incorporation, dated April 6, 1801, gave the name of the new
church as "The African Methodist Episcopal Church of the
City of New York." But the New York black Methodists were
usually referred to as the Zionites, after the original Zion
Chapel. [33]

In Wilmington, Delaware, another group of Negro
Methodists, under the leadership of Peter Spencer, founded
the African Union Church in 1813. These black Christians
obtained complete control of their church. [34] Negro Baptists
likewise achieved independence more rapidly than did Negro
Methodists in Philadelphia, Baltimore or New York. In
Boston, the first independent Negro Baptist church was organized in 1805 as the African Baptist Church, later known
as the Joy Street Church, pastored by Thomas Paul. * Several years later, probably in 1809, Paul helped to form the
Abyssinian Baptist Church for Negro Christians who had been

Mother Bethel A.M.E. Church, Philadelphia (in recent years).

---

granted letters of honorable "dismission" from a white congregation in New York. About the same time Negroes in
Philadelphia were forming the First African Baptist Church.[35]
These Negro Baptists did not have strong ecclesiastical organizations to contend with and could simply depart with their
religious privileges intact. But the Bethelites and Zionites
had a long uphill struggle before they obtained complete organizational freedom.

Independence Comes at Last

While they did want to worship by themselves and be
free to minister more effectively to the Negro community,
neither the Bethelites nor the Zionites originally intended to
form distinct denominations. Total separation from the
Methodist Episcopal Church came only as a result of the
interference of whites in the internal affairs of both groups.
The "Articles of Agreement" which were drawn up for the
Bethelites and the Zionites consigned their church property
over to the elders and bishops of the Methodist General
Conferences in, respectively, Philadelphia and New York.
The trustees were to be black, but they could not transfer
or mortgage their property without the consent of the white
elder who was assigned to oversee the Negroes. He nominated the preacher and had a right to occupy the pulpit.
Both Negro groups pledged to continue forever in union with
the Methodist Episcopal Church "subject to the governance
of the present Bishops and their successors in all their ecclesiastical affairs and transactions. "[36]

As long as the white elders refrained from pursuing
their prerogatives too vigorously, the Negroes did not have
cause for concern. But in 1805, the Rev. James Smith,
newly appointed to the Philadelphia circuit, came and "waked
us up" as Richard Allen, still only a deacon, recalled. After a disagreement with the black leaders at Bethel over admitting a certain woman to the communion table, Smith demanded the keys and books of the church, intent on closing
it down. Allen protested that Bethel belonged to the blacks,
but Smith contended that it belonged to the General Conference. "We took counsel on it, " Allen recalled, "and counsel
informed us we had been taken in; according to the incorporation it belonged to the white connection. "[37]

In 1807, although it caused a "considerable rumpus, "
the blacks drew up a supplement to the original articles.
This gave them control of Bethel property, the power to
elect their own exhorters, and a veto over whomever the
white Methodists appointed as their elder in charge. The
African Supplement, as it was called, still gave the white
elder the right to administer the sacraments. When a dispute over the fee demanded by the visiting elder arose, the
Bethelites argued that the assessments should not be paid
directly to St. George's and that the white clergy were ne-
glecting their duties. In the ensuing years aggressive white
elders attempted to enlarge their prerogatives at the expense

of Allen's people. Finally the issue was forced by the Rev.
Mr. Burch who took legal action in 1815 "to know why the
pulpit was denied to him." A writ of mandamus by the
Pennsylvania Supreme Court decided the question on January
1, 1816. The church belonged to Richard Allen and his associates. [38] Now there was no turning back.

Four months later Richard Allen, Daniel Coker, Peter
Spencer, and delegates from several other Negro churches
came together in Philadelphia to draw up an "Ecclesiastical
Compact" that would unite them in an independent conference.
Spencer, rebuffed in his attempt to include the presiding el-
dership in the new organization, went back to his own African Union Church, but the others formed the African Methodist Episcopal Church. Coker and Allen were elected to a
dual bishopric when Allen was not present. Upon returning,
Allen declared that such a small group did not need two
bishops. Coker then declined the office. [39] Another version,
which Daniel Alexander Payne recounted in his Recollections
of Seventy Years, states that Coker was first elected but the
"pure blacks, led by Jonathan Tudas, a friend in council with
Richard Allen," objected to Coker's light color. A man of
high feeling, Coker, whose mother was English and father an
African slave, immediately resigned. [40] Allen was consecrated on April 11, 1816; one of those who assisted was an
Episcopalian priest, the Rev. Absalom Jones.

The movement toward independence by the Zionites
was more gradual and less dramatic than that of the Bethelites. John Street Church continued to supply Zion Chapel
with preachers for nearly a decade after its organization.
Abraham Thompson and June Scott, licensed black preachers,
felt that they ought to be compensated by the trustees of
Zion. When a renegade Quaker offered them a lot for their
own church they left the Zion Society. In 1813 Thomas Sip-
kins, a trustee of Zion, was expelled "for being somewhat
headstrong and rather ungovernable." He went off to establish Asbury Church. [41] These internal troubles caused
the white elders to attempt closer supervision over the affairs of Zion Chapel.

Then in 1819 the blacks were made pastorless as a
result of a lay-clergy dispute within the John Street Church.
The Rev. William Stilwell, who was serving both Zion and
Asbury, participated in a secession movement from the New
York Conference. The Zionites supported the Stilwell move-
ment and met together on July 21, 1820, to decline "receiving

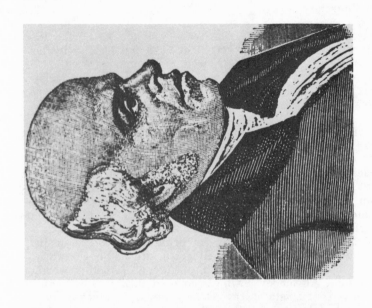

Left: the Rev. Thomas Paul (1773-1831), leader of Negro Baptists in Boston and New York; right: Bishop James Varick (1750?-1828), first bishop of the A.M.E. "Zion" Church.

any further services from them [the John Street authorities]
as respecting our church government." Several weeks later
another meeting was held at which two critical questions
were raised--first, "Shall we join Bishop Allen?" and second,
"Shall we return to the white people?"[42]

Had the Zionites joined with Richard Allen's African
Methodists the story of the Negro church in America would
be vastly different. As it was, the Zionites were resentful
of incursions made into New York City by William Lambert,
a one-time member of the Zion Chapel who had defected to
the Allenites and then returned to establish a missionary
society of the A.M.E. Church. Some time later an Allenite
elder organized a church in New York, and Richard Allen
came to dedicate it. During his visit he met with a committee of Zionites, led by James Varick* and Abraham
Thompson. The meeting of August 17, 1820, did not go well.
"After some conversation with the old man," wrote Christopher Rush, "they found that the interview only served to let
them know that he 'was not a child, that he knew his business,' (as he said)...."[43]

Allen, strong-willed and zealous for the Bethelites,
declared that he would not ordain clergy for the Zionites unless they subordinated themselves to his authority. This
was a severe setback for the New York group, for without
a legitimate ministry, according to the Methodist pattern,
independence was impossible. The New York Conference
also refused to ordain elders for the Zionites except at the
price of a return to their old status. About this same time
Negro Methodists at such places as New Haven and Philadelphia were also seeking independence and looking to the
Zion and Asbury groups for leadership. There were 22
preachers and 1410 members associated with the movement.
The Zionites had their own Discipline, adapted from the old
Methodist one, and were meeting as early as June of 1821
in a separate conference.[44]

But their status was still uncertain. The white
bishops claimed authority over the Zionites and assumed
that they were still in formal connection with the General
Conference. Finally on July 17, 1820, William Stilwell and
two other elders from the secessionist Methodist group ordained Abraham Thompson, James Varick, and Leavin Smith
as elders for the Zionites. Varick, one of the original
founders of Zion Chapel, became the first bishop of the
"African Methodist Episcopal Church in America." The quali-
fier "Zion" was not officially added until 1856.[45]

It is fashionable today to discern in the Allenite and, to a lesser degree, in the Zionite stories, the first examples of black nationalism and black separatism.[46] By 1816 and 1822, respectively, the Bethelites and the Zionites did take the position that full organizational separatism was the only means by which Negro Christians could maintain the integrity of their own religious lives and their witness to the black community. Black separatism, however, does not satisfactorily describe the events of the 1780s and 1790s.

Neither Richard Allen nor the leaders of Zion Chapel claimed to be separatists. In a statement addressed to the public in 1794, Allen and his associates gave three reasons why they wanted their own place of worship: (1) to lessen the chances of offense which arose in mixed worship, (2) to preserve "from the crafty wiles of the enemy our weak-minded brethren" who rejected the Gospel because of the prejudice they experienced, and (3) to "build each other up in our most holy faith."[47] Even at the time when they supplemented the "Articles of Agreement" so as to obtain control of their own church property, the Bethelites declared that they had no purpose or intention of separating themselves from the Methodist Conference. They wanted only, as the Bethelite trustees declared, "to regulate our affairs, temporal and spiritual, the same as if we were white people."[48]

In a "Founders' Address" published in 1820, the leaders of the Zionites did argue that independence was necessary in order to give black preachers full ecclesiastical privileges and to make them more useful "for the advancement of the Redeemer's kingdom among our brethren."[49] But the questions of racial autonomy and social control were first thrust upon the Zionites by happenstance because of the Stilwell secession. To be sure, the seeds of institutional separtism, as distinct from doctrinal loyalty, were sown in the first attempts by blacks both in New York and in Philadelphia to worship by themselves. Yet they flowered and bloomed as a result of the refusal of white authorities to leave the initial planting unmolested.

A Season for Growing

Once established as independent denominations, the A.M.E. Zion Church and the A.M.E. Church began to organize conferences, establish a network of local congregations with deacons, preachers, and elders, and, in general,

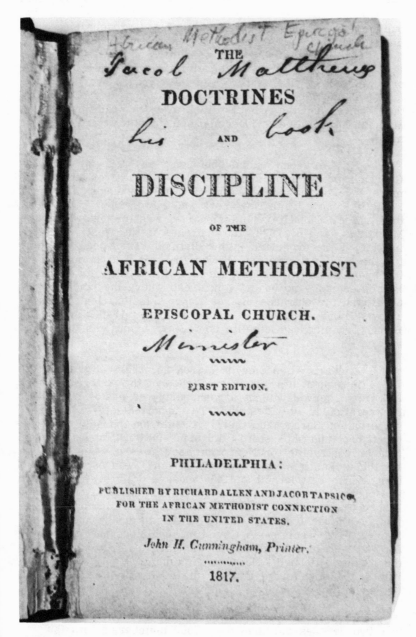

First edition of the African Methodist Episcopal Discipline (1817).

duplicate the ecclesiastical machinery and proselytizing
methods of the white Methodists.   In doctrinal matters
there was little difference between them and the Methodist
Episcopal Church.   Except for eliminating the role of the
presiding elder with its threat of interference over local affairs and including a stronger denunciation of slavery, both
the Zionites and the Allenites took over the traditional
Methodist Discipline and accompanying theological frame of
mind.

At its second annual conference in 1818, the A.M.E.
Church reported 1066 members.   Most were from the Baltimore and Philadelphia areas, but in the ensuing years the
Bethelites moved into New York and New England.   By 1822,
the A.M.E. Church had missionaries west of the Alleghany
Mountains, and by 1828, the churches in the West, chiefly
in Ohio, were organized into a distinct conference.   Except
for the brief existence of Morris Brown's church in Charleston and for several congregations in the border states, the
Bethelites made no headway in areas where the black codes
prohibited the entrance of free Negro missionaries.   They
enjoyed more success in Canada, where in 1840 Morris
Brown organized a Bethelite conference among the fugitive
slaves. 50

Richard Allen died on March 26, 1831, at the age of
72.   Throughout his tenure as Bishop of the A.M.E. Church,
Allen also served without a cash salary as pastor of Bethel
congregation in Philadelphia.   To support his wife, an ex-
slave named Sarah, and their six children, he sold groceries,
ran a boot and shoe store, did blacksmithing, and served as
a labor contractor for Negro chimney sweeps.   His entire
estate, including several parcels of land, was estimated as
being worth between 30 and 40 thousand dollars. 51   Allen
had been a respected member of the Philadelphia community.
Bishop Thomas Coke, other prominent white Methodists, and
Benjamin Rush frequently dined at Allen's house and had
learned to appreciate his Christian manliness and courage. 52
As was said of a local deacon who died a few months before
the Bishop, Richard Allen was a "venerable patriarch" who
"labored almost to the last for the vindication of the Gospel
of Peace, and went down to Jordan's stream rejoicing."53

Five years after Allen's death, the A.M.E. Church,
now two decades old, had over 7000 members in its four
conferences.   Of these, 743 were in the stronghold of the
Zionites at eight different locations in the New York City

"Praising the Lord," African Methodist Episcopal Church,
Cincinnati, Ohio.

---

area.[54] The A.M.E. Zion Church, which since the death
of James Varick had been led by Christopher Rush, grew
more slowly. In 1831, only 1016 members were reported
in the New York Conference and 673 in the Philadelphia.
This was an increase of only 270 members in ten years.
Despite their small numbers, the Zionites could claim such
famous names as Harriet Tubman, Sojourner Truth, Jermain
Loguen, and Frederick Douglass as having been, at one time
or the other, in association with them.[55]

Internal troubles plagued the Zionites and tended to
retard their growth. After Richard Allen's death there was
little disruption in the A.M.E. Church. Morris Brown,
who had become a bishop in 1828, assumed the position of
leadership which Allen had occupied.[56] But when Christopher
Rush retired due to old age and near blindness, the Zionites
became involved in a controversy over the ranking of the
assistant superintendents. A faction of the membership withdrew to form the Wesleyan Methodist Church. Compounding
the A.M.E. Zion Church's difficulties was the loss of the
Asbury congregation to the Bethelites and competition from

Left: Bishop Morris Brown (1770-1849), leader of African Methodists in Charleston, S. C., and in Canada; right: the Rev. Christopher Rush (dates unknown), second bishop and historian of the Zionites.

white Methodists who established separate churches, such as
Zoar in Philadelphia, for Negroes to keep them from going
over to the all-black denominations.[57]

These factors, along with a slowness in extending
their connection into the West, account for the fact that by
1864 the Zionites had only 13,704 members and 132 churches.
There were 97 preachers, 16 deacons, and 19 exhorters to
serve these churches. After the Civil War the Zionites made
an inroad into the South, heretofore forbidden territory, but
the great strength of the Zionites was still in the region where
they had first begun--in the Eastern and Middle Atlantic
States.[58] Her numbers may have been small, but the existence of the A.M.E. Zion Church spoke eloquently for the
cause of Negro self-assertion in the antebellum period. Her
doors were open to black Christians when others were closed.
"Many seasons of peace and joy I experienced among them, "
wrote Frederick Douglass of the Zionites in New Bedford,
Massachusetts. After having tasted the bitter fruit of prejudice among the white Methodists, Douglass came to appreciate the sweet savor of brotherhood in little Zion of New
Bedford.[59]

When Douglass sat down in 1848 to answer in essay
form the question, "What are the Colored People Doing for
Themselves?", the black churches immediately came to mind.
There were three Negro pulpits, he claimed, "which have
the power to produce a revolution in the condition of the
colored people in this land." The first was Mother Bethel
of Philadelphia, the second was Zion Church in New York
City, and the third was St. Philip's Church, also of New
York.[60] St. Philip's was a Negro Episcopalian church which
had achieved prominence under the leadership of Peter
Williams.*[61] Douglass might also have mentioned the black
Baptist churches of the North. Although they lacked the denominational framework that unified and aided the Methodists,
the black Baptist churches were making headway and ministering to many Negroes, especially those who had fled the
South.[62]

The Era of Bishop Daniel Alexander Payne

In the winter of 1841 a frail but determined Negro by
the name of Daniel Alexander Payne joined the Philadelphia
Conference of the A.M.E. Church. Although he would not be
elected bishop until 1852, Payne's arrival inaugurated a new

Left: Bishop Daniel Alexander Payne (1811-1893), historian and educator of the Bethelites; right: the Rev. William Paul Quinn (?-1873), the "Peter Cartwright" of African Methodists.

era in the history of the Bethelites. Born in Charleston, the
son of free parents, Payne had taught school until 1835 when
a South Carolina statute took effect which exacted 50 lashes
and a fine not exceeding 50 dollars of any free Negro who
taught slaves to read and write. Payne came North and enrolled at the Evangelical Lutheran Seminary in Gettysburg,
Pennsylvania. [63]

While a student, Payne had been supplying a small
A. M. E. congregation. In spite of his Methodist predilec-
tions, he was reluctant to join the African Methodists because of their animosity toward an educated clergy. After
being assured that he would not be sent to Liberia, Payne
sought ordination in 1839 from the antislavery Franckean
Synod (Lutheran). As his first charge, he held a pro tem-
pore pastorate among mostly white Presbyterians in East
Troy, New York. Payne then returned to the A. M. E.
Church and was assigned to Carlisle, Pennsylvania. In
1843 he became the pastor of the Israel congregation in
Washington, D. C. [64]

Payne witnessed the great growth of the A. M. E.
Church which began after the Evangelical communion split
over the slavery issue in the middle 1840s. On free-soil
territory in the West, the Bethelites carried on an effective
mission to the Negroes. William Paul Quinn was the Peter
Cartwright of the African Methodists, carrying the Gospel
to frontier settlements and helping to establish footholds of
the A. M. E. Church in such unlikely places as St. Louis,
Missouri, and Louisville, Kentucky. [65] The Negro Methodists of Canada grew so rapidly that they were given a
peaceful dismissal in 1856 in order to organize the British
Methodist Episcopal Church. [66]

In 1852 Payne finally bowed before the wishes of his
colleagues and "the manifest will of the Great Head of the
Church." He was elected to the office of bishop, to serve
with William Quinn and Willis Nazrey, despite a great feeling
of personal inadequacy. The A. M. E. Church was at that
time divided into three episcopal jurisdictions. Payne was
assigned to the Philadelphia and New England areas, where
he immediately began a program of reform and of educational progress. He promoted an organizational newspaper,
was instrumental in establishing a church college, and
nurtured Negro Methodism in countless ways for over fifty
years. Richard Allen lit the torch of the black church, but
it was Daniel Alexander Payne who kept it burning and who

passed it on, with an even brighter light, to the generations that followed. [67]

At the General Conference of 1860, Payne reported that the A.M.E. Church was in "a very flourishing condition--much improvement very noticeable, the ministry fast increasing, the missions very hopeful."[68] The westward migration to California had opened promising mission stations, and a thriving Missouri District had been established. On the eve of the Civil War, the A.M.E. Church was poised to enter the South, the last remaining area where it had had little success.

Almost as soon as the Union forces cleared the way, the Bethelites sent laborers to bring in the Southern harvest. On April 27, 1863, the Rev. C. C. Leigh, a leader in the Methodist Episcopal Church and the National Freedman's Association, requested Bishop Payne to accept a Macedonian call to the Sea Island region of South Carolina.[69] Here many newly freed slaves were in need of moral, social, and religious guidance.[70] About a month later, the Rev. James Lynch and the Rev. James D. S. Hall sailed for South Carolina. They began working in the Port Royal, Edisto, and Beaufort regions, but as soon as Savannah and Charleston were captured, these representatives of the A.M.E. Church moved inland.[71]

On May 13, 1865, Bishop Payne himself stood on board the ship Arago gazing at the destruction of Charleston. Thirty years earlier he had been forced to flee this city for the crime of teaching black children to read. Now he returned as the leading bishop of the nearly fifty thousand member A.M.E. Church. Two days later he presided over the formation of the South Carolina Conference. In the coastal and sea island regions of the Carolinas and Georgia, about four thousand Negroes joined Payne and his associates. In Nashville, Tennessee, several years earlier, Payne had had the opportunity of bringing into the A.M.E. Church two Negro chapels named Caper's and Andrew's. The names were immediately changed to St. John's and St. Paul's. Thus did the church that the ex-slave Richard Allen founded come into its rightful heritage.[72]

"The Negro Church," Booker T. Washington wrote in 1909, "was the first institution to develop out of the life of the Negro masses and still retains the strongest hold upon them."[73] "The Negro church of to-day," W. E. B. Du Bois had written six years earlier, "is the social center of Negro life in the United States, and the most characteristic expression of the African character."[74] These observations, of course, reflected the phenomenal growth and influence of the black Baptists and Methodists in the decades after the Civil War. But what Du Bois and Washington wrote is also applicable to the Negro churches in the antebellum period.

The Negro denominations were the only significant organizations which blacks controlled in the free North for several generations. Thus by analyzing how these institutions responded to the great issues of the day, such as slavery, education, social reform, colonization, and the like, we shall have gone a long way towards understanding black history before the Civil War. The burden of functioning as religious center, political forum, social hall, school room, and vehicle of race pride, may have been the Achilles' heel of the black church in the United States. But this tremendous burden may also have been the dynamic which shaped and prepared the black churches for the task they face today.

Chapter VI

THE BLACK CHURCHES CONFRONT THE WORLD

> I want you to set me down as a Liberator
> man. Whether you will call me so or not,
> I am with you in heart. I may not be in
> hands and head--for my hands will fight a
> slaveholder--which I suppose the Liberator
> and some of its good friends would not
> do.... I am a fugitive slave, and you
> know we have strange notions about many
> things.
> > --The Rev. Jermain W. Loguen of the
> > African Methodist Episcopal Zion
> > Church[1]

Throughout the history of Christianity, the institutional church has divided its energies between reforming the world and retreating from it. The black churches in the antebellum North, like the monasteries of Christendom, were islands of serenity and seclusion for many. Yet they also felt compelled to push the battle to the gates so that the world might more perfectly conform to the Kingdom of God. The Bethelites, for example, were extremely upset by the accusation that they were, as Charles B. Ray claimed in The Coloured American in 1840, not sufficiently concerned about "the great questions of the day." In their opinion, the A.M.E. Church was not "a whit behind any body of our people in measures of general improvement."[2]

Black Christians in the antebellum North used their churches as vehicles for spiritual uplift, social relief, and social protest. Christian charity, moral reform and education were endeavors which were of an internal nature. The problems of prejudice, colonization, and slavery, however, demanded that the black Christians speak to the larger society. Had the churches been content with internal matters

only, the Negro voice of protest would have been severely
muted. Fortunately, the black churches attempted to be
true to the Biblical injunction to be in the world but not of
the world.

A Time for Service and Self-Help

The community which the African churches ministered
to was almost entirely composed of Negroes. Because they
knew what the demon of race prejudice could do within the
Christian church, the early African churches subscribed to
John Wesley's egalitarian motto--"If thy heart be as my
heart, then give me thy hand."[3] Once established, the
A.M.E. and A.M.E. Zion Churches kept their doors open
to any who might wish to join them. Bishop Payne was
principally responsible for the inclusion of a number of white
members and at least one white minister in the Bethelite
connection.[4] But the independent black churches were neither
more nor less what historical circumstances and social
pressures allowed them to be. While not exclusivist, they
were racial churches. Their constituency was principally
made up of blacks who resided outside of the slave states.
To the larger public, the black churches were a visible and
tangible witness against the continuance of "the Negro Pew."
Their very existence was a kind of political statement.

Richard Allen believed that as free blacks moved
toward establishing their own social and religious organizations, they had to act so as not to provide grist for the anti-
emancipationist mill. This was an old concern. In 1787
Jupiter Hammon had pointed out that the proslavery forces
were fond of the notion that if the slaves were freed they
would "take to bad courses; that we should be lazy and idle,
and get drunk and steal."[5] Allen was aware of the power
of this common assumption and urged the Negro community
to conduct itself so as not to "strengthen the bands of oppression and keep many in bondage who are more worthy
than ourselves."[6] He was constantly alert for any false
aspersions which were cast upon free blacks by prejudiced
whites, such as had been done during the great plague of
yellow fever in Philadelphia in 1793, when members of the
Free African Society were accused of demanding exorbitant
prices for nursing care and of stealing beds from the houses
of the dead.[7] In 1808 he again had the opportunity of ad-
dressing Philadelphia Negroes on the urgency of the upright
life. In a gallows sermon, with two killers of a white shop-

keeper as the object lesson, he moralized, "See the tendency
of dishonesty and lust, of drunkenness and stealing...."[8]

Of the many causes which the black churches took up
in order to help themselves and set a good example, the
most important were moral reform, education, and missions.
Except in the case of the antislavery crusade, black Christians worked independently of the white Evangelicals. There
were no Negro members on the numerous boards and commissions of the so-called "benevolent empire." Education,
missions, and moral reform were internal matters of self-
help. Blacks were serving blacks.

The black churches adopted the Evangelical notion of
progressive sanctification and the customary standards of
Christian piety, such as cleanliness, thrift, industry, honesty,
temperance, marital fidelity, and charity for the less for-
tunate. Negro clergymen divided their time and energies between "saving souls" and ministering to the physical needs of
their parishioners and the community at large. Benevolent
Societies, composed of church women, offered the destitute
food for the stomach along with food for the soul. The
Bethelites met the needs of their senior citizens by forming
special classes for the aged and for the infirm. A.M.E.
Conferences memorialized their constituency in behalf of the
sacredness of marriage and against the evils of divorce.[9]

In 1809 Allen, Absalom Jones, and James Forten, an
Episcopal layman, helped to organize the Society for the
Suppression of Vice and Immorality for the purpose of eradi-
cating what the A.M.E. Church later termed "a disease that
is both pestilential and contagious." Preachers who imbibed
were to be disciplined and the general membership was prohibited from "the buying, selling, distilling, or using of
ardent spirits in any way ... unless prescribed by a phy-
sician." Total abstinence was the ideal, for intemperance
was said to be "the seed of sedition, the life of mobocracy,
the scourge of the Church and the arch-enemy of God and
man." The black clergy believed that intemperance not only
degraded the Negro but also that it provided fodder for those
who were already prejudiced against him and suspicious of
his freedom.[10]

The black churches also supported Sabbatarian reform, chiefly in opposing the delivery of the mail on Sunday.
They joined the campaign to expunge from Christian use that
noxious weed, the tobacco plant.[11] Their members were

encouraged to avoid a slovenly and ragged appearance, which was thought "to perpetuate the prevailing aversion and prejudice against color." Yet a pietistic animosity toward ostentatious dress was also evident. The A.M.E. Discipline, for example, urged preachers not to give tickets of admission to the Lord's Supper to any that wore "high heads, enormous bonnets, ruffles, or rings." The reluctance of the people to adopt the plain look, according to the Christian Recorder, was to be blamed on the clergy themselves, some of whom dressed "more like sportsmen, than preachers of the Gospel." The New York Conference levied a fine of 25 cents upon any minister who appeared "ungenteely dressed."[12]

The greatest challenge and, indeed, the greatest success was experienced not in the crusade against intemperance or the quest for pietistic reform, but in education. Here the black pulpit, as Frederick Douglass recognized, had the power, if it so wished, "to speak the right word--the word of progress--the word for mental culture."[13] The doors of the Northern classrooms were as reluctantly opened to blacks as were the doors of the white churches. When the Negro student did gain admittance, he was generally forced to attend segregated schools with inadequate facilities and materials and a poorly trained staff.[14] Most of the free blacks in the North were as far removed from a good education as the slaves of the South.

Many of the first generations of black preachers were poorly trained. This was partially due to their animosity toward an educated clergy and partially due to the influx of men into their ranks who had never had the opportunity to learn to read and write. Several of the founders of the A. M.E. Church simply made their mark on the original "Articles of Association." Richard Allen, Jr., the 15-year-old son of the Bishop, had to be engaged as the secretary of the General Conference of 1818, because, as Payne supposed, "he was the best scholar that the Conference could obtain." Many of the Negro clergy who came out of the slave cabin into the pulpit brought as their only credentials a self-authenticated "call to preach."[15]

The educational backwardness of the early black clergy cannot be attributed solely to a lack of opportunity. When Payne inquired about joining the A.M.E. Church, Bishop Morris Brown warned him that many of its preachers customarily introduced their sermons by declaring that,

... they had 'not rubbed their heads against col-
lege-walls, ' at which the people would cry, 'Amen, '
they had 'never studied Latin or Greek, ' at which
the people would exclaim, 'Glory to God!' they had,
'never studied Hebrew, ' at which all would shout.[16]

Anyone who has examined the style of old-time Negro preaching will recognize this anti-intellectual appeal as a common
feature, a means of identification with the hearers, many of
whom were illiterate.[17] It was also true to the spirit of
Peter Cartwright and the other Evangelical mechanic-preach-
ers who pitted the pursuit of piety against the pursuit of
learning.

There were, of course, a number of Negro clergymen
in the North who possessed excellent educational credentials.
Henry Highland Garnet* and Alexander Crummell attended the
Oneida Institute of Beriah Green. Crummell later studied at
Cambridge University in England. James W. C. Pennington
so impressed the European academic community that he was
awarded a Doctor of Divinity degree by Heidelberg University.
Of the prominent black clergy whom Martin Delany lauded in
1852, several had been educated at Jefferson College in
Pennsylvania or at Hanover College in Indiana. With the exception of Payne, none of the early African Methodist clergymen received seminary training. No African Baptist ministers seem to have obtained specialized training for the
ministry.[18]

     In the light of the prevailing bias against formal
training, we can begin to appreciate the personal achievement of Daniel Alexander Payne, known to the A.M.E.
Church as its Christian educator par excellance.[19] He took
up the fight against clerical ignorance by publishing five
"Epistles on the Education of the Ministry" in 1843. This
triggered a "struggle between darkness and light, between
baptized superstition and Christianity...." "The enemies
of Christian culture belched and howled forth all vitupera-
tion against me, " Payne recalled. The opposition to his
proposals came not from the bishops but from the rank and
file preachers.[20]

     In 1843 at the Baltimore Annual Conference, Payne
was instrumental in having those present deny ordination to
three licentiates who evidenced a poor knowledge of the
Discipline. Resolutions were passed in favor of a more
thorough training for prospective clergy. The next year, in

spite of considerable opposition at the General Conference,
Payne introduced a four-year course of studies which included such works as Joseph Butler's Analogy of Religion,
J. A. W. Neander's History of the Christian Religion,
William Paley's Evidences of Christianity, and D'Aubigne's
History of the Reformation. 21 In 1845 eight more essays
on the education of the ministry appeared. Payne's fervor
reached inspirational heights. The last essay in the series
invoked the spirit of Richard Allen, called upon the "beloved
young brethren" to "swear eternal hatred to ignorance," and
summoned the "venerable mothers of Israel" to dedicate
their sons Hannah-like to God and teach them "from infancy
to value learning more than silver and wisdom more than
gold."22

     Payne's elevation to the episcopacy in 1852 further
enhanced the cause of ministerial education. His conference
messages invariably contained exhortations to greater educational achievements and for the formation of literary and historical societies. The report of the Committee of Education
of the Baltimore Annual Conference in 1857 reflected the
changing atmosphere. Education, the Committee asserted,
was the "only means that will ever elevate our race to distinguished positions amongst other nations on the earth."23
The same spirit had infected the Zionites. In 1858 the
Genesee A.M.E. Conference declared: "We fully believe
that education, intellectual and moral, is the lever by which
the elevation of Blacks is to be accomplished." Industry,
economy, and temperance were not to be ignored, but "education is the great instrument that will render effectual all
other means."24

     Payne knew that unless his campaign was carried to
the level of the local church, total victory was not possible.
In 1845 he was appointed to Baltimore. In addition to
pastoral duties at Bethel (Daniel Coker's old church) and
Ebenezer congregations, Payne conducted a school for about
fifty children with a curriculum that "embraced all the English studies now taught in the best graded schools" and Greek
and Latin. He soon saw the necessity of reforming the class
structure and improving the worship services of his charges.
Many of the members loved to sing what were known as
"corn-field ditties." Payne was opposed to such extrava-
gances in the A.M.E. Church, as was the Ohio Conference,
which resolved to eliminate "the singing of fugue tunes, and
hymns of our own composing in our public meetings and congregations."25 Payne attempted to introduce regular choral

Left: the Rev. Henry Highland Garnet (1815–1882), Presbyterian clergyman and abolitionist; right: the Rev. Peter Williams, Jr. (d. 1849?), Episcopalian priest and critic of the American Colonization Society.

singing and instrumental music. Resentment was great. He
was once refused a local pulpit by the people themselves.
The stewards had no complaints as to Payne's character.
But they informed him, as Payne wrote in his Recollection
of Seventy Years, "that I had too fine a carpet on my floor,
and was too proud; that if one of the members should ask
me to take tea with them, I would not; and lastly, that I
would not let them sing their 'spiritual songs'."[26]

So, temporarily defeated, Payne left in 1850 to begin
his researches for an authorized history of the A.M.E.
Church. But all was not lost. The use of choir and organ
soon became the rule rather than the exception in the larger
black churches. Progress in the education of the laity had
been made. In 1844 the Baltimore Conference reported that
there were 869 scholars in its nine Sabbath schools and 129
in three common schools. Israel A.M.E. Church in Washington, D.C., even boasted a small library, no doubt the work
of Payne.[27]

In 1845 the Ohio Conference of the A.M.E. Church
opened a manual labor school on a tract of land outside of
Columbus. Union Seminary, as the school was called, was
a misadventure from the start, plagued by financial problems and an insufficiency of students.[28] Nine years later,
with a membership approaching 50,000, the Bethelites were
invited to join with the white Methodists in Ohio in establishing a collegiate institution which would train Negro
teachers. The proposal was abandoned because a majority
of the delegates to the General Conference viewed the plan
as a scheme "to ensnare us into measures for our expatria-
tion." Payne was no advocate of "the hated scheme of African colonization," but he saw merit in cooperating with the
white Methodists. In 1856 he moved his family to the vicinity
of Xenia and became one of the original trustees of Wilberforce University.[29]

As many of the students at Wilberforce were "the
natural children of Southern planters," the outbreak of the
Civil War brought an end to the school's financial support.
The doors were closed and the trustees informed Bishop
Payne that they would let him have the school for 10,000
dollars. There was no time for Payne to seek pledges from
the A.M.E. Church membership. With but a ten-dollar bill
in his pocket he made a bid and declared: "In the name of
the Lord I buy the property of Wilberforce for the African
Methodist Episcopal Church." This was Payne's greatest

Wilberforce University, Shorter Hall, as rebuilt after fires in 1865 and 1867.

triumph. On March 11, 1863, Wilberforce University became the first black-controlled college in the United States.[30]

Not all the black clergy were as forward-looking in
matters of education as was Payne. Peter Spencer, the
founder of the African Union Church in Wilmington, Delaware, had a special dislike of the educated ministry and opposed it whenever he could. The Zionites of New York had
no Payne amongst them and moved slowly towards establishing educational institutions. In 1848 Rush Academy, a manual
labor school, was proposed for Essex County, New York.
Like the Bethelite Union Seminary, this venture did not fare
well. Twenty years later the Zionites moved their academy
to Fayetteville, North Carolina, and renamed it the Zion Hill
Collegiate Institute. After a decade of little progress it was
removed to Salisbury, North Carolina, where today Livingston College is. The black Baptists had no schools of their
own before the Civil War.[31]

As the general Negro population became better educated, the black ministers were obliged to do likewise. Samuel
R. Ward, * reflecting upon the situation of the African
churches in the United States, wrote in 1855 that a great
thirst for knowledge on the part of free blacks had forced
the African clergy to give them better instruction than formerly. "Now many of them, " Ward said of the black preachers, "compare very favorably in education with white preachers; and as honest expositors of God's holy Word, they by
illimitable odds excel them. "[32]

Convictions on Colonization and Missions

The black churches had nothing against converting
Africans to the Gospel of Christ, but they were not about
to be drawn into a colonization enterprise under the guise
of missionary work. The American Colonization Society,
founded in 1816 by the Presbyterian cleric Robert Finley,
attracted white support for various reasons. Africa was
seen as a refuge for manumitted slaves, as an outlet for
free blacks who were viewed as an economic threat and a
troublesome people, and as a mission field.[33]

In January 1817, leaders of the free Negro community met at Absalom Jones' in Philadelphia at the request of
Finley. He apparently hoped that by gaining their support
the masses of the free blacks would come along. But a

146   Black Religion

protest meeting at Mother Bethel shortly thereafter indicated
that Finley had misjudged the Negro community. In a letter
from James Forten to Paul Cuffee, dated January 25, 1817,
we are informed that of the three thousand who attended,
"there was not one soul that was in favor of going to Africa. "34 Those who met in Allen's church saw colonization
as a scheme whereby the slaveholders sought to tighten the
shackles of human bondage.

We do not know if Richard Allen specifically influenced the mass meeting in the direction of opposing Finley's
colonization plans. But in 1827 the pioneer black paper in
America, Freedom's Journal, published a letter from Allen
in which he declared:

> I have no doubt that there are many good men who
> do not see as I do; and who are for sending us to
> Liberia, but they have not duly considered the sub-
> ject--they are not men of colour. This land, which
> we have watered with our tears and our blood, is
> now our mother country; and we are well satisfied
> to stay where wisdom abounds and the Gospel is
> free. 35

Allen recognized that it was in the interests of the slaveholders to have the free blacks exported to Liberia and
he had no intention of aiding and abetting such a scheme.
Martin Delany wrote in 1852 that because of the leadership
of Richard Allen, among others, blacks gave little credence
to the colonization scheme and "in a word, the monster was
crippled in its infancy, and has never as yet recovered from
the stroke. "36 In the 1850s the Christian Recorder, the
church paper of the Bethelites, was still damning the colonizing of blacks to any country under the patronage of the A.C.S.
Colonization could never succeed, stated the editor, "for this
reason--the whole scheme is not natural; it is the bastard
spawn of prejudice. "37

The Rev. Peter Williams, Jr., also opposed colonization to Africa. In an address delivered on July 4, 1830
in New York City, he skillfully exposed the self-serving and
hypocritical motives of some white supporters of transporta-
tion to Liberia. How ironic, he argued, was the assertion
that colonization would improve Africa when the whites were
claiming that free blacks in the United States were "the most
vile and degraded people in the world." Williams suggested
that if the promoters of colonization wished to benefit the

black race so much, they might lay aside their own prejudice and begin to exercise justice at home. [38]

A few Negroes, slave and free, did wish to go to
Africa. Bureell W. Mann, for example, wrote repeatedly
to Finley's Society, asking that it purchase him so that he
might "be the instrument of the hand of God in turning Many
to Righteousness. "[39] As the A.C.S. had no intention of
purchasing slaves for this purpose, no matter how deeply
Africa was in need of the Gospel, Mann's pathos-filled letters went unanswered. Mann, and those like him, were no
doubt sincere in wishing to be sent to Africa as missionaries. But as they were frantically seeking any means to
obtain their freedom and to exercise their religious obligations without harassment, their support of the A.C.S. was
a case of special pleading. Even the famous Lott Cary, the
pioneer black missionary to Liberia, whose religious sin-
cerity we cannot question, was motivated by the desire "to
go to a country where I shall be estimated for my merits
not by my complexion. "[40] Thus the support which some
blacks gave to the American Colonization Society was, in
part, also a means of obtaining their own freedom. [41]

One of the free blacks in the North who went to Liberia was Daniel Coker, Allen's associate and the early
leader of Baltimore African Methodists. After his rejection
of the episcopate in 1816 and expulsion from the Baltimore
Conference two years later, on grounds unknown to us today,
Coker joined a contingent of free blacks sailing for West
Africa under the auspices of the Maryland Colonization Society. "I can say, " he wrote in 1820, "that my soul cleaves
to Africa.... This land only wants industrious, informed,
and Christian people, to make it one of the greatest nations
in this world. "[42]

Coker was not officially sponsored by the Bethelites,
although historians of the African Methodist Episcopal Church
include his story when discussing the missionary enterprise
of their denomination. John Boggs went to Africa about 1824,
but if he accomplished anything there is no record of it today.
Not until 1856 was Africa set apart as a distinct mission field.
Unfortunately, the individual who was appointed to begin the
work went over to a splinter group, the Zion Wesleyan A.M.E.
Church. Once again the cause of African missions fell dor-
mant. It was not until 1878 that the first A.M.E. Church
was established in Liberia among a group of black American
emigrants. [43]

The tardiness with which the A.M.E. Church arrived
in Africa should certainly not be interpreted as a lack of
concern by the black Christians in America for the potential
mission harvest. The problem was that the English and
American white churches had preempted the field; the work
was supported by those who desired to cover attempts to ex-
patriate free blacks with pious rhetoric about bringing the
light of the Gospel to the benighted millions of Africa. The
black churches concentrated their mission work in other
areas--the West Indies and Canada.

In 1824 Richard Allen wrote a letter to President
Jean-Pierre Boyer of Haiti thanking him for opening a refuge
for the oppressed and informing him that over five hundred
American Negroes had enrolled for emigration. "The greater
part of them," Allen assured Boyer, "are respectable and
industrious, who I trust will give a favourable report of the
land they will inhabit."[44] In 1827 the Rev. Scipio Beanes
was commissioned by the Baltimore Conference to begin mission work on the French part of the island. About the same
time the Rev. Nathaniel Paul was sent by the Baptist Missionary Society of Massachusetts. Beanes soon returned to
the United States, leaving several Methodist societies to establish a ministry of their own. Although Paul wrote home
about "powerful precious soul reviving seasons," neither of
these adventures, because of linguistic and organizational
problems, seems to have prospered in any way statistically
remarkable.[45] Their importance was more symbolic. As
the Committee on Missions of the A.M.E. Church reported
in 1860, Haiti loomed up in the Atlantic Ocean as a "very
inviting field ... already ripe for harvest" for here had been
"demonstrated the truth that colored men are capable of self-
government."[46]

Peter Williams strongly urged American blacks to
consider Canada as a haven from prejudice and discrimination. He argued that a plan to purchase a tract of land
around Lake Huron "has a peculiar claim upon our patronage,
because it has originated among our own people. It is not
of the divising of the white man...."[47] The African Methodists were quick to see the missionary potential in the provinces of Canada in which thousands of fugitive slaves and
free Negroes were settling. Many African Methodists were
among those who were forced to flee Ohio when the state
revitalized its Black Codes. Societies were organized in
Canada as early as 1827 and by 1840 they were set aside as
the Upper Canada Conference.[48] Sixteen years later, having

grown in number and "feeling free from the American abomi-
nation--colorphobia, " as Payne reported, the Canadian missions organized as the independent British Methodist Episcopal Church. The word "African" was not prefixed because
it was felt that the British were "too wise and good to enact
laws based upon the color of a man's skin, and the texture
of his hair. "49

    Emigration to Haiti, Canada, Central America, or
even Africa was not, of course, economically feasible or
desirable to the vast majority of the Negroes in the United
States. Their destiny was to be decided under the Constitution of a country that counted them as but three-fifths of a
man. The rationale employed by leaders of the free black
community in urging moral reform, self-help, and educational uplift was that, in part, blacks had to prove something
to the dominant society, namely, that they were worthy of
emancipation and equal treatment. But there came a time
and an issue when some black spokesmen decided that there
had been enough of such talk.

The Voice of Protest

    In 1855 a contributor to the Christian Recorder drew
the ire of the editor by stating once again the old argument
about moral uplift. Citing the Richmond Examiner, the
anonymous individual claimed that whites would grant blacks
their rights if only "we show our oppressors that we are
worthy of having our rights, by assuming a nationality, and
cultivating the arts and sciences among us. " To which the
Rev. J. P. Campbell, the editor, replied: "We have to wait
for nothing. The right is a natural one. The Examiner is
not the light from heaven to us. "50 There was little disagreement within the black churches on the question of
slavery. With a unanimous voice they declared that freedom
was a God-given and natural right of every man.

    Richard Allen, although he had been favored with a
kinder master than most, knew how strongly the desire for
freedom burned in the hearts of his brethren in chains. Yet
he could not bring himself to urge the violent overthrow of
slavery. He counseled the slaves to have the patience of
Job--to have "an affectionate regard towards your masters
and mistresses, so-called, " and a reliance upon the consolation that no one could deprive them of the hope of heaven. 51
Allen extended forgiveness to the slaveholders and appealed

to them to rid themselves, their children, and their country
of the burden of slavery. [52]

On January 2, 1800, the House of Representatives
took up for debate a petition from three prominent Philadelphia Negroes. Richard Allen, Absalom Jones, and James
Forten memorialized Congress to adopt measures "as shall
in due course emancipate the whole of their brethren from
their present situation." They also petitioned for emendation
of laws relating to fugitive slaves and the slave trade. This
first effort by a group of American Negroes to bring about a
redress of their grievances by directly petitioning the federal
government was overwhelmingly defeated. Only one congress-
man, George Thatcher, of Massachusetts, voted in behalf of
the proposal. [53]

Eight years later, however, there was some cause for
rejoicing. On January 1, 1808, the 20-year period of grace
during which Congress was prohibited from interfering with
the migration and importation of slaves in the thirteen original slave states came to an end. Absalom Jones celebrated
the occasion by preaching a thanksgiving sermon in St. Thomas' African Episcopal Church. He began by comparing the
end of the slave trade with the deliverance of the Hebrews
from Egyptian bondage. He told his congregation not only to
be thankful for past mercies but to continue praying for further reforms, especially the amelioration of the sufferings
of those who were still in bondage. [54]

The position which Richard Allen and Absalom Jones
took pertaining to slavery was not an especially radical one.
Both men were gradual emancipationists. Putting their trust
in the wise providence of God, they looked to that day when
all men would be free, and urged the slaves to take comfort
in the Gospel promises until that time. David Walker, a
free Negro who had seen much of the South before going to
Boston where he became a storekeeper, took a more strident
position with respect to slavery, but he did not dismiss the
great contributions of Richard Allen. When Walker's Appeal
in Four Articles appeared in 1829, it was found to include
the complete text of Allen's letter, opposing colonization,
which had appeared two years earlier. Walker heartily en-
dorsed Allen's position on this issue. He could barely re-
strain himself in praise of Allen's efforts to teach true Christianity:

Richard Allen! O my God!! the bare recollections

of the labours of this man, and his ministers
among his deplorably wretched brethren (rendered
so by the whites) to bring them to a knowledge of
the God of heaven, fills my soul with all those
very high emotions which would take the pen of an
Addison to portray.[55]

Walker was not content to wait upon the sure but slow providence of God. His pamphlet was a trumpet call to the bondsmen to take history into their own hands, even if this neces-
sitated the use of force.[56]

The Rev. Henry Highland Garnet was even more forthright in calling for rebellion against the slaveholders. In
1843 this militant Presbyterian clergyman, once a slave, delivered a fiery speech before the National Negro Convention
in Buffalo. Because of its incendiary rhetoric, the speech
was not published until 1848 when Garnet included it with
David Walker's Appeal. Invoking the spirit of Denmark
Vesey and Nat Turner, Garnet called the slaves to "RESIS-
TANCE! RESISTANCE! RESISTANCE!" "However much all
of us may desire it, " he told the slaves, "there is not much
hope of Redemption without the shedding of blood. "[57]

Individual black clergymen, like Garnet, were more
militant than the black churches themselves. The African
Methodists, for example, employed the same language with
respect to slavery as had the antislavery Evangelicals at the
turn of the nineteenth century. The first Disciplines of the
A.M.E. Church (1816) and the A.M.E. Zion Church (1820)
employed, word for word, the same restrictions against admitting slaveholders as members as did the early white
Methodists.[58] It is significant, however, that when the
African churches organized under their own governance the
Methodist Episcopal Church had already compromised itself
by admitting a slaveholding member except "where the laws
of the state in which he lives will admit emancipation. "[59]

At the A.M.E. General Conference of 1856, the first
one to give the debate on slavery a central place, the Bethelites discovered that some among them had obtained slaves
on what were known as "conditions, " the slaves being freed
as soon as the purchase price was repaid. The Rev. M. M.
Clark reported that among the A.M.E. membership there
were several who lived off the profits of slaves they owned
in the South. A controversy arose as to whether or not the
A.M.E. Discipline currently in use was proslavery because

152   Black Religion

it allowed the slaveholder to be given "due-notice by the
preacher in charge" to liberate his slaves.

    The majority of the Committee on Slavery felt that the
times demanded a stronger statement, one that would rid the
church of the compromising due-notice provision. They recommended rewriting the Discipline so as to require immediate
emancipation and urged the adoption of the following resolution:

        Resolved, 1st. That the sin of slaveholding, as
        practiced in the American churches, is a sin of
        the first degree, and the greatest known in the
        catalogue of crimes--the highest violation of God's
        law--a shameful abuse of God's creatures, shocking
        to enlightened humanity, and should unchurch, and
        does unchristianize every man and woman who is
        a slaveholder. [60]

A minority of the committee argued that the Discipline was
adequate on the matter of slavery. In more subdued language,
the minority did "deprecate" and "deplore" the sin of slavery.
Much was made in the minority report of phrases such as
"we can do no more than pray, " "we have no voice in the
affairs of the nation, " and "we, as a denomination, have no
power, so far as our political rights are concerned. " The
floor debate between proponents of the majority report and
those of the minority one was long and heated, extending
over several days. Charges of "ultraism" and "pro-slavery"
were exchanged. After the defeat of the move to change the
Discipline, the minority resolutions were adopted amidst
cries of "Give us the question--the question! the question!"
and general confusion all around. [61]

    In view of the status of the black churches in the
United States before the Civil War, we must conclude that
the minority report was right. The A.M.E. Church was
composed of individuals who were but nominally free. They
had even less access to the seats of power and influence in
Washington and Richmond than did the white Methodists.
Both the white and the black churches had to fall back upon
moral persuasion and pious talk about the will of Providence
and the demands of Christian charity. Thus further examination of denominational debates and resolutions will not tell us
much about how free black Christians met the challenge of
slavery. We must narrow our focus to sentiments and activities of individuals.

During the great 1856 debate among the Bethelites, the name of Daniel Alexander Payne was invoked by the party desiring a hard line approach in the Discipline. In 1839, the same year Payne was ordained by the Lutherans, he addressed the Franckean Synod on the necessity of their adopting a strong antislavery platform. He eloquently rehearsed the evils of slavery, how it brutalized both master and slave, subverted the moral government of God, perverted the Gospel, and, as in his own case, even caused the slave to question the very existence of a merciful and just God. In the final peroration, Payne exclaimed:

> O, Brethren of the Franckean Synod! awake!
> AWAKE! to the battle, and hurl the hottest thunders of divine truth at the head of this cruel monster, until he shall fall to rise no more; and the groans of the enslaved are converted into the songs of the free!![62]

To this day the Franckean Synod is remembered for its courageous stand against slavery, something unique among antebellum Lutherans. Perhaps Payne's address in the crucial convention of 1839 influenced them in this direction.[63]

When Payne later joined the A.M.E. Church he enlisted in the ranks of numerous spokesmen of black Christianity who had been and were making their individual protestations. Daniel Coker, for one, published a fictitious account of a dialogue between a Virginia slaveholder calling on business in Baltimore and an African Methodist minister, obviously Coker himself. The Virginian tried to convince the minister that the evils of general emancipation would be greater than were those of slavery itself. The two men discussed the Biblical basis for slavery, the matter of miscegenation, and the effect of the "peculiar institution" upon the moral agency of the slave. The African minister revealed that he favored Thomas Jefferson's plan of fixing a period after which no one should be born a slave in the United States and children now in bondage would be set free upon reaching a certain age. The Virginian, convinced by the minister that the Bible did not justify chattel slavery, that the Negro abhorred intermarriage as much as he did, and that human bondage had dreadful consequences on slave morality, seemed satisfied that this plan of gradual emancipation might be accomplished. The two men parted amicably.[64]

Coker won an easy victory in this debate with the

Virginian, written as it was, from the security of his study.
To confront slaveholders face to face from the pulpit was
another matter. The Rev. William Paul Quinn, the pioneer
missionary of African Methodists in the West, was convinced
that slavery, like all sins, needed to be denounced from the
pulpit. His favorite remark about a slaveholder was "May
God have mercy on him; I never will." Once in St. Louis
he was arrested for disturbing the peace when a proslavery
crowd took offense at such remarks. A large man, standing
6 feet 3 inches and weighing over 200 pounds, Quinn could
more than hold his own against hecklers. But on one occasion, at a campmeeting in Ohio, a fanatic proslavery sympa-
thizer stabbed him in the thigh. After some first aid, Quinn
hobbled to the speaker's stand and proceeded to flay the
slavery crowd in such strong terms that his friends, fearful
of further violence, spirited him out of town. [65]

Men like Quinn, who represented independent black
denominations and moved freely along the frontier, could
lash out at slavery and then, when threatened, simply shake
off the dust of that locality which would not hear them, as
Jesus told his disciples to do, and move on. But for those
ministers in charge of black congregations within white-controlled denominations, the freedom to protest was often circumscribed. Early in his career Peter Williams, Jr., had
spoken out forcefully in favor of the abolition of the slave
trade and against colonization. Williams was also one of
four Negroes on the Board of Managers of the American
Anti-Slavery Society. In 1834 Bishop Benjamin T. Onderdonk
of the Protestant Episcopal Church advised Williams to resign. The usual business about "the Christian side of meek-
ness, order, and self-sacrifice to the common good, and the
peace of the community" was given as necessitating Williams'
resignation. [67] St. Phillip's outspoken pastor was an embar-
rassment to the conservative-minded Episcopalians. Williams
did as he was told. His reputation in the free black community was no doubt damaged as a result of this incident. [68]

Unwilling to jeopardize their membership in the white-
controlled denominations, some Negro Christians accepted the
racial status quo. Such was the case with the "colored
branch" of the Methodist Episcopal Church in Cincinnati. The
local African Methodist Episcopal congregation petitioned for
the repeal of the obnoxious black codes which Ohio had enacted to control free blacks. But the "colored branch" issued
a public disclaimer of any such action, asking only "a con-
tinuation of the smiles of the white people as we have hitherto
enjoyed them. "[69]

The Struggle Against Slavery

The occasions when the black churches publically bowed before racism in the United States were relatively rare. We cannot know how many kept silent in order to avoid trouble. But we can get an indication of the sentiment of black Christians from their organized involvement in three areas: (1) the convention movements, (2) abolitionism, and (3) the underground railroad.

In Spetember of 1830 Austin Steward, an ex-slave and outspoken opponent of slavery, make his way through Philadelphia to Bethel A.M.E. Church. Although struck by the beauty and symmetry of the city of the "peaceable, just, and merciful William Penn," he had journied to Philadelphia not to see the sights but in answer to an appeal from Bishop Allen, with whose reputation as an enemy of prejudice Steward was well acquainted. [70] Forty delegates, many of them prominent Negro clergymen, likewise responded to the Bishop's appeal, which had been issued in the wake of the repressive laws against blacks in Ohio. The first national Negro convention elected Allen as its president, Steward as its vice-president, and took the official title of "The American Society of Free Persons of Colour, for Improving their Condition in the United States; for Purchasing Lands; and for Establishing of a Settlement in Upper Canada." Steps were taken to organize local societies, gather monies for the purchase of land in Canada, give moral support to all who were forced to abandon their homes, and to establish the convention as an annual affair. [71]

Richard Allen died three months before the second annual meeting in June 1831. Men of kindred spirit continued the conventions up to 1835, using them as a public platform to condemn involuntary colonization and racism and to proclaim the virtues of temperance, education, and moral reform. More conservative Negroes, largely wealthy laymen from Philadelphia, succeeded in abandoning the all-black conventions in favor of the American Moral Reform Society, which adopted William Lloyd Garrison's moral suasion tactics and a diversified program of reform. The Rev. Samuel Cornish, Presbyterian minister from New York and co-editor of Freedom's Journal, opposed any attempt to substitute "Oppressed Americans" for "colored people" and to dilute and divert the stream of black protest. The National Negro Convention movement was reestablished in Buffalo in 1843. Despite differences over tactics and ideology, which split the

white antislavery societies, many Negro clergymen were
active in the conventions, including, among others, Thomas
Paul, Hosea Easton, William Douglass, J. W. C. Pennington, Theodore Wright, Alexander Crummel, Amos G.
Beman, Henry Highland Garnet, John Gloucester, William C.
Munro, and Charles B. Ray. The name of Daniel Alexander Payne,
as are those of many other A.M.E. and A.M.E. Zion church
leaders, is missing.[72]

In 1838 Payne first met Theodore Dwight Weld and
Lewis Tappen. They tried to persuade him to mount the
public platform in behalf of the American Anti-Slavery Society, with a salary of 300 dollars and traveling expenses.
Payne refused. His call, he felt, had been to the pulpit
not to the lecture hall. "Frederick Douglass was fitted for
his speciality; Daniel Alexander Payne for his," he reasoned.[73]
In view of the contrasting personalities of Payne and Douglass, one can only conclude that each was suited best for the
task assigned them.

Although Payne never took an active role in the abolitionist organizations, he lent them his moral support and
used the pulpit as his platform from which to condemn
slavery. On April 14, 1862, Payne had an audience with
President Abraham Lincoln. The bill that would emancipate
the slaves in the District of Columbia was awaiting executive
signature. Payne, as a leading spokesman of the Negro
churches, sought to persuade the President to act immediately. Although Lincoln gave him no promises, Payne left
with an impression of Lincoln's greatness and "of his fitness
to rule a nation composed of almost all the races on the
face of the globe."[74]

A number of black clergymen had joined ranks with
the American Anti-Slavery Society, but in 1840, because of
a desire to move from moral suasion to political pressure,
they withdrew with the Tappenites to form the American and
Foreign Anti-Slavery Society. Peter Williams, Jr., who
was eventually forced to resign, Samuel E. Cornish and
Theodore S. Wright, both Presbyterians, together with
Christopher Rush, the second bishop of the A.M.E. Zion
Church, belonged to the American Anti-Slavery Society.
Cornish, Rush, and Wright went over to the American and
Foreign Anti-Slavery Society in 1840 and there joined five
other black clergymen--Henry Highland Garnet, Stephen H.
Gloucester, Andrew Harris, and Jehiel C. Beman and his
son Amos, as founders. Cornish, Rush, Charles B. Ray,

and James W. C. Pennington were on the Executive Committee.[75]

One cannot read a detailed history of blacks involved in the organized and integrated antislavery campaign without running across these names constantly, along with those of other black clergymen, such as Robert Purvis, Nathaniel Paul, Alexander Crummell, and Samuel Ringgold Ward.[76] The striking fact about this group of men is that, with the exception of Rush, all were clergymen ordained in the white denominations and, generally, associated with Negro churches within those bodies. The majority were Congregationalists or Presbyterians, operating chiefly in the New England area. Leaders of the independent black denominations did not assume prominent roles in the integrated abolitionary societies. Perhaps they shied away from the Garrisonians and the Tappenites because they were afraid that their churches in the border states and in such hotbeds of anti-Negro sentiment as New Orleans and St. Louis would suffer if the abolitionist label were attached to them. Indeed, during the great debate at the General Conference of 1856, the Bethelites were informed that "ultra-slavery action" would damage the A.M.E. Church's work below the Mason and Dixon Line.[77]

The Bethelites and the Zionites ought to be termed, as Benjamin Quarles has suggested, "emancipationist" rather than "abolitionist."[78] But the Bethelites and Zionites did help the crusade against slavery. They opened up their churches to such speakers as William Lloyd Garrison and Frederick Douglass. And, even more importantly, the A.M.E. and A.M.E. Zion Churches, dotted as they were along the traditional routes of the underground railroad, became lifesaving waystations for fugitive slaves following the North Star.

When Harriet (Brent) Jacobs finally escaped to free territory, after an agonizing confinement in the garret of her grandmother's house in Charleston, she was immediately introduced to the Rev. Jeremiah Durham, pastor of Mother Bethel in Philadelphia. Durham took her home, put her in contact with other friends, and finally arranged for her to flee to New York.[79] Durham, in giving aid to "the poor, flying slave, trembling and panting in his flight," was simply continuing a practice that Sarah Allen was noted for. Her husband knew firsthand the fears which went with the fugitive slave no matter how far removed he was from the clutches of the slaveholder. Once Allen himself had to file a civil

suit against a slave speculator who had come to Philadelphia
claiming that he was a runaway. [80]

    We sense something of the significance that Mother
Bethel had for the fugitive slaves in the autobiography of
John Thompson. After escaping from Maryland to Philadelphia, Thompson was directed to Mother Bethel. A revival
was going on. He took a seat in a dark corner of the church
while the congregation was singing. A tall man soon entered
the pulpit and read out a hymn which spoke of the Savior's
love for poor wandering sinners, how He delivered them
when bound, healed their wounds, and turned their darkness
into light. Then the congregation began to raise another
hymn. Thompson was overpowered by the suitability of the
hymn to his own case. "My mind," he tells us, "was forcibly carried back to the state of bondage from which I had
just escaped, and the many manifestations of God's mercies
to me throughout the journey." The preacher, the Rev.
Josiah Gilbert of Baltimore, next read out his text, "O
praise the Lord, for He is good, and His mercies endure
forever." Gilbert's sermon had great effect upon the fugitive slave in the dark corner. Thompson felt as if a great
load had been removed from his heart. He found himself
standing up in church, praising God, and sensing "a heaven
upon earth" in his soul. That very night he joined Mother
Bethel. [81]

    The Rev. Jermain W. Loguen, a close friend of Fred-
erick Douglass, was stationed by the A.M.E. Zion Church at
Syracuse, New York. Here he fitted up an apartment for
fugitive slaves and aided them on their way to Canada. In
the same region of western New York, Harriet Tubman made
use of the Rochester Zionite Church as a shelter for the
bands of fugitive slaves she was spiriting to Canada. In Chicago, the Quinn Bethelite Chapel, named after the pioneer
missionary William Paul Quinn, served as another station on
the underground railroad. These black churches, and many
more we shall never know of, offered temporary havens to
the fugitive slave when all else boded the prospect of recap-
ture. [82]

    The Fugitive Slave Act of 1850 intensified the terrors
confronting blacks hoping to get to Canada and increased the
dangers for those who aided them. Many fugitive slaves who
had lived relatively unmolested were now, as Frederick Douglass wrote, "suddenly alarmed and compelled to flee to Canada for safety as from an enemy's land--a doomed city--and

take up a dismal march to a new abode empty-handed, among strangers. "83 Payne came to Douglass asking his advice as to whether blacks ought to flee to Canada or stand their ground. Douglass told Payne that he could not desert his post and would not leave his abolitionist friends, Henry Highland Garnet and Samuel Ringgold Ward, to carry on alone. Payne told Douglass that he had seen Ward crossing from Detroit to Windsor and that he himself felt whipped and ready to retreat. Payne's abjection was a stunning blow to Douglass, who felt the black clergyman "had power to do more to defeat this inhuman enactment than any other colored man in the land, for no other could bring such brain power against it. "84

Other black ministers, however, stepped forward to try to render the Fugitive Slave Law ineffective. Ward and Loguen were both involved in the successful rescue of a fugitive slave by the name of Jerry, a cooper living in Syracuse. He was dramatically snatched by an angry crowd from the clutches of the federal marshals and spirited to Canada. Both Ward and Loguen publically condemned the Fugitive Slave Act. Loguen declared, "I don't respect this law--I don't fear it--I won't obey it! ... I shall make preparations to meet the crisis as becomes a man. "85 Ward cried out in a speech in Boston's Faneuil Hall, "... I pledge you there is one fugitive slave whose name is Sam Ward, who will never be taken alive. "86

The passage of the Kansas-Nebraska Act in 1854 further incensed the black community. Opponents of the bill felt that it was a plot to keep free labor out of the territories and populate them with slaves. The Philadelphia Annual Conference of the A.M.E. Church boldly damned the Act "as another stretch of that power, which like the horse-leech, still cries 'Give, give!' or like the grave, 'is never satisfied'. "87 Indeed, the flames of sectionalism were already consuming the slender tendrils of the Union. Soon the whole country would become a "Bleeding Kansas."

In 1857 Chief Justice Roger Taney handed down the infamous Dred Scott Decision, which deprived blacks of slave ancestry of the rights of citizenship. In October of 1859 John Brown led a small band of blacks and whites against the federal arsenal at Harper's Ferry, Virginia. Less than three months later he, along with six others, was hanged. Among Brown's papers was found the name of the Rev. Thomas W. Henry, a clergyman of the A.M.E. Church. An attempt was made to arrest him, but it proved futile. 88

Left: the Rev. Jermain W. Loguen (1814–1872), Zionite minister and friend of the fugitive slave; right: the Rev. Samuel Ringgold Ward (1817–1866?), Congregational clergyman and antislavery orator.

In 1860 a spectacular comet appeared in the skies over the Eastern United States. Coming at a time when rumors of war were abroad in the land, "the star with a tail" was seen as a harbinger of great importance. Levi J. Coppin recalled that many black Christians turned to their Bibles and found in the prophet Daniel the words, "So the King of the North shall come and cast up a mount, and take the most fenced cities, and the arms of the South shall not withstand." The presence of the comet in conjunction with Biblical prophecy was taken as a sign that the King of the South would soon be conquered and slavery destroyed. [89]

The Civil War had providential, even apocalyptic, meaning not only for a few slaves on the Eastern shore of Maryland, where Coppin resided in 1860, but for black Christians generally. While the battle raged, they were told that the Lord's "avenging chariot is now moving over the bloody fields of the doomed South, crushing beneath its massive wheels the very foundations of the blasphemous system" and that slavery like old Pharaoh of Moses' day would "sink to rise no more forever."[90] The New York Annual Conference of the A.M.E. Church declared in 1865 that in "the recent great struggle between union and disunion" the "mighty power of an Allwise Providence" had been the rod of correction "chastening this nation for the guilt of oppression, opening the way of redemption, for the enslaved."[91] As the Christian Recorder had prophesied in 1855, no nation could "with impunity sin against God, by the practice of injustice and oppression and afterward escape with all its crimes and iniquities unpunished."[92] Ten years later, on December 18, 1865, the Thirteenth Amendment prohibiting slavery in the United States went into effect, a partial atonement for the sins of the past.

The scars of the Civil War, in which black Christians saw the chastening rod of God, would take a long time to heal. The Negro churches, however, were ready to take on the task of binding up the wounds of both North and South and of ministering to the Freedmen. "When slavery was overthrown, all eyes of thoughtful men," wrote the A.M.E.'s Bishop Payne, "were turned toward this church, and she was found to be in possession of more talent, more pluck, and more general intelligence than in other combinations of colored men then existing within the Republic."[93]

Chapter VII

BLACK RELIGION THROUGH THE PRISM OF HISTORY

> The antiquarian fallacy is not confined to
> antiquarians. Whenever a professional his-
> torian deliberately tries to cut himself off
> from his own time in order to study some-
> body else's, he commits the same mistake.
> --David Hackett Fischer, Historian's
> Fallacies[1]

Unlike the antiquarian, who mouselike secretes himself in some tiny chamber of the past, the historian cannot
completely ignore the demands of the present. Because of
the challenges raised by the Black Revolution of the 1960s,
there is renewed debate as to the form and function of religion in the lives of black Americans. Curiosity, the search
for a useable past, pride in all things black, a desire to tell
the whole story, all serve as motivating factors. A kaleido-
scope of images, some factual, some fanciful, has come into
focus. Controversy about the character of Negro religion is
not new and, like arguments about the cause of the Civil War,
it seems to have gone through a number of well-defined
stages. As the images pass in review, the observer notices
that, regardless of ethnic or religious identification, inter-
preters of the religious life of the American Negro have not
been able to extricate analysis of the subject from the intricate and entrapping web of black-white relationships.

The Crucible of the Controversy

The religion of the Negro was a contested issue in
the ideological debate between the antebellum North and South.
Proponents of the "peculiar institution" piously pronounced
that in enabling hundreds of thousands of the slaves to listen
to the glad tidings of the Gospel, Southern Christians were

doing more for black souls than all the "freedom shriekers"
of the North. In search of higher ground, abolitionist clergymen struck out at the inherent contradiction between Christian
freedom and human bondage and professed deep skepticism of
the vaunted missionary claims of the Southern clergy. In
taking the Bible from the hands of the slaves, in controlling
their consciences with the lash, and in forcing them from the
true Gospel, the South, according to its Northern critics, had
developed the "darkest features of the spirit of Romanism."[2]

Southern Christians cited numbers, great numbers,
of slave conversions in evidence of their concern for the
Negro. They were met with the counterargument that the
plantation missions were designed to make the Negro "a good
slave, not a bold soldier of Jesus Christ."[3] Shifting the debate to the issue of quality rather than quantity, Northern
critics contended that it was absurd to think that one could
improve a slave's respect for Christianity by telling him that
the Bible sanctioned his being whipped and driven all his life
in the cotton field without pay. Overlooking the continued
existence of the segregated pew in their own midst, these
voices professed disbelief as to how the slaves could lead
the fully moral life while continuing as the chattel property
of alleged Christians who prayed with them on Sunday and
beat them on Monday.[4]

Jones, Meade, Capers, and their associates in the
plantation missions were well aware of the performance gap
between deed and creed. Frederick Douglass once remarked
that a pharisaic Southerner would think the abuse of a slave
baby less serious than a doubt about Predestination.[5] Such
an accusation is out of place with regard to these men.
They ought not be blamed for the cruelties which some whites
manifested toward blacks under the guise of piety. Many of
the missionaries did, wittingly or unwittingly, lend their
moral support to the slave system by preaching a "safe"
gospel. To this extent they were also captives of the evil
forces of racism, self-interest, and fear that undergirded
slavery. In attempting to shackle the Gospel, white Christians of the South brought themselves to personal grief, to
the scorn and ridicule of their critics, black and white, and
to the eternal bar of justice as depicted in the very Book
they kept from the Slave cabin.

The Myth of the Pious Old-time Negro

Almost as soon as the Union armies liberated portions

of the Confederacy, newly freed blacks deserted the churches
and plantation chapels of their former masters. This gave
the lie to the claim by the Southern denominations that, as
of 1860, they were effectively caring for the spiritual welfare
of almost a half million slaves. The exodus continued unabated throughout the Reconstruction years. After 1870, for
example, only 8000 Negroes remained under the auspices of
the white Methodists. Of the more than 200, 000 members
claimed by the Southern Methodists in 1861, most had drifted
away, joined the black denominations, or were "set off" in
1870 as the Colored Methodist Episcopal Church. 6

Few white observers saw the exodus as a positive
assertion by the Freedmen of their desire to worship under
their own vine and fig tree. Writers sympathetic to the
"lost cause" have charged that the Freedmen were seduced
away from the Southern churches "by fanatical carpetbaggers,
who inflamed the worst passions of the illiterate blacks."
The Freedmen were accused of conducting "religious orgies"
under the leadership of preachers who could be categorized
as "good, bad, and indifferent." Had the South been left
alone, the Rev. James McNeilly contended, "every right and
privilege to which the Negro was justly entitled by his nature
and capacity would have been freely given him."7

Many white Southerners, threatened by the presence
of de jure free Negroes, spun the myth of the pious old-time
Negro, "the frank, honest, simple, old servant," as Du Bois
wrote, "who stood for the earlier religious age of submission and humility."8 How wise of God, the mythmakers said,
that an entire race had been rescued from the mudsill of a
religion "animistic, oppressed and infinitely crude" and introduced to Christianity and civilization.9 Forgetful of Denmark
Vesey, James W. C. Pennington and the countless now forgotten slaves who found a mandate for resistance and covert
protest in the Gospel, the mythmakers focused upon the pious
old-time "uncles" and the venerable but servile "colored
preachers" who had found special favor with their masters.
James Battle Avirett, once a Confederate chaplain, bemoaned
the loss of the old fashioned colored men who, unlike "the
later products of the race, " in childlike faith evidenced loyalty
and gratitude to their white benefactors.10 The pious old-
time Negro was the stereotype Uncle Tom, loaded as that
epithet is with the freight of a century of abuse and miscasting of Mrs. Stowe's original character.

Old myths were resurrected and given pseudo-scien-

tific status during the Jim Crow era and well into the twentieth century. Apologists for white supremacy found the
Negro wanting in almost every capacity except that of a pro-
pensity for religion, particularly an otherworldly one. "Im-
perfectly as they may express themselves," wrote the Rev.
Charles M. Melden, "everyone who knows the Negro people
must admit that they are naturally religious."[11] Whites,
had, of course, always been foolishly speculating about
unique characteristics of blacks as a "race." In his Notes
on Virginia, Thomas Jefferson had given credence to the
belief that the Negro was more emotional and sensual than
the white man. It is interesting that in an era much taken
with pseudo-scientific racial myths and new patterns of white
superiority established upon old premises, a preeminence in
religious sensibility should still be given to the Negro.[12]

I suspect that this was done without upsetting traditional notions of the inferiority of the Negro and his need for
white paternalism. Religious enthusiasm, if kept within
reasonable bounds, was not felt to threaten the racial status
quo. Ludicrous and misguided according to white standards,
Negro religion was not particularly upsetting as long as it
siphoned off discontent that would ordinarily spill over into
the social or political realm. Those who were enamoured
of the notion of a uniquely Negro religiosity had little appreciation for the fact that, as the black orator J. Sella Martin
declared, the slaves were inclined to religion because, having
been driven by whites from the family hearth, the seat of
justice, and the church, they had "to make an appeal from
these unfaithful exponents of Christianity to the author of
Christianity Himself."[13] As Timothy L. Smith has stated,
the dehumanizing pressures of their daily lives caused the
slaves "to discover in the religion of their white oppressors
a faith whose depths few of the latter had ever suspected."[14]

Negro Religion: Functional or Dysfunctional?

Several black writers, with no intention to shore up
the props of racism, have given attention to certain features
of the memory portrait, the most glaring defect of which was
that it was composed of what whites wanted to believe about
the Negro. George Freeman Bragg, Negro historian and
Episcopalian clergyman, described the slave gallery as the
"most convenient testing and proving ground for the unex-
plored ignorance" of Africans fresh from the "barbarism of
their native land." George Arnett Singleton, historian and

pastor in the A. M. E. Church, described the African as a
worshipper of sticks and stones and the American slave as
"docile, forgiving, highly imitative, and anxious to learn."
Slave religion, he argued, had no social meaning, no particular interest in earthly matters; it focused upon heavenly
consolation. G. R. Wilson, another Negro scholar, wrote
in 1923 that during slavery the African "became a decidedly
different person, having a new religion, a primitive Christianity, with the central emphasis, not upon this world but
upon heaven." In the midst of pain and sorrow, the slave
looked to a future time when "he would be rich and free to
sing, shout, walk, and fly about carrying the news." The
slaves' idea of God, claimed Benjamin E. Mays, author of
the influential The Negro's God As Reflected in His Literature (1938), was a compensatory one, based upon the belief
that the harder the cross, the brighter the crown.[15]

Revisionist scholars, such as W. E. B. Du Bois and
Carter G. Woodson, were of no mind to portray the slave's
religion simply as a mutant variety of that of the master and
the mistress. Du Bois, even though he described the Negro
as "a religious animal," parted company with the memory
portrait by tracing "the faith of the fathers" back to its
African roots.[16] Carter G. Woodson saw much affinity between African beliefs and certain Christian teachings and
went so far as to say "that about the only change that the
black slave made was to label as Christian what he had
practiced in Africa."[17] Even Franklin Frazier, who took
the opposite viewpoint, namely that "it was not what remained of African culture or African religious experience
but the Christian religion that provided the new basis of
social cohesion," gave more autonomy to slave religion in
the form of the "invisible institution."[18]

The revisionist scholars were unable to veil their
disappointment in the allegedly escapist nature of slave religion. Frazier used portions of various spirituals to illus-
trate what he called "the predominantly other-worldly outlook in the Negro's religion." Du Bois, in his Souls of
Black Folk, expressed the opinion that emotionalism, fatal-
ism, and submission characterized slave Christianity. He
wrote that the bondsmen, "losing the joy of this world,
eagerly seized upon the offered conceptions of the next."
Woodson discerned the relationship between discontent and
protest in a number of slave songs but described them as
basically lamentational in character.[19]

Herein was the dilemma. Revisionist writers, perhaps having soured on the institutional Negro church of their
day, were not able to view the Christianity which the slaves
expressed as other than useful for psychic survival. Those
features of "hush-arbor" religion which did serve the cause
of liberation and black self-identity were traced back to the
African heritage, even though there might be, as was the
case with the prophetic style of Nat Turner's preaching,
kindred ties to the Bible. There seemed to be no way to
put together an interpretation that would stress the theme of
resistance against oppression with a view of Christianity that
was functional toward that end. Miles Mark Fisher, in his
groundbreaking study of slave songs, resorted to robbing the
spirituals of their essentially religious content in order to
relate their coded messages to the quest of secular, that is,
earthly freedom. [20]

Psychic survival or the ability to stand up under the
crushing yoke of slavery, to keep on keeping on, even if
that was all that the Negro found in Christianity, is not, of
course, to be gainsaid. One wonders what else can be said.
Much more has been said as a result of the events since
Martin Luther King, Jr., made the Bible "a flaming source
of inspiration" in the Civil Rights struggle. Dr. King, with
his prophetic summons for love in action and for concretized
justice, stripped away the myth of the docile, other-worldly
Negro preacher. During the turbulent 1960s, some blacks
moved beyond the strategy of passive civil disobedience and
attempted to further radicalize the Negro churches. Searching for a useable past, they began to emphasize the historic
protest strain in Negro religion and cast out the compensatory thesis in favor of the revolutionary one. The secret
religious meetings of the slaves, the "invisible institution"
on the plantations, were viewed as planning sessions for rebellion. Correlations between religious fervor and resistance began to be stressed, as in the case of Nat Turner. [22]
The story of the rise of the independent Negro churches in
the North was interpreted so as to fit the contemporary demands of Black Nationalism. [23]

Black Religion: The Search for a Useable Past

In searching for a useable past, perhaps too much of
the mood of the 1960s has been read back into the history of
the pioneer period of the independent Negro churches. Can
the actions of Allen, Jones, Varick, Williams, Payne, and

the like, be best understood by measuring them against the
demands of Black Nationalism, Black Power, and Black
Separtism, as these concepts are currently used? I think
not. Clio, the muse of history, can be roughly handled by
many different kinds of groups who seek her blessing upon
present struggles.

While the garb of the Black Christian Nationalist
would but poorly fit Richard Allen and his compatriots, we
by no means intend to underestimate their accomplishments
as "race men." They were making a positive assertion of
black pride and black self-reliance. As Lerone Bennet, Jr.,
wrote, Allen, Jones, and their followers discovered a new
sense of themselves--"the idea of an African-Methodist per-
sonality."[24] By seeking religious freedom in their own
house, these Negro churchmen were making a public affirmation of black dignity, but they by no means intended to
found an exclusivist or separatist fellowship based solely on
race.[25] It was the caste nature of white religion that contributed to the rise of the independent black churches. Frederick Douglass's North Star scorned the separated Negro
churches as "negro pews, on a higher and larger scale."[26]
As blacks engaged in a long drawn out struggle for racial
assimilation and church integration in the twentieth century,
the legitimacy of all-black denominations and the reputation
of Richard Allen were again called into question. Douglass's
remark was certainly conditioned by his passionate concern
that no excuse be given the dominant society to further maintain any institution, be it the colored school or the Negro
car on the railroad, based on the pigmentation of a man's
skin. The more recent miscasting of the character of the
antebellum Negro denominations arises from a misunderstand-
ing of their nature and purpose.

The varied movements which brought the independent
Negro churches into existence were not an attempt to re-
create or revive a special kind of African religious per-
sonality. There is little evidence that the first generation
of pioneer black churchmen abandoned their customary forms
of worship, Christian traditions, theological beliefs, patterns
of piety, or organizational structures for an indigenous African one. What they did do was to establish black churches
under black leadership. In a sense they were only doing
what, out of practical necessity and out of their understanding
of the true spirit of Christianity, they had to do in order to
meet the whole needs, physical and spiritual, of black people.
Thus, by circumstance and not be design, they became ethnic

churches. But had not the white denominations already become ethnic churches, by circumstances and by design?[27]

"Methodism," Bishop Daniel Payne wrote in response
to an accusation that it degraded the Negro, "is Christianity
in earnest." Five decades after the founding of the A.M.E.
Church, Payne declared that there was "no essential difference between the Methodism that came from the hand of
Wesley--or as it assumed the American form, under the
presiding minds of Coke and Asbury--and that which was
chosen by the Founders of the A.M.E. Church."[28] The
genius of the independent black churches, be they Baptist or
Methodist, was that they held true to the egalitarian principles of the likes of a Wesley or a Roger Williams while at
the same time providing blacks with a more adequate platform for expressing their religious and racial views. Even
though the white churches had been captivated by the spirit
of exclusiveness, Allen and his co-laborers hoped for a visible expression of religious fellowship between white and black
and, like Martin Luther King, Jr., valued reconciliation
more than separatism. The unabated intransigence, paternalism, and intolerance of white Christians made the hoped-
for fellowship impossible.

The current quest for a Black Theology is perhaps
the most publicized result of the effect of the post-Civil
Rights black experience upon Negro religious thought. The
craftsmen are still at their benches, their handiwork varies,
and the end product is not yet in sight. But enough of its
features have been formed so as to discern something of the
nature and purpose of Black Theology. More concentration
on the here and now, Jesus as the liberator of the oppressed,
power for black people, which is described as more than the
espousal of correct Christian dogmatics, a disdain for a
white piety that is a mask for racism, and a celebration of
the folk element in Negro religion are some of the important
features of Black Theology. It flows out of the experiences
of the black community, is given substance by the contribution of Negro voices from the past, such as Payne, Garnet,
and Turner, and has cultural ties to African traditional religions. Black Theology condones neither resignation nor
accommodation but views liberation and black dignity as the
acid test of the Gospel. Traditional eschatology or talk
about heaven and the hereafter is given little attention. The
focus is on ways in which religious beliefs can serve to increase power and freedom in the here and now. To some
exponents, such as Albert Cleage, Jr., Black Theology means

black religious ethnocentrism. But Black Theology for others
has universal overtones, so that oppressed and oppressor are,
regardless of ethnic identification, both confronted by judgment and hope. [29]

    "To preserve the spiritual in realistic secular power
communities," writes Joseph R. Washington, Jr., "is a task
whereby black theologians would be faithful to the tradition
of black religion in the past and add a much needed dimension
to all religious life in this society. "[30] There certainly are
parallels between strands in the developing tapestry of Black
Theology and the common purposes that united the pioneer
Negro churchmen in service to the black community. Social
cohesion, justice, liberation, racial elevation, and self-help
are goals shared by both nineteenth-century and contemporary
Negro churchmen. But Allen should not be dragged into the
present and forced to fit a mode of pragmatic spirituality
which finds both its authentication and fulfillment strictly in
the here and now. Allen was able to retain both a thisworldly and an otherworldly frame of reference. His pietistic self and his socially conscious self were not in tension.
For him, as for most of the Negro churchmen who picked
up his mantle after his death, a gospel that was not both
eminently personal and social was not the Gospel. Perhaps
it is only the obscured vision of the modern mind, with its
ready habit of distinguishing between the sacred and the secular, that would ask Allen to choose between a religion that
is otherworldly and compensatory and one that is pragmati-
cally and socially conscious. [31]

    "To have hope," Major J. Jones has written quoting
Jürgen Moltmann, is "not only a consolation in suffering,
but also the protest of divine promise against suffering. "[32]
The genius of black Christians, slave and free, was that they
were able to forge a faith that enabled them to both endure
and oppose oppression. Having traveled through the valley
of shadows, they sensed something of the irony and mystery
of God's rule over history. In the Evangelical message,
cleansed of the stains of prejudice, they discovered a reason
to hope. This hope was grounded in the belief that there
was an eternal order of justice and love that called into
question all earthly institutions which were an affront to
human dignity. As Timothy L. Smith has written, with respect to slave prayer meetings and revivals, the ecstasy of
black Christians "represented not so much a flight from
reality as a celebration of their discovery of the strength
with which to face it. "[33]

Kyle Haselden has detected a tendency among whites
to cleave Christian piety into two parts. They apply the
active, positive virtues to themselves--noble, manly, wise,
strong, and courageous. Black Christians are left with the
passive and supposedly negative adjectives, such as patient,
long-suffering, humble, self-effacing, childlike, and submis-
sive. [34] Christian piety, at least in its classic formulations,
cannot be so easily divided, nor are the two sets of characteristics to which Haselden refers necessarily in conflict.
Much depends on the circumstances. Given the rigidity of
American racism and the severity of slavery, patient en-
durance on the part of black Christians may have been both
an expression of strength and nobility as well as the better
part of valor. Grace under pressure is still grace.

Negro Christians responded in many different ways to
the Gospel. In some it fostered the cry of protest, the discovery of collective power, and the struggle for self-deter-
mination. To others it gave a new sense of self, of history,
of the presence of the spirit of God even in the valley of the
shadow of death. In life, as in a battle, each man and
woman draws a line beyond which he or she will not yield.
The location of that last redoubt varies with the individual.
Some erect it in close proximity to the enemy, vulnerable
and exposed, but on the outer edge of all that is worth protecting and preserving. Others place that last safehold much
closer to home, concentrating their meager resources in
defense of personal dignity and the sanctity of their own
souls. Negro Christians did both. In the first instance,
they have been described as thisworldly and manly; in the
second, they have been portrayed as otherworldly and compromising. But the judgments have not always been valid
nor the conclusions well-drawn.

"A careful examination of any man's life, " writes
Howard Thurman in Deep Is the Hunger, "would reveal that,
at one point, he bends with the wind and keeps on living,
while at another point he defies the wind and is quite prepared to be brought crashing to the ground. "[35]

POSTSCRIPT

"Use not vain repetitions, " Scriptures say. With this admonition in mind, I shall not try to conclude this study with redundant remarks about the many issues surrounding the theme of American Evangelicalism and black religion. I wish to let a voice from the past have the final word. Occasionally a historian encounters a piece of evidence that so effectively focuses many of the problems with which he has dealt that it is worthy of special attention. Such is the case with two letters that James W. C. Pennington wrote in 1844, one to his family and one to his former master.[1]

Pennington was surely one of the most remarkable of the Negro churchmen before the Civil War. While still technically a slave, he was awarded an honorary Doctor of Divinity degree by the prestigious University of Heidelberg during one of his visits to Europe as an abolitionist lecturer. He authored the first history textbook on the American Negro, designed for the use of school children. From 1848 to 1856, he served as pastor of the First Colored Presbyterian Church in New York City. His ministry was of a peripatetic nature, as Negroes were forbidden by city ordinances to ride the public conveyances. Pennington was active in the convention movement for the improvement of Negroes and was well respected in the black community. The fugitive blacksmith, as he called himself, died in 1871.

In 1844 Pennington wrote two revealing letters, one to those of his family still in bondage and one to his former master. Seventeen years earlier he had left his parents, six sisters, and four brothers on a plantation in Maryland and with the North Star as his only guide, walked a hundred miles to freedom. During years of preaching from Sabbath to Sabbath in the North, Pennington often thought of his family, many of whom had been sold into the deep South after his escape. When he baptized Negro children in his church in New

172

York, he was reminded of those of his family in slavery who
remained without the blessings of this Holy Ordinance. And
many times as he taught the Gospel to hundreds of children
in freedom, Pennington longed to be able to instruct his own
brothers and sisters. It is exceedingly difficult to give expression to the agony of soul which Pennington experienced.
To his family he wrote: "While visiting the sick, going to
the house of mourning, and burying the dead, I have been a
constant mourner for you."[2]

Pennington's master had made no special provision for
the religious instruction of the slaves on his plantation. But
two important figures, the slave exhorter and the Methodist
preacher, were part of Pennington's religious experience
while a slave. From Sabbath to Sabbath the Negro exhorter
went to the various parts of the neighborhood, usually conducting funeral services, praying, singing, and preaching.
The Methodist preacher was arrested, Pennington recalled,
for telling the slaves, "You have precious immortal souls,
that are worth far more to you than your bodies are to your
masters"--or words to that effect. Pennington was converted
while living with a Presbyterian family in New York City.[3]

Pennington's letter to his master gives voice to the
fundamental meaning that Christianity gave to the Negro's
understanding of slavery. Pennington declared that slavery
had no divine sanction but was the invention of wicked men,
instigated by the devil. To his master, Pennington wrote:
"And I verily believe that I have performed a sacred duty
to God and myself, and a kindness to you, in taking the
blood of my soul peacably off your soul." There would come
a day, Pennington warned, when the slaveholder must appear
before "the awful bar of the impartial Judge of all who doeth
right." At that time all accounts would be settled. Master
and slave would stand as equals before the bar of God.
Pennington warned his master that he would have a complaint
against him for 20 years of suffering. As for himself, Pennington declared: "I have nothing to fear when we both fall
into the hands of the just God."[4]

Pennington wrote to his family of his abiding concern
for their welfare and of his prayer that because of his actions they would not suffer additional cruel treatment. To
his aged parents, who had borne the yoke of slavery for so
long, he offered the hope of a blessed rest in heaven where
the wicked would cease troubling them and where the oppressed no longer hear the voice of their oppressors. "The small

and great are there," Pennington reminded them, quoting
from Job, "and the servant is free from his master." This
was to be their consolation. Christianity was to be their
buoyant principle. True, slaveholders had perverted the
Christian message and made it a gospel of oppression. But
Pennington urged his family to cling to the fundamental truths
of the Gospel of the Son of God. We do not know if his family ever received this letter of 1844. In a sense, it was
more than a letter to one slave family; it was the voice of
the Negro church trumpeting the good news of freedom in
Jesus Christ to the bondsmen. Pennington eloquently exclaimed:

> The gospel rightly understood, taught, received,
> felt, and practised, is anti-slavery as it is anti-
> sin. Just so far and so fast as the true spirit of
> the Gospel obtains in the land, and especially in
> the lives of oppressed, will the spirit of slavery
> sicken and become powerless like the serpent with
> his head pressed beneath the fresh leaves of the
> prickly ash of the forest. [5]

CHAPTER NOTES

PROLOGUE

[1]Will Herberg, Protestant-Catholic-Jew (rev. ed.; Garden City, N.Y.: Anchor Books, 1960), p. 114. Vincent Harding, "Religion and Resistance Among Antebellum Negroes, 1800-1860," in The Making of Black America, Vol. I of The Origins of Black Americans, ed. by August Meier and Elliott Rudwick (New York: Atheneum, 1969), p. 179. Robert T. Handy, "Negro Christianity and American Church Historiography," in Reinterpretations in American Church History, ed. by Jerald C. Brauer (Chicago: University of Chicago Press, 1968), pp. 91-92.

[2]Carter G. Woodson, The History of the Negro Church (1st ed.; Washington, D.C.: The Associated Publishers, 1921). A second edition was published in 1945.

[3]Carter G. Woodson, "The Negro Church, an All-Comprehending Institution," The Negro History Bulletin, III, 1 (October, 1939), 7.

[4]Robert Baird, Religion in America, a critical abridgment with introduction by Henry Warner Bowden (New York: Harper & Row, 1970), p. 301. Originally published in unabridged form in 1856 by Harper & Brothers, Publishers, New York.

[5]Solomon Northup, Twelve Years a Slave, in Puttin' On Ole Massa, ed. by Gilbert Osofsky (New York: Harper & Row, 1963), p. 275. Northup's narrative was first published in 1853 by Derby and Miller in Auburn, New York.

[6]Benjamin Drew, The Refugee: A North-Side View of Slavery (Boston: John P. Jewett and Company, 1856), p. 108.

[7]Timothy L. Smith, "Slavery and Theology: The Emergence of Black Christian Consciousness in Nineteenth-Century America," Church History, XLI, 4 (December, 1972), 497.

[8]Benjamin Quarles, Black Abolitionists (New York: Oxford University Press, Inc., 1969), p. ix.

[9]A recent survey of the union efforts of the three major black

denominations of the Methodist persuasion is Roy W. Trueblood's "Union Negotiations Between Black Methodists in America, " Metho- dist History, XIII (July, 1970), 18-29. The first serious proposal for uniting the Bethelites and the Zionites came in 1864, but long- standing hard feelings born of disputes over Richard Allen's attempt to force the Zionists to join with the A.M.E. Church in 1820 and serious structural differences brought the endeavor to naught. The formation of the Colored Methodist Episcopal Church in 1870 for black members from the Methodist Episcopal Church, South, added a new divisive factor to the discussions.

[10]Edwin S. Gaustad, "America's Institutions of Faith: A Statistical Postscript, " in Religion in America, ed. by William C. McLoughlin and Robert N. Bellah (Boston: Beacon Press, 1968), pp. 115-17.

[11]Smith, "Slavery and Theology, " 502.

CHAPTER I

[1]Francis Grund, The Americans in Their Moral, Social, and Political Relations (1837), excerpted in The Voluntary Church, ed. by Milton Powell (New York: The Macmillan Company, 1967), p. 81.

[2]Quoted by Sidney E. Mead, "The 'Nation with the Soul of a Church', " Church History, XXXVI, 3 (September, 1967), 262. Using the term "line" instead of "wall, " Prof. Mead has perceptively ana- lyzed the relationship between State and Church in post-Revolutionary America. The debate was not, he argues, between State and Church in the Old World fashion, but between the particularistic theologies of the sects and the cosmopolitan theology of the Republic. See his "Neither Church nor State: Reflections on James Madison's 'Line of Separation', " The Journal of Church and State, X, 3 (Autumn, 1968), 349-68.

[3]Leonard Woolsey Bacon, A History of American Christianity, Vol. XIII of The American Church History Series, ed. by Phillip Schaff, et al. (New York: The Christian Literature Company, 1897), p. 230.

[4]Quoted by Winthrop Hudson, Religion in America (New York: Charles Scribner's Sons, 1965), p. 131.

[5]The crowds attending services were frequently three times as large as the official rolls of churches which required a con- version experience for membership. In 1800 the total church audi- ence may have been as much as 40 per cent of the national popula- tion. In 1860, when the religious constituency of the country was nearly 70 per cent, the membership rolls accounted for about 20 per cent. It is only with the broadening of the concept of church mem- bership in the post-Civil War era that official statistics began to

convey some idea of the strength of organized religion. Franklin H. Littell, "The Churches and the Body Politic," in Religion in America, ed. by William G. McLoughlin and Robert N. Bellah (Boston: Beacon Press, 1968), pp. 25, 28. H. Shelton Smith, Robert T. Handy, and Lefferts A. Loetscher, American Christianity: An Historical Interpretation with Representative Documents (2 vols.; New York: Charles Scribner's Sons, 1966), I, 519. Hudson, Religion in America, pp. 129-30. Edwin S. Gaustad, Historical Atlas of Religion in America (New York: Harper & Row, 1962), p. 42.

[6]Benjamin Trumbull, A Complete History of Connecticut, Civil and Ecclesiastical, From the Emigration of Its First Planters from England, in the Year 1630, to the Year 1764 (2 vols.: New Haven, Conn.: Mattby, Goldsmith, and Company, 1818), II, 18.

[7]G. Adolf Koch, Religion of the American Enlightenment (New York: Thomas Crowell Company, 1968), pp. 244-47. Hudson, Religion in America, p. 110. Bacon, History of American Christianity, p. 230. Sydney E. Ahlstrom, A Religious History of the American People (New Haven, Conn.: Yale University Press, 1972), pp. 364-79.

[8]Quoted by Charles Roy Keller, The Second Great Awakening in Connecticut (New Haven, Conn.: Yale University Press, 1942), p. 26. This cleric, a certain Thomas Robbins, had formerly referred to Jefferson as that "howling atheist."

[9]Nathan Bangs, A History of the Methodist Episcopal Church (2 vols.; New York: Mason and Lane, 1840), II, 21. See also, Koch, American Enlightenment, pp. 239-84. In the antebellum era the Evangelicals continued to exploit the image of the infidel, both as a foil to their campaigns to save America and as a means of shoring up internal discipline. See Albert Post, Popular Freethought in America, 1825-1850 (New York: Columbia University Press, 1943), pp. 199-225. The technique of exploiting the infidel threat was no longer useful or necessary when the Evangelicals achieved national prominence. Martin E. Marty, The Infidel (New York: The World Publishing Company, 1961), pp. 108-18, 179-93.

[10]Quoted by William Warren Sweet, Religion in the Development of American Culture, 1765-1840 (New York: Charles Scribner's Sons, 1952), p. 135.

[11]Rush Welter, "The Frontier West as Image of American Society: Conservative Attitudes before the Civil War," The Mississippi Valley Historical Review, XLVI, 4 (March, 1960), 597. Hudson, Religion in America, p. 130.

[12]Baptists and Methodists were making vigorous efforts in behalf of the multitudes in Virginia before the Revolution. But the revival among students at Hampden-Sydney and Washington Colleges in 1787 is usually taken as inaugurating the Second Great Awakening.

178   Black Religion

The story is told in Wesley M. Gewehr's The Great Awakening in
Virginia, 1740-1790 (Durham, N.C.: Duke University Press, 1930).
At about the same time, the rise to power of the New Divinity group
in Connecticut began an awakening in New England. See Keller,
Second Great Awakening in Connecticut. Presbyterians, Methodists,
and Baptists, despite some significant doctrinal differences, cooper-
ated in fostering "quickened interest" in the Carolinas, Kentucky,
and Tennessee. The account of the Great Revival of 1800 in the
Cumberland River region is told in Catherine C. Cleveland's The
Great Revival in the West, 1797-1805 (Chicago: University of Chicago Press, 1916). For the activities of Charles G. Finney, see
Bernard A. Weisberger, They Gathered at the River (Chicago:
Quadrangle Books, Inc., 1966), Chapters IV, V; and Whitney R.
Cross, The Burned-Over District (New York: Harper & Row, 1965),
especially pp. 151-160, 173-84, 238-51.

13Donald G. Mathews, "The Second Great Awakening as Or-
ganizing Process, 1780-1830: An Hypothesis," American Quarterly,
XXI, 1 (Spring, 1969), 27-30. William Warren Sweet, with the
Turner thesis in mind, has made much of the meliorating and civi-
lizing influence of the church on the frontier. See his Religion in
American Culture, particularly Chapter IV, "Religion Follows the
Frontier," and Chapter V, "Barbarism Versus Revivalism." Also
see his "The Churches As Moral Courts of the Frontier," Church
History, II, 1 (March, 1933), 3-21.

14Quoted by W. D. Blanks, "Corrective Church Discipline in
the Presbyterian Churches of the Nineteenth-Century South," The
Journal of Presbyterian History, XLIV, 2 (June, 1966), 91.

15In Methodist circles most laymen were tried at the local
level by the congregation, class meeting, or ad hoc committee. The
clergy were more often given hearings before the quarterly conferences. Baptists had a very unstructured kind of church discipline.
A great deal of it was taken care of by the local congregation; the
Baptist associations were advisory only. In the Presbyterian and
Episcopalian denominations, a system of lower and higher courts
made it possible for the alleged offender to carry his case as far as
the synod and convention level. See Cortland Victor Smith, "Church
Organization As an Agency of Social Control: Church Discipline in
North Carolina, 1800-1860" (unpublished Ph.D. dissertation, Uni-
versity of North Carolina, 1966), passim; Wade Crawford Barclay,
To Reform a Nation, Vol. I of Early American Methodism, 1769-
1844 (2 vols.; New York: Board of Missions & Church Extension of
the Methodist Church, 1950), pp. 347-67; Ernest Trice Thompson,
Presbyterians in the South, 1607-1861 (Richmond, Va.: John Knox
Press, 1963), pp. 314-22; and William Manross, The Episcopal
Church in the United States, 1800-1840 (New York: Columbia University Press, 1938), pp. 138-40.

16Timothy L. Smith, Revivalism and Social Reform (New
York: Harper & Row, 1965), pp. 63-79. This is a most informed

and well-documented study of the system of organized benevolence on the eve of the Civil War. It is a needed corrective to Charles I. Foster's An Errand of Mercy: The Evangelical United Front (Chapel Hill, N.C.: University of North Carolina Press, 1960) in which a case was made for the dissolution of united benevolence after the 1830s.

[17]Smith, Revivalism and Social Reform, p. 79. This accounts for the inordinate amount of attention, Smith argues, which is usually given to such groups as the Mormon theocrats, Shakers, Millerites, and numerous other fringe religionists in such works as Alice F. Tyler's Freedom's Ferment: Phases of American Social History to 1860 (Minneapolis: University of Minnesota Press, 1944). I would add The Stammering Century (New York: The John Day Company, Inc., 1928) by Gilbert Seldes as an example of the kind of history which has focused on the minor movements and manias in nineteenth-century American religion and ignored mainstream Evangelical Protestantism. Also see Richard Hofstadter, Anti-Intellectualism in American Life (New York: Vintage Books, 1963), p. 87. Hofstadter traces the anti-intellectual strain in American Evangelicalism from Charles Finney to Dwight Moody and Billy Sunday. Ibid., pp. 81-116.

[18]William G. McLoughlin, ed., The American Evangelicals, 1800-1900, An Anthology (New York: Harper & Row, 1968), p. 12.

[19]Ahlstrom, Religious History of the American People, pp. 438-39, 452-54. Sydney E. Ahlstrom, "The Scottish Philosophy and American Theology," Church History, XXIV, 3 (September, 1955), 257-72.

[20]Ralph H. Gabriel, "Evangelical Religion and Popular Romanticism in Early Nineteenth Century America," Church History, XIX, 1 (March, 1950), 34-47. H. Shelton Smith, Changing Conceptions of Original Sin (New York: Charles Scribner's Sons, 1955), Chapters V, VI. Sydney E. Ahlstrom, ed., Theology in America (New York: The Bobbs-Merrill Company, Inc., 1967), pp. 41-45.

[21]Lyman Beecher, "The Faith Once Delivered to the Saints," from his Sermons Delivered on Various Occasions (Boston, 1828), reprinted in McLoughlin, ed., American Evangelicals, p. 71.

[22]Robert Baird, Religion in America, ed. and abridged by Henry Warner Bowden (New York: Harper & Row, 1970), p. 183. Originally published in unabridged form in 1856 by Harper & Brothers, New York.

[23]Smith, Revivalism and Social Reform, pp. 225-37. The millennial theme in American history is expanded upon in Ernest Lee Tuveson's Redeemer Nation (Chicago: University of Chicago Press, 1968).

[24]Kenneth Scott Latourette, The Great Century in Europe and

180   Black Religion

the United States of America, A.D.1800-A.D.1914, Vol. IV of A
History of the Expansion of Christianity (4 vols.; New York and
London: Harper & Brothers, 1946), p. 7.

[25]The organization in England of the Particular Baptist Society for Propagating the Gospel amongst the Heathen on October
2, 1792, at the urging of William Carey, is usually cited as marking
a new era in the history of Protestant missions, an unprecedented
period both in organized activity and in concrete results. See
Latourette, The Great Century, pp. 65-69. When reports of Carey's
work in India reached America, students at Andover Theological
Seminary requested that as New World Christians they be allowed
to carry the Gospel to heathen lands. As a consequence, the American Board of Commissioners for Foreign Missions was formed in
1812, and five men sailed for India, the most famous being Adoniram
Judson and Luther Rice. Rice soon returned but Judson went up to
Burma and there founded the great model of mission fields. The
best survey of America's early foreign mission impulse is the dissertation of Clifton Jackson Phillips, recently reproduced by the
East Asian Research Center of Harvard University Protestant America and the Pagan World: The First Half Century of the American
Board of Commissioners for Foreign Missions, 1810-1860 (Cambridge, Mass.: Harvard University Press, 1969). See especially,
pp. 13, 19-23, 34-35.

[26]Jerald C. Brauer, Protestantism in America (Philadelphia:
The Westminster Press, 1953), pp. 140-46. The American Home
Missionary Society did not disband officially until 1892 and left
voluminous records of its activities. Colin Brummit Goodykoontz
has written its history in his Home Missions on the American Frontier, With Particular Reference to the American Home Missionary
Society (Caldwell, Idaho: Caxton Printers, Ltd., 1939).

[27]William Capers, "Letter," Southern Christian Advocate,
XIII (January 18, 1850), 130, as cited by Thomas Leonard Williams,
"Methodist Mission to the Slaves" (unpublished Ph.D. dissertation,
Yale, 1943), p. 92. Luther Porter Jackson, "Religious Instruction
of Negroes, 1830-1860, with Special Reference to South Carolina,"
The Journal of Negro History, XV, 1 (January, 1930), 102.

[28]Letter, Henry Ruffner to William S. Plumer, June 17,
1834, Presbyterian Historical Society, Plumer Letter File.

[29]"Philander" [James O. Andrew], "Miscellanies," Wesleyan
Journal, I (July 1, 1826), 159. Cited by Williams, "The Methodist
Mission to the Slaves," p. 29. This plea for domestic missions
pricked the conscience of the Rev. John B. Adger, a Presbyterian
missionary to the Armenians, to such an extent that he returned
home to work among "the colored population," confessing that he felt
that it was "time for me to cast in my lot with my own people."
Adger, The Religious Instruction of the Colored Population, A Sermon, May 9, 1847 (Charleston, S.C.: T. W. Haynes, 1847), p. 5.

[30]Charles C. Jones, Suggestions on the Religious Instruction
of The Negroes in The Southern States; Together with an Appendix
Containing Forms of Church Registers, Form of a Constitution, and
Plans of Different Denominations of Christians (Philadelphia: Presbyterian Board of Publication, 1847), p. 9.

[31]Charles C. Jones, Report of the Committee to Whom Was
Referred the Subject of the Religious Instruction of the Colored Population of the Synod of South Carolina and Georgia at its Sessions in
Columbia, South Carolina, December 5th-9th, 1833 (Charleston,
S.C.: Observer Office Press, 1834), p. 4. In addition to this
synodical report, Jones was the author of 13 annual reports, from
1833 to 1848, on the work of the Association for the Religious Instruction of Negroes, which he organized in Liberty County, Georgia,
in 1831. We shall have occasion in Chapter II to comment frequently
on the contributions of this important Presbyterian missionary.

[32]Quoted by Lorenzo Johnston Greene, The Negro in Colonial
New England, 1620-1776 (New York: Columbia University Press,
1942), p. 257.

[33]Greene, Negro in Colonial New England, pp. 257-89. Mar-
cus W. Jernegan, "Slavery and Conversion in the American Colo-
nies," The American Historical Review, XXI, 33 (April, 1916), 504-
27. Edgar L. Pennington, "Thomas Bray's Associates and Their
Work Among the Negroes," Proceedings of the American Antiquarian
Society, New Series, XLVIII (1938), 311-418. Henry J. Cadbury,
"Negro Membership in the Society of Friends," The Journal of Negro
History, XXI, 2 (April, 1936), 151-213. Carter G. Woodson, The
Education of the Negro Prior to 1861 (2nd ed.; Washington, D.C.:
The Associated Publishers, Inc., 1919), pp. 18-50.

[34]In 1664 Maryland enacted a law which specifically stated
that Christian Baptism did not alter the condition of black slaves,
who were to serve "for life." The other colonies subsequently
passed similar laws. See Winthrop D. Jordan, White Over Black
(Baltimore: Pelican Books, 1969), pp. 180-87. See also, David
Brion Davis, The Problem of Slavery in Western Culture (Ithaca,
N.Y.: Cornell University Press, 1966), pp. 197-222.

[35]Jernegan states: "We must conclude from all the evidence
that the struggle between the contending forces had on the whole resulted in the victory for those who were antagonistic to the conversion of the Negroes." "Slavery and Conversion," 526. See also,
Greene, Negro in Colonial New England, p. 289.

[36]Jernegan, "Slavery and Conversion," 523, note 123. There
are no reliable statistics on Negro members of white churches at the
outbreak of the American Revolution. My estimate is based on the
fact that the figure of 4 to 5 per cent for Negro church membership
was not reached until 1800. Gaustad, Historical Atlas, p. 150.

[37]Department of the Commerce, Bureau of the Census, Negro Population, 1790-1915 (Washington, D.C.: Government Printing Office, 1918), p. 25.

[38]Manross, Episcopal Church in the United States, pp. 48-53, 63-65.

[39]Quoted by Margaret Burr Des Champs, "The Presbyterian Church in the South Atlantic States, 1801-1861" (unpublished Ph.D. dissertation, Emory University, 1952), p. 18. Robert Ellis Thompson, A History of the Presbyterian Church in the United States (New York: The Christian Literature Co., 1895), p. 68.

[40]Wade Crawford Barclay, Missionary Motivation and Expansion, Vol. I of Early American Methodism, 1769-1844 (2 vols.; New York: Board of Missions and Church Extension of the Methodist Church, 1949-50), pp. 124, 127. Gaustad, Historical Atlas, pp. 56-57, 76, 78.

[41]The Presbyterians were represented in the South in 1830 by about 38,000 members. But their strength was largely outside the slave states, as evidenced by the fact that in 1830 they had 49,741 communicants in the state of New York alone. The Lutheran Churches, principally located in the Middle Atlantic states, had a total of 45,000 members in 1830. After that time their membership increased markedly by a wave of German immigrants, but few of these settled in the South. Despite signs of recovery, the Protestant-Episcopal Church could not claim any statistical victory by 1830, as it numbered only some 30,000 across the entire country. Slow progress was being made in South Carolina and Virginia. Thompson, Presbyterians in the South, p. 175. Abdel Ross Wentz, A Basic History of Lutheranism in America (rev. ed.; Philadelphia: Fortress Press, 1964), p. 109. Gaustad, Historical Atlas, p. 67.

[42]William M. Wightman, Life of William Capers, D.D., One of the Bishops of The Methodist Episcopal Church, South, Including an Autobiography (Nashville, Tenn.: Southern Methodist Publishing House, 1858), p. 206. The first 228 pages of this volume comprise Caper's account of his own life up to and including his thirty-first year. The autobiographical portion will henceforth be cited as Wightman, Life of Capers. The kind of faith which Capers described has been passed down to the present day and can be found in the so-called Bible-belt region of the South. See Wilbur J. Cash, The Mind of the South (New York: Alfred A. Knopf, Inc., 1941), p. 58.

[43]Minutes of the Annual Conferences of the Methodist Church, 1773-1828 (2 vols.; New York: T. Mason & G. Lane, 1840), I, 26.

[44]Charles C. Jones, The Religious Instruction of the Negroes in the United States (Savannah, Ga.: Thomas Purse, 1842), pp. 40, 56. This account, by a central figure in the plantation mission movement, is a most important historical source. It was the first attempt to survey the subject of Negro missions and covered the

period from 1620 to 1842. Jones discovered that only the Methodists had preserved records of Negro membership and that most of
their success during the first quarter century after their organization in the United States was in the Middle and Southern states.

[45]Robert B. Semple, A History of the Rise and Progress of
the Baptists in Virginia, revised and extended by G. W. Beale
(Philadelphia: American Baptist Publications Society, 1894), p. 290.

[46]Garnett Ryland, The Baptists in Virginia, 1699-1926 (Richmond, Va.: The Virginia Board of Missions and Education, 1955),
p. 281.

[47]William S. Plumer, Thoughts on the Religious Instruction
of the Negroes of this Country (Savannah, Ga.: Edward J. Purse,
1848, p. 14. Jones reported that the situation of the Baptists was
as follows: "The Baptists have no societies in existence expressly
for evangelizing the Negroes; although their associations and conventions do from time to time call up the subject and act upon it.
There are more Negro communicants, and more churches regularly
constituted, exclusively of Negroes, with their own regular houses
of public worship, and with ordained Negro preachers, attached to
their denomination than to any other denomination in the United
States." Religious Instruction of the Negroes, p. 91.

CHAPTER II

[1]Letter, Mrs. M. J. Davis to Richard T. Davis, January
26, 1854, University of Virginia, Archives, Preston-Davis Manuscripts. Supplied to me by Ann Stauffenberg, Manuscripts Division,
University of Virginia Library.

[2]Carter G. Woodson, The Education of the Negro Prior to
1861 (2nd ed.; Washington, D.C.: The Associated Publishers, Inc.,
1919), p. 93 and passim.

[3]Ernest Trice Thompson, Presbyterians in the South (Richmond, Va.: John Knox Press, 1963), p. 175. Other examples of
individuals who preached to Negroes while ministering chiefly to a
white congregation are the Rev. John Jacob Tschudy in Berkeley,
South Carolina; the Rev. John Bachman in Charleston; and the Rev.
Henry Patillo in Greenville County, North Carolina. See Edgar
Legare Pennington, The Reverend John Jacob Tschundy, Dalcho
Papers, No. 6 (Charleston, S.C.: The Dalcho Historical Society,
1954), p. 5. William Wohler, John Bachman: Letters and Memories of His Life (Charleston, S.C.: Evans & Cogwell, 1888). William S. Plumer, Thoughts on the Religious Instruction of the Negroes of this Country (Savannah, Ga.: Edward J. Purse, 1848),
pp. 13-14. Andrew E. Murray, Presbyterians and the Negro--A
History (Philadelphia: Presbyterian Historical Society, 1966), pp.
11-12, 15-16.

184 Black Religion

Charles C. Jones, The Religious Instruction of the Negroes in the United States (Savannah, Ga.: Thomas Purse, 1842), p. 61.

Ibid. See also, Samuel J. Baird, A Collection of the Acts, Deliverances, and Testimonies of the Supreme Judicatory of the Presbyterian Church (Philadelphia: Presbyterian Board of Publication, 1855), p. 817.

William Pope Harrison, ed., The Gospel Among the Slaves (Nashville, Tenn.: Publishing House of the Methodist Episcopal Church, South, 1893), p. 137. For this survey of mission work among the slaves, Harrison edited materials gathered by a certain Annie Maria Barnes. Harrison was at the time the book editor of the Southern Methodists. No mention of the activities, planned or realized, of Mallard and Glenn was made by Charles C. Jones in his Religious Instruction of the Negroes.

Francis Asbury, The Journal and Letters of Francis Asbury, ed. by Elmer T. Clark, J. Manning Pitts, and Jacob S. Payton (3 vols.; Nashville, Tenn.: Abingdon Press, 1958), II, 591. Ezra S. Tipple, Francis Asbury, The Prophet of the Long Road (New York: Methodist Book Concern, 1916).

William M. Wightman, Life of William Capers, D.D., One of the Bishops of The Methodist Episcopal Church, South, Including an Autobiography (Nashville, Tenn.: Southern Methodist Publishing House, 1858), p. 408. Joseph B. Earnest, The Religious Development of the Negro in Virginia (Charlottesville, Va.: The Michie Company, 1914), p. 52.

Robert Emory, History of the Discipline of the Methodist Episcopal Church (New York: G. Lane and P. P. Sanford, 1844), pp. 274-79.

Wightman, Life of Capers, p. 139.

Cited by Thomas Leonard Williams, "The Methodist Mission to the Slaves" (unpublished Ph.D. dissertation, Yale, 1943), p. 37.

Lionell H. Kennedy and Thomas Parker, An Official Report of the Trials of Sundry Negroes, Charged with an Attempt to Raise An Insurrection in the State of South Carolina, in The Trial Record of Denmark Vesey, with an introduction by John Oliver Killens (Boston: Beacon Press, 1970), pp. 31, 16, 58, 85-86, 130.

Herbert Aptheker, American Negro Slave Revolts (New York: Columbia University Press, 1943), pp. 101-02, 224-25. Donald G. Mathews, Slavery and Methodism (Princeton, N.J.: Princeton University Press, 1965, p. 31.

Edwin C. Holland, A Refutation of the Calumnies Circulated Against the Southern and Western States, Respecting the Institution

and Existence of Slavery Among Them (Charleston, S.C.: A. E.
Miller, 1833), p. 11.

[15]William Sumner Jenkins, Pro-Slavery Thought in the Old
South (Chapel Hill, N.C.: University of North Carolina Press,
1935), p. 72.

[16]Richard Furman, Exposition of the Views of the Baptists
Relative to the Colored Population of the United States in a Com-
munication to the Governor of South Carolina (Charleston, S.C.:
A. E. Miller, 1823), p. 15.

[17]Frederic Dalcho, Practical Considerations Founded on the
Scriptures Relative to the Slave Population of South Carolina
(Charleston, S.C.: A. E. Miller, 1823), p. 6.

[18]Plumer, Thoughts on the Religious Instruction of the
Negroes, p. 4.

[19]These societies were principally concerned with domestic
missions among whites in the newly settled areas of the West and
among the Indians.   Little effective work was done among the
slaves.   As the political controversy over slavery increased sectional tensions, the South complained that the national boards did
not understand its peculiar problems.   It became exceedingly difficult for the societies to gain access to the slaves.   For example,
in 1841 the Annual Report of the American Baptist Home Missionary
Society stated: "Attempts have been made by the committee to
erect the standard of the gospel, but their want of success in finding
a suitable man willing to go is humiliating."   Cited by Robert Andrew Baker, "The American Baptist Home Mission Society and the
South, 1832-1894" (unpublished Ph.D. dissertation, Yale, 1947),
p. 52.   Some success, however, was had in the border states, particularly Kentucky.   See Augustus Field Beard, A Crusade of Brotherhood (Boston: The Pilgrim Press, 1909), pp. 97-102.   Beard tells
the story of the American Missionary Association, which was formed
in 1846.   The history of the American Home Missionary Society is
told by Colin Brummitt Goodykontz, Home Missions on The American
Frontier (Caldwell, Idaho: The Caxton Printers, Ltd., 1939).   The
American Baptist Missionary Society conducted no missionary work
between 1832 and 1862 among Negroes in the South "on account of
the general situation throughout the nation."   Charles L. White, A
Century of Faith (Philadelphia: The Judson Press, 1932), p. 102.

[20]Letter, Francis Asbury to Christopher Frye, July 23, 1814,
in Journals and Letters of Francis Asbury, III, 506-07.   Between
1810 and 1815 the white Methodists increased from 139,836 to
167,928 and the blacks from 34,727 to 43,187.   However, in the
previous five-year period the national growth rate had been not less
than 40 per cent, and from 1815 to 1820, despite losses to the
African Methodists, it was nearly 50 per cent.   These figures are
based on those published for the period from 1790 to 1825 in the

Wesleyan Journal of January 14, 1826, as cited by Williams, "Methodist Mission to the Slaves, " p. 25.

[21]Jones, Religious Instruction of the Negroes, pp. 59-60. Daniel Alexander Payne, A History of the African Methodist Episcopal Church, ed. by Charles Spencer Smith (Nashville, Tenn.: Publishing House of the A.M.E. Sunday School Union, 1891), p. 26.

[22]Mathews, Slavery and Methodism, p. 69. Williams, "Methodist Mission to the Slaves, " p. 35. Wightman, Life of Capers, p. 292. Luther P. Jackson, "Religious Instruction of Negroes, 1830-1860, With Special Reference to South Carolina, " The Journal of Negro History, XV, 1 (January, 1930), 81.

[23]Charles Cotesworth Pinckney, An Address Delivered in Charleston before the Agricultural Society of South Carolina at its Anniversary Meeting (Charleston, S.C.: A. E. Miller, 1829), pp. 10, 13.

[24]Wightman, Life of Capers, p. 292.

[25]Susan Markey Fickling, Slave-Conversion in South Carolina, 1830-1860, published as the Bulletin of the University of South Carolina, September, 1924 (Columbia, S.C.: University of South Carolina Press, 1924), pp. 43-44. Albert M. Shipp, The History of Methodism in South Carolina (Nashville, Tenn.: Southern Methodist Publishing House, 1884), p. 458.

[26]The statistics for the plantation missions of the Methodists for the years from 1829 to 1844 are conveniently gathered in Table I of the Appendix. The source is J. C. Hartzell, Methodism and the Negro in the United States (New York: Hunt & Eaton, 1894), p. 16. Hartzell's table is based on the annual reports of Capers' Missionary Society. Shipp, Methodism in South Carolina, p. 468. Jackson, "Religious Instruction of Negroes, " pp. 81-82.

[27]Charles C. Jones, Annual Report of the Missionary to the Negroes, in Liberty County, (Ga.): Presented to the Association, for the Religious Instruction of the Negroes in Liberty Co., Ga., November, 1833 (Charleston, S.C.: Observer Office Press, 1834), p. 5. These reports will henceforth be cited only in relation to the year to which they actually pertain. All were written by Jones with the exception of the eighth one, which was drawn up in 1843 by the Rev. Issac S. K. Axson, president of the Liberty County Association. No report seems to have been published for the year 1836.

[28]Ralph Quarterman Mallard, Plantation Life Before Emancipation (Richmond, Va.: Whittet & Shepperson, 1892). Mallard's recollections are a valuable contemporary witness to the activities of Jones. Mallard's father owned a plantation to which Jones came frequently to preach to the slaves, and he was one of the organizers of the Liberty County Association. The younger Mallard himself

became a missionary to the slaves. He dedicated this volume as follows: "To the Memory of Charles Colcock Jones, D.D., who, Whether His Work as a Missionary to the Blacks, or the Wider Influence of His Example, and Writings in Their Behalf, Be Considered, is Justly Entitled to the Name of the Apostle to the Negro Slaves; and of His Many Fellow Workers in the Gospel Ministry in the Same Field, Only Less Conspicuous, Self-denying and Useful; And of the Host of Masters and Mistresses, Whose Kindness to the Bodies, and Efforts for the Salvation of the Souls of the Subject Race Providentially Placed under Their Rule and Care, Will Be Read Out, With Their Names, in the Day when 'The Book Shall be Opened', and 'God shall bring Every Work into Judgment, with Every Secret Thing, Whether it be Good or Whether it be Evil'."

[29]Robert Manson Myers, The Children of Pride (New Haven, Conn.: Yale University Press, 1972), pp. 16-18. Myers selected and put in chronological order some 1200 letters from a total of over 6000. The reader is thus able to follow the fortunes of the family and their associates in minute and fascinating detail from 1854 to 1868, including the last decade of the life of the Rev. Dr. Charles C. Jones, the destruction of his beloved plantation in the wake of Sherman's march to the sea, and the bitter fruits of the war itself.

[30]Jones, First Annual Report for 1833, p. 6. Mallard, Plantation Life, pp. 74, 92-93, 101.

[31]Jones, First Annual Report for 1833, pp. 7-11.

[32]Jones, Second Annual Report for 1834, pp. 10-11. Jones, Third Annual Report for 1835, p. 1.

[33]Mallard, Plantation Life, pp. 126-127.

[34]Jones, Thirteenth Annual Report for 1848, pp. 45-55.

[35]Mallard, Plantation Life, p. 98.

[36]Charles C. Jones, The Religious Instruction of the Negroes--A Sermon, Delivered Before Associations of Planters in Liberty and M'Intosh Counties, Georgia (4th ed.; Princeton, N.J.: D'Hart & Connelly, 1832), p. 14.

[37]Letter, Charles C. Jones to William S. Plumer, June 28, 1834, Presbyterian Historical Society, Plumer Letter File. See also Jones' Third Annual Report for 1835 (p. 21) in which he states: "The religious instruction of the Negroes, with its accompanying blessings is the security and the present and future prosperity of the Southern States; and that individual who thinks differently has either never studied the subject, or is a disbeliever in revelation."

[38]Jones, Third Annual Report for 1835, p. 20.

188   Black Religion

Pinckney, Address, p. 13.

Mathews, Slavery and Methodism, pp. 82-87. Mathews
argues that religious instruction for the Negroes was idealized as
"the Mission" of the Southern churches in the middle 1840s when
the Methodists, in particular, divided. I contend that from the very
beginning one of the motives of the plantation mission supporters
was to placate the consciences of pious Southerners who were sensitive to Northern charges that at their very doorsteps they were
allowing the Negroes to remain in a more spiritually barren state
than the heathen of Africa. In sum, the plantation missions became
"Africa at home. "

Herbert Aptheker, Nat Turner's Slave Rebellion (New York:
Humanities Press, 1966), pp. 36-38. As a result of this reactionary
situation and because of the laws which prohibited the use of printed
matter in the instruction of the slaves, the mission work now entered
into a period which Carter G. Woodson has called "religion without
letters. " Education of the Negro, pp. 161-62, 179-204.

Jones, Religious Instruction of the Negroes, A Sermon, pp.
19, 27.

Jones, Religious Instruction of the Negroes, p. 96.

Ibid., p. 97. Statistics for the Methodist plantation missions indicate that for 1835 there was a loss of six stations and
about 100 members over the previous year. The station count was
not regained until 1837 and only by 1839 had the Methodists opened
up a significant number of new preaching locations on the plantations.
See Table I in the Appendix.

Stanley M. Elkins, Slavery (New York: Grosset & Dunlap,
1963), pp. 199-200.

The intricate nature of the debates and the mixed motives
of the spokesmen from the presbyteries in the slave states are
examined in Elwyn A. Smith, "The Role of the South in the Presbyterian Schism of 1837-38, " Church History, XXIX, 1 (March, 1960),
44-63. Smith makes the useful observation that no simple connection
can be made between Old School theology and slavery, on the one
hand, and New School theology and abolitionism, on the other. There
were politically conservative churchmen in the New School party,
both in the North and in the South, who disliked the radicals as
much as did the James Henry Thornwells of the slave states. And
there were Old School supporters, mostly in the West, who were
hostile to slavery.

This interpretation is stressed by C. Bruce Staiger in
"Abolitionism and the Presbyterian Schism of 1837-38, " The Mississippi Valley Historical Review, XXXVI, 3 (December, 1949),
391-414.

[48]One of the issues in debate between the Old and New School Presbyterians was the question of participation in the American Home Missionary Society. The Old School faction withdrew entirely in 1838, leaving the New School Assembly to carry on the work of domestic missions in cooperation with the Congregationalists. Even though the A.H.M.S. refused to expel slaveholders from its membership and aided churches of which slaveholders were members, little access was had to the slaves in the South. Clifford S. Griffin, "Cooperation and Conflict: The Schism in the American Home Missionary Society, 1837-1861," The Journal of the Presbyterian Historical Society, XXXVIII, 4 (December, 1960), 213-33.

[49]W. G. Williams, "James Osgood Andrew," in Lives of Methodist Bishops, ed. by Theodore L. Flood and John W. Hamilton (New York: Phillips & Hunt, 1882), p. 540. Donald G. Mathews explains Andrew's delicate situation as follows: "He had been bequeathed at the death of his first wife in 1842 a young Negro girl whom he could have freed and sent either to Liberia or a free state. But the law forbade manumission within the state of Georgia where Andrew lived, and the girl preferred to remain with him. Sometime later, he received a Negro boy in the same manner as the girl although he expected to send the youth to the North when he was old enough to go. Thus Andrew was a slaveholder twice over when he married his second wife. Because Mrs. Andrew owned slaves, and because the bishop did not want to be their master, he secured them to her by a deed of trust. But neither Andrew's reticence nor his legal arrangements could satisfy the abolitionists." Slavery and Methodism, pp. 256-57.

[50]Quoted from the Journal of the General Conference of 1844 by Mathews, Slavery and Methodism, p. 264. The most detailed discussion of the complicated political maneuvering at the 1844 Assembly is John Nelson Norwood's The Schism in the Methodist Episcopal Church, 1844: A Study of Slavery and Ecclesiastical Politics (Alfred, N.Y.: The Alfred University Press, 1923). For the growth of the new abolitionism in Methodist circles prior to 1844 see Mathews, Slavery and Methodism, pp. 113-47.

[51]Quoted by A. H. Redford, History of the Organization of the Methodist Episcopal Church, South (Nashville, Tenn.: Publishing House of the M.E. Church, South, 1871), p. 273.

[52]Andrew, Speech of May 28, 1844, partially reprinted in Redford, Organization of the Methodist Episcopal Church, South, pp. 272-73. See also, Gross Alexander, History of the Methodist Episcopal Church, South, The American Church History Series, Vol. XI (New York: The Christian Literature Company, 1894), p. 34.

[53]Capers, Speech of May 28, 1844, partially reprinted in Redford, Organization of the Methodist Episcopal Church, South, pp. 301-02. Wightman, Life of Capers, pp. 403-08.

[54]Quoted by Mathews, Slavery and Methodism, p. 191.

[55]Quoted by Redford, Organization of the Methodist Episcopal Church, South, p. 303.

[56]Albert H. Newman, A History of the Baptist Churches in the United States (6th ed.; New York: Charles Scribner & Sons, 1915), pp. 445-47. In 1835 the Charleston Baptist Association petitioned the South Carolina State Legislature to the effect that "the said Association does not consider that the holy scriptures have made the fact of slavery a question of morals at all." On the question of South Carolina's right to regulate slavery within her territorial limits, the Association stated: "We would resist to the utmost, every invasion of THIS RIGHT, come from what quarter and under whatever pretense it may." Cited by William Goodell, Slavery and Anti-Slavery; A History of the Great Struggle in Both Hemispheres; With A View of The Slavery Question in the United States (New York: William Harned, 1852), p. 184. A good survey of the Baptist response to the sectional controversy is the dissertation by Willie Todd Grier, "The Slavery Issue and the Organization of the Southern Baptist Convention" (unpublished Ph.D. dissertation, University of North Carolina, 1964).

[57]Mathews, Slavery and Methodism, pp. 66-67. Albert H. Newman, ed., A Century of Baptist Achievement (Philadelphia: American Baptist Publication Society, 1901), p. 218. Department of Commerce, Bureau of Census, Negro Population, 1790-1915 (Washington, D.C.: Government Printing Office, 1918), p. 55. According to the census of 1840, there were 2,641,977 Negroes in the "southern divisions," of whom only 213,991 were freemen.

[58]Capers, Speech of May 24, 1844, p. 301.

[59]Proceedings of the Meeting in Charleston, S.C., May 13-15, 1845, on The Religious Instruction of The Negroes, Together with the Report of The Committee, And The Address to The Public (Charleston, S.C.: B. Jenkins, 1845), p. 72.

[60]Jones, Second Annual Report for 1834, p. 19. Letter, Charles C. Jones to William S. Plumer, June 28, 1834, Presbyterian Historical Society, Plumer Letter File.

[61]Proceedings of the Meeting in Charleston, pp. 9, 14-15.

[62]Ibid., p. 69 and passim.

[63]Ibid., p. 72.

[64]Quoted by Williams, "Methodist Mission to the Slaves," p. 205.

[65][William Capers?], "Report of the Missionary Society of the South Carolina Conference, of the Methodist Episcopal Church, South;

for the Year Ending January, 1847, " The Quarterly Review of the Methodist Episcopal Church, South, I, 3 (July, 1847), 333-34.

[66]Fletcher M. Green, "Northern Missionary Activities in the South, 1846-1861, " The Journal of Southern History, XXI, 2 (May, 1955), 154-61.

[67]Ibid., pp. 161-70. The Southern churches took advantage of an auxiliary status in which they simply had to report on any missionary activity which they had organized and pay their surplus funds into the general treasury. This meant that the Southern societies, for all practical purposes, operated autonomously with financial support from the intersectional Southern Aid Society.

[68]The increasing radicalism within the Methodist Episcopal Church, North, is discussed in Donald G. Mathews, "The Methodist Schism of 1844 and the Popularization of Antislavery Sentiment, " Mid-America, LI, 1 (January, 1968), 3-23. Men of the abolitionist temper within the Baptist fold found that the American Baptist Free Mission Society, organized in 1843, was a useful antislavery platform, as it admitted no slaveholders. Goodell, Slavery and Anti-Slavery, pp. 507-08.

[69]Thompson, Presbyterians in the South, pp. 530-50. Murray, Presbyterians and the Negro, pp. 106-26.

[70]Quoted by Green, "Northern Missionary Activities, " 171.

[71]Harrison, Gospel Among the Slaves, p. 302. Eugene P. Southall, "The Attitude of the Methodist Episcopal Church, South, Toward the Negro From 1844 to 1870, " The Journal of Negro History, XVI, 4 (October, 1931), 365.

[72]Table II, Appendix.

[73]Quoted by Fickling, Slave-Conversion in South Carolina, p. 40.

[74]William Warren Sweet, The Story of Religion in America (New York: Harper & Brothers), p. 445.

[75]Walter Brownlow Posey, Frontier Mission: A History of Religion West of the Southern Appalachians to 1861 (Lexington, Ky.: University of Kentucky Press, 1966), p. 202.

[76]Quoted by Stiles Bailey Lines, "Slaves and Churchmen: The Work of the Episcopal Church Among the Negroes, 1830-1860" (unpublished Ph.D. dissertation, Columbia University, 1960), p. 65.

[77]Fickling, Slave-Conversion in South Carolina, pp. 38-39.

[78]John B. Adger, The Religious Instruction of the Coloured Population. A Sermon, May 9, 1847 (Charleston, S.C.: T. W.

192   Black Religion

Haynes, 1847), pp. 4-5. Murray, The Presbyterians and the
Negro, p. 60.

[79]Daniel Robinson Hundley, Social Relations in Our Southern
States (New York: Henry B. Price, 1860), p. 297. Hundley broke
down the total figure as follows: Methodist Episcopal Church,
South--200,000; Methodist Episcopal Church, North, (in Virginia
and Maryland)--15,000; Missionary and Hard Shell Baptists--
175,000; Old School Presbyterians--15,000; New School Presby-
terians--20,000; Protestant Episcopalians--7000; Disciples of Christ
--7000; and other sects--20,000. The same figures, except with
regard to the Baptists, were reported in the Christian Observer in
February of 1861. See W. Harrison Daniel, "Southern Protestantism and the Negro, 1860-1865," The North Carolina Historical Review, XLI, 3 (July, 1964), 338. It is impossible to reconcile the
different claims made for the Baptists. According to one source,
the Home Mission Board of the Southern Baptist Convention was itself reaching some 400,000 Negroes in 1860. See Newman, Century
of Baptist Achievement, p. 218. W. E. Burghardt Du Bois accepted the figure of 468,000 as representative of black church members in the South in 1859. The great bulk of this total was made up
of 215,000 black Methodists and 175,000 black Baptists. See his
The Negro Church (Atlanta, Ga.: Atlanta University Press, 1903),
p. 29.

[80]Henry Alexander White, Southern Presbyterian Leaders
(New York: The Neale Publishing Company, 1911), p. 306.

[81]Jackson, "Religious Instruction of the Negroes," 107.
Jackson, "Religious Development of the Negro in Virginia from 1760
to 1860," The Journal of Negro History, XVI, 2 (April, 1931), 234.

[82]Department of Commerce, Bureau of the Census, Negro
Population, 1790-1915, p. 33.

[83]Charles C. Jones, Suggestions on the Religious Instruction
of the Negroes in the Southern States; Together with an Appendix
Containing Forms of Church Registers, Form of A Constitution, and
Plans of Different Denominations of Christians (Philadelphia: Presbyterian Board of Publication, 1847), p. 6.

                        CHAPTER III

[1]Charles C. Jones, The Religious Instruction of the Negroes
in the United States (Savannah, Ga.: Thomas Purse, 1842), p. xi.

[2]James Henry Thornwell, The Rights and Duties of Masters.
A Sermon Preached at the Dedication of A Church Erected in
Charleston, S.C., for the Benefit and Instruction of the Coloured
Population (Charleston, S.C.: Walker & James, 1850), pp. 11, 14.
See also, Frederick A. Ross, Slavery Ordained of God (Philadel-
phia: J. B. Lippincott & Co., 1857), p. 6.

[3]Donald G. Mathews, Slavery and Methodism (Princeton: Princeton University Press, 1965), p. 85. See the review of Thornwell's The Rights and Duties of Masters in The Christian Examiner and Miscellany, XLIX, 4 (November, 1850), 482-87. The author of this review says about Thornwell's comments on the theories of the origin of the races, "We will not, however, digress to discuss the question where there is the lesser measure of faith and humanity in regarding blacks as men and women, descended from a distinct human stock, or in maintaining their unity of descent with ourselves, while we treat them as beasts."

[4]Charles C. Jones, The Religious Instruction of the Negroes. A Sermon, Delivered Before Associations of Planters in Liberty and M'Intosh Counties, Georgia (4th ed., Princeton, N.J.: D'Hart & Connolly, 1832), p. 14.

[5]Jones, Religious Instruction of the Negroes, p. 178.

[6][William Capers], "Report of the Missionary Society of the South Carolina Conference, of the Methodist Episcopal Church, South; for the year ending January, 1847," The Quarterly Review of the Methodist Episcopal Church, South, I, 3 (July, 1847), 322.

[7]Andrew Flinn Dickson, Lessons About Salvation: From the Life and Words of the Lord Jesus, Being a Second Series of Plantation Sermons (Philadelphia: Presbyterian Board of Publication, 1860), p. 13.

[8]William Andrew Smith, Lectures on the Philosophy and Practice of Slavery, as Exhibited in the Institution of Slavery in the United States: with the Duties of Masters to Slaves (Nashville, Tenn.: Stevenson and Evans, 1856), p. 321.

[9]Quoted by William S. Plumer, Thoughts on the Religious Instruction of the Negroes of this Country (Savannah, Ga.: Edward J. Purse, 1848), p. 19. Dr. Rice was one of the early proponents of a seminary which would be established in the South for the express purpose that a "ministry might be educated at home and fitted for the field composed as it is, of masters and servants, bond and free." The Prince Edward Theological Seminary did not get built, but somewhat later a school was established at Columbia, South Carolina, by the Presbyterians. See Jones, Religious Instruction of the Negroes, p. 70.

[10]Letter, Henry Ruffner to William S. Plumer, June 17, 1834, Presbyterian Historical Society, Plumer Letter File. See evidence of a similar concern in Charles C. Jones, Third Annual Report of the Missionary to the Negroes in Liberty County, Ga. Presented to the Association, Riceborough, Jan. 1836 (Charleston, S.C.: Observer Office Press, 1836), p. 13.

[11]Charles Cotesworth Pinckney, An Address Delivered in Charleston before the Agricultural Society of South Carolina at its

Anniversary Meeting (Charleston, S.C.: A. E. Miller, 1829), p. 10.

12Jones, Religious Instruction of the Negroes, p. 209.

13William Meade, Pastoral Letter to the Ministers, Members, and Families, of the Protestant Episcopal Church on the Duty of Affording Religious Instruction to Those in Bondage. Delivered in the Year 1834 (Richmond, Va.: H. K. Ellyson, 1853), p. 20. A good discussion of the Southern appropriation of the medieval two-kingdom theory and the formulation of "a Christian Doctrine of slavery" is H. Shelton Smith's "The Church and the Social Order in the Old South as Interpreted by James H. Thornwell," Church History, VII, 2 (June, 1938), 115-24.

14See, for example, Victoria V. Clayton, White and Black Under the Old Regime (Milwaukee, Wis.: The Young Churchman Co., 1899), p. 59. John McDonogh, a Louisiana slaveholder, included in his will the following directive: "See to it that the overseers, every morning and evening, assemble the people in prayer ... have them taught (little children and all) the Ten Commandments, the Lord's Prayer, and the Creed, and (if permitted by law) hold Sunday schools ... for old and young and they may be made to attend the whole day. Let there be a house erected on each plantation for a church." Quoted by Joe Taylor Gray, Negro Slavery in Louisiana (Baton Rouge, La.: The Louisiana Historical Association, 1963), p. 150.

15Jones, Religious Instruction of the Negroes, p. 249.

16Ibid., p. 243.

17Holland Nimmons M'Tyeire, Duties of Christian Masters, ed. by Thomas O. Summers (Nashville, Tenn.: Southern Methodist Publishing House, 1859), p. 167.

18Nash Burger, "A Side-Light on an Ante-Bellum Plantation Chapel," Historical Magazine of the Protestant Episcopal Church, XII, 1 (March, 1943), 72.

19Charles C. Jones, First Annual Report of the Missionary to the Negroes, in Liberty County, (Ga.). Presented to the Association for the Religious Instruction of the Negroes in Liberty Co., Ga., November, 1833 (Charleston, S.C.: Observer Office Press, 1834), p. 12. Jones, Religious Instruction of the Negroes, p. 243. Ralph Quarterman Mallard, Plantation Life Before Emancipation (Richmond, Va.: Whittet & Shepperson, 1892), p. 104. References to other planters who built chapels can be found in William Pope Harrison, ed., The Gospel Among the Slaves (Nashville, Tenn.: Publishing House of the M.E. Church, South, 1893), pp. 220, 225-29, 254.

20Charles C. Jones, Second Annual Report, of the Missionary

to the Negroes, in Liberty County, Ga.   Presented to the Association, Riceborough, Jan. 1835 (Charleston, S.C.: Observer Office Press, 1835), p. 19.

[21]Mallard, Plantation Life Before Emancipation, pp. 102-03. A similar description of Jones' personal labors has been provided by his brother-in-law, the Rev. John Jones.   Cited by Robert Manson Myers, The Children of Pride (New Haven, Conn.: Yale University Press, 1972), pp. 14-16.

[22]John B. Adger, The Religious Instruction of the Coloured Population.   A Sermon, May 9, 1847 (Charleston, S.C.: T. W. Haynes, 1847), p. 12.

[23]Letter, Mrs. M. J. Davis to Richard T. Davis, January 26, 1854, University of Virginia, Preston-Davis manuscripts.   This was supplied to me by Ann Stauffenberg of the Manuscripts Division, University of Virginia Library.

[24]Margaret Douglass, Educational Laws of Virginia; The Personal Narrative of Mrs. Margaret Douglass, A Southern Woman, Who Was Imprisoned for One Month In the Common Jail of Norfolk, Under the Laws of Virginia, For the Crime of Teaching Free Coloured Children to Read, included in Legal and Moral Aspects of Slavery: Selected Essays (New York: Negro Universities Press, 1969), p. 22.   Mrs. Douglass and her daughter actually had been careful that the children whom they instructed belonged to free Negro families, for she knew that the laws of Virginia prohibited teaching slaves to read and write.   When Mrs. Douglass informed the mayor that "all the churches in Norfolk were actually instructing from books both slave and free colored children, and had done so for years without molestation," he pleaded ignorance of these violations.   In 1848 the penalties for teaching slave children to read and write were increased for whites to a maximum fine of $100 and six months in prison.   Mrs. Douglass, because of the acute embarrassment which her imprisonment caused, spent but one month in the Norfolk jail. Her experience caused her to conclude that the "grand secret of the opposition to the instruction of the colored race" was the fear of amalgamation.

[25]Frederick Douglass, Life and Times of Frederick Douglass (rev. ed. of 1892; rpt. London: The Crowell-Collier Publishing Co., 1962), p. 83.

[26]For information on the passage of laws regarding the instruction of Negroes with written materials see Carter G. Woodson, The Education of the Negro, Prior to 1861 (2nd ed.; Washington, D.C.: The Associated Publishers, Inc., 1919), pp. 159-71.   The principal purpose of these laws was to buttress the police control of the slaves by making it difficult for Negroes to learn of abolitionary activities and to gather together for mutual religious instruction or worship.   See Howell M. Henry, The Police Control of the Slave in South Carolina (1914; rep. New York: Negro Universities Press,

196   Black Religion

1968), pp. 133-38, and John Codman Hurd, The Law of Freedom
and Bondage in the United States (2 vols.; New York: D. Van Nostrand, 1862), II, 7, 9, 81, 101, 106, 147, and passim.
On the
restrictions against distributing Bibles, see Samuel Ringgold Ward,
Autobiography of A Fugitive Negro (London: John Snow, 1855), pp.
64-65, 67. The comments of Frederick Douglass on the laws
which made it a crime to leave the Bible at the door of the slave
cabin are also instructive. See Douglass, "Bibles for Slaves,"
from The Liberty Bell (June, 1847), reprinted in Philip S. Foner,
ed., The Life and Writings of Frederick Douglass (4 vols.; New
York: International Publishers, 1950), I, 254-55.

[27]William H. Heard, From Slavery to the Bishopric in the
A.M.E. Church (Philadelphia: A.M.E. Publishing House, 1924),
pp. 31-32. Sarah Grimke, daughter of a wealthy Episcopalian
planter in South Carolina, recalled how "with almost malicious
satisfaction" she would defy the laws of the state by teaching her
Negro waiting-maid at night, with the light out, the keyhole
screened, and the spelling book before them. When the Grimke
family later moved to Philadelphia both Sarah and Angelina taught
a Sunday school for Negro children. See Catherine H. Birney, The
Grimke Sisters, Sarah and Angelina Grimke (Boston: Lee and
Shephard, 1885), p. 12.

[28]Albert Barnes, An Inquiry into The Scriptural Views of
Slavery (Philadelphia: Perkins & Purvis, 1846), p. 319. Charles
C. Jones, Third Annual Report of the Missionary to the Negroes,
in Liberty County, Ga. (Charleston, S.C.: Observer Office Press,
1836), p. 9. Letter, Ruffner to Plumer, June 17, 1834. M'Tyeire,
Duties of Christian Masters, p. 158.

[29]John Mines, The Evangelical Catechism, or A Plain and
Easy System of the Principal Doctrines and Duties of the Christian
Religion, Adapted to the Use of Sabbath Schools and Families, with
a New Method of Instructing Those Who Cannot Read (Richmond, Va.:
N. Pollard, 1821), p. 10.

[30]William D. Capers, A Catechism for Little Children (and
for use on) The Missions to the Slaves in South-Carolina (Charleston,
S.C.: Printed by J. S. Barges, 1833). This also appeared as A
Short Catechism for the Use of the Colored Members on Trial of
the Methodist Episcopal Church in South Carolina (Charleston, S.C.:
Observer Office Press, 1833). The only extant copy is in the li-
brary of the University of South Carolina. For a sample of the
third edition see Thomas O. Summers, ed., Catechisms of the
Wesleyan Methodists (rev. ed.; Nashville, Tenn.: Publishing House
of the Methodist Episcopal Church, South, 1860). Charles C. Jones,
A Catechism of Scripture Doctrine and Practice for Families and
Sabbath-Schools Designed Also For the Oral Instruction of Colored
Persons (Philadelphia: Presbyterian Board of Publication, 1852).
The first edition was published in Charleston in 1834. Jones made
the following comment about the origin of his catechism: "A diffi-
culty presented itself at the very beginning of my Sabbath-School

instruction. There were no books! I tried all the catechisms.
Necessity forced me to attempt something myself. I prepared lessons, weekly, and tried them and corrected them from the schools,
and the result was; 'The Catechism of Scripture Doctrine and Practice...'." See his Tenth Annual Report of the Association of the
Negroes, in Liberty County, Georgia (Charleston, S.C.: Observer
Office Press, 1845), p. 8. On translations, see Myers, Children
of Pride, p. 16.

[31]Letter, Mary Jones to Ev. B. Jones, August 5, 1865, contained in Myers, Children of Pride, pp. 1286-87.

[32]Isaac Watts, The First Sett of Catechisms and Prayers
Or, The Religion of Little Children Under Seven or Eight Years of
Age (7th ed.; Boston: Rogers and Fowle, 1748). Mention is made
of the use of Watt's catechism among the slaves in John F. Hoff,
A Manual of Religious Instruction, Specially Intended for The Oral
Teaching of Colored Persons, But Adapted to General Use in
Families and Schools (rev. ed.; Richmond, Va.: P. B. Price,
1857), p. 4. Mather's resolutions on the subject of the religious
instruction of Negroes can be found in the Appendix of Woodson's
The Education of the Negro Prior to 1861, pp. 337-39.

[33]Letter, Charles C. Jones to William S. Plumer, June 28,
1834, Presbyterian Historical Society, Plumer Letter File. See
also, Jones, Religious Instruction of the Negroes, pp. 256-61.
Here he illustrates how a missionary might teach the doctrine of
election by using the account of St. Paul's conversion on the road
to Damascus.

[34]Letter, Ruffner to Plumer, June 17, 1834.

[35]Jones, Suggestions on the Religious Instruction of the
Negroes, p. 15. Jones recounts his pleasure at being told by "an
aged and native African," "Sir, you preach to our understanding.
You preach as clear as the water in the well." Jones, Third
Annual Report for 1835, p. 12.

[36]Jones added: "He must not treat them as if they were a
parcel of children, or a people perfectly stupid. Poor people have
feelings as well as rich people; and if people are ignorant, and, if
you please, fools, yet they do not like to be told of it. No good
comes of it. It is enough for the minister to know what they are;
let him go on and make them better." Religious Instruction of the
Negroes, p. 255. Jones, Suggestions on the Religious Instruction
of the Negroes, p. 13. Jones, Third Annual Report for 1835,
p. 12.

[37]Malcolm X, The Autobiography of Malcolm X, with the
assistance of Alex Haley and an introduction by M. S. Handler
(New York: Grove Press, Inc., 1965), p. 162.

[38]William E. Channing, Slavery in Slavery and Emancipation

198   Black Religion

(New York: Negro Universities Press, 1968), pp. 112-13. Slavery
was originally published in 1836 by James Munroe & Co., Boston.

39[George Washington Carleton], The Suppressed Book About
Slavery (New York: Published by the Author, 1864), p. 78. Carleton had prepared this book in 1857 as part of the abolitionists'
assault on slavery. He was a New York artist, book dealer, and
printer.

40George D. Armstrong, The Christian Doctrine of Slavery
(New York: Charles Scribner, 1857), pp. 131-32.

41Richard Nisbit, The Capacity of Negroes for Religious and
Moral Improvement Considered: With Cursory Hints, To Proprietors
and To Government For the Immediate Melioration of the Condition
of Slaves in the Sugar Colonies: To Which Are Subjoined Short and
Practical Discourses to Negroes, on the Plain and Obvious Principles
of Religion and Morality (London: James Phillips, 1789), p. vii.
Jones, Catechism of Scripture Doctrine and Practice, p. 31. Alexander Glennie, Sermons Preached on Plantations to the Congregations
of Negroes (Charleston, S.C.: A. E. Miller, 1844), p. 75.

42Hoff, Manual of Religious Instruction, p. 11.

43William Meade, Sermons, Dialogues and Narratives For
Servants, To be Read to Them in Families; Abridged, Altered, and
Adapted to Their Conditions (Richmond, Va.: James C. Walker,
1836), pp. 5-6, 23.

44Meade, Sermons, Dialogues and Narratives for Servants,
pp. 77-78.

45Clayton, White and Black Under the Old Regime, p. 59.

46Smith, Lectures on the Philosophy and Practice of Slavery,
p. 323.

47Jones, Suggestions on the Religious Instruction of Negroes,
p. 21. Of one slave, Jones wrote to his wife: "Caesar came in
after tea. Says he wishes to go with me in joining the church.
Appears in spirit very well, but deficient in clear views of the plan
of salvation. Recommended him to wait another Communion for
further instruction. Perfectly willing." Letter, Charles Jones to
Mary Jones, November 18, 1859, included in Myers, Children of
Pride, p. 536.

48Jones, Suggestions on the Religious Instruction of Negroes,
p. 42. The records of the Grace Methodist Episcopal Church of
Wilmington, North Carolina, indicate that cases of discipline involving Negroes in a mixed congregation were higher in proportion
to their numbers than for white members. From 1832 to 1845 cases
involving whites represented 2.2 per cent of the total white membership each year. For blacks the figure was 3.6 per cent. From

1846 to 1852 the figure for Negroes was 2.7 per cent, but that for whites was only .6 per cent. See Cortland Victor Smith, "Church Organization As An Agency of Social Control: Church Discipline in North Carolina University, 1800-1860" (unpublished Ph.D. dissertation, University of North Carolina, 1966), p. 102. Proceedings of the Meeting in Charleston, S.C., May 13-15, 1845, on The Religious Instruction of the Negroes, Together with The Report of The Committee, And The Address to The Public (Charleston, S.C.: B. Jenkins, 1845), p. 61.

[49]M'Tyeire, Duties of Christian Masters, pp. 97-98.

[50]Ibid.

[51]Jones, Religious Instruction of the Negroes, p. 233.

[52]Plumer, Thoughts on the Religious Instruction of the Negroes, pp. 6-7. See also, Haven P. Perkins, "Religion for Slaves: Difficulties and Methods," Church History, X, 3 (September, 1941), 238-39.

[53]Walter Brownlow Posey, Frontier Mission (Lexington, Ky.: University of Kentucky Press, 1966), p. 215. See also, Address to the Presbyterians of Kentucky, Proposing a Plan for the Instruction and Emancipation of Their Slaves (Cincinnati, Ohio: Taylor & Tracy, 1835), p. 14.

[54]Jones, Suggestions on the Religious Instruction of Negroes, pp. 36-37. See also Jones' Catechism of Scripture Doctrine and Practice, pp. 128-29.

[55]George F. Pierce, A Sermon Delivered Before the General Assembly at Milledgeville, Georgia, on Fast Day, March 27, 1863 (Milledgeville, Ga.: Boughton, Nisbet and Barnes, 1863), pp. 14-15. Other examples are cited in W. Harrison Daniel, "Southern Protestantism and the Negro, 1860-1865," The North Carolina Historical Review, XLI, 3 (July, 1964), 351-52.

[56]Frank Tannenbaum, Slave and Citizen (New York: Alfred A. Knopf, Inc., 1946), pp. 49, 64, 75-78.

[57]Jones wrote in 1842: "It is too much the fashion of late years, for ministers (I speak not of all) to consider themselves, ex-officio, the supervisors of human affairs; the conservators of theological, the civil, and the political interests of society, and of course, as posessing wisdom, experience, and observation sufficient 'to entitle them to be heard'." Religious Instruction of the Negroes, p. 271.

[58]Quoted by Philip S. Foner, ed., The Life and Writings of Frederick Douglass, I, 50. Also see the criticisms of Harriet Beecher Stowe in her A Key to Uncle Tom's Cabin: Presenting the

200   Black Religion

Original Facts and Documents Upon Which the Story Is Founded
(Boston: J. P. Jewett & Co., 1853), pp. 244-50.

⁵⁹Quoted by John Vickers, Thomas Coke (Nashville, Tenn.:
Abingdon Press, 1969), p. 69.

⁶⁰Jones, Third Annual Report for 1835, p. 10.

⁶¹Proceedings of the Meeting in Charleston, p. 42.

⁶²Mines, Evangelical Catechism, p. 59.

⁶³Glennie, Sermons Preached on Plantations, p. 21. The
duties of servants to masters are usually discussed in the catechisms in conjunction with the obligations of other states in society,
such as that of children to parents, and of wives to husbands. See
Hoff, Manual of Religious Instruction, pp. 135-37; Mines, Evangelical Catechism, pp. 56-61; Jones, Catechism of Scripture Doctrine and Practice, pp. 120-31; and Robert Ryland, A Scripture
Catechism for the Instruction of Children and Servants (Richmond,
Va.: Harrold and Murray, 1848), pp. 135-39.

⁶⁴William Andrew Smith wrote: "The attempts which are
sometimes made to prove that doulos of the Septuagint, and servus,
of the Vulgate version, translated indifferently servant or slave
means only a hired servant, need only to be mentioned to be re-
futed. That these terms defined an actual state of slavery among
the Greeks and Romans no one acquainted with the facts will deny."
Lectures on the Philosophy and Practice of Slavery, pp. 141-44.
Augustus B. Longstreet wrote a lengthy rebuttal to claims by
Northern Methodists that Onesimus was not a slave in the same
sense as were those of the South. See his Letters on the Epistle of
Paul to Philemon, or the Connection of Apostolical Christianity with
Slavery (Charleston, S.C.: B. Jenkins, 1845). The abuse given
the term "servant" as an euphemism for "slave" reached its zenith
when Bishop Meade told the blacks that they ought to be content
with their situations because Jesus had been born a "servant" and
took the part of a "servant" in his relationship to the disciples.
Meade, Sermons, Dialogues and Narratives for Servants, p. 23.

⁶⁵Jones, Religious Instruction of the Negroes. A Sermon,
p. 28.

⁶⁶M'Tyeire, Duties of Christian Masters, p. 57.

⁶⁷Ibid., pp. 146, 233-34. Glennie, Sermons Preached on
Plantations, p. 23. Meade, Sermons, Dialogues and Narratives
for Servants, p. 7. Other examples of the exploitation of religion,
and, specifically, of "the fear of God," to induce obedience and
docility in the slaves are: Jones, Catechism of Scripture Doctrine
and Practice, p. 130; Nisbit, Capacity of Negroes for Religious and
Moral Improvement, pp. 81, 88; and Hoff, Manual of Religious Instruction, p. 23.

[68]M'Tyeire, Duties of Christian Masters, p. 234.

[69]Stowe, Key to Uncle Tom's Cabin, pp. 249-50.   Mrs.
Stowe was probably citing from the sermons of Bishop Meade as
she found them in Samuel Brooke's Slavery and the Slaveholder's
Religion, as Opposed to Christianity (Cincinnati, Ohio: The Author,
1846).

[70]Plumer, Thoughts on the Religious Instruction of Negroes,
p. 23.   Letter, Henry Ruffner to William S. Plumer, June 17, 1834.

[71]Jones, Religious Instruction of the Negroes, p. 252.

[72]Jones, Third Annual Report for 1835, p. 14.

[73]Jones' account of this second incident also deserves to be
quoted in full.   In his Tenth Annual Report for the year 1845, he
wrote: "Allow me to relate a fact which occurred in the spring of
this year, illustrative of the character and knowledge of the negroes
at this time.   I was preaching to a large congregation on the
Epistle to Philemon; and when I insisted upon fidelity and obedience
as Christian virtues in servants, and, upon the authority of Paul,
condemned the practice of running away, one-half of my audience
deliberately walked off with themselves, and those that remained
looked anything but satisfied, either with the preacher or his doctrine.   After dismission, there was no small stir among them:
some solemnly declared that there was no such epistle in the Bible;
others, 'that it was not the gospel, ' others, 'that I preached to
please masters'; others, 'that they did not care if they ever heard
me preach again'. "   Jones, Tenth Annual Report for 1845, pp. 24-
25.   Antislavery writers cited this incident to prove that the slaves
recognized a perversion of the Gospel when they heard one.   See
Stowe, Key to Uncle Tom's Cabin, pp. 245-46, and Barnes, Inquiry
into the Scriptural Views of Slavery, p. 319.

[74]Jones, Third Annual Report for 1835, p. 8.

[75]Ibid.

[76]C. F. Sturgis, Melville Letters; or, The Duties of Masters
To Their Servants, included together with essays by Holland N.
M'Tyeire and A. T. Holmes in Duties of Masters to Servants:
Three Premium Essays (Charleston, S.C.:   Southern Baptist Publication Society, 1851), pp. 104-10, 126-27, 142-51.   The Melville
Letters was a fictional exchange between two brothers, one a professor of religion and one a lawyer, about the duties of owners of
slaves.   It was written by the Rev. C. F. Sturgis, a Baptist clergyman, in competition for a prize of 200 dollars which was offered
for the best essay on the duties of Christian masters by the Baptist
State Convention of Alabama in 1849.

[77]Isaac S. K. Axson, Eighth Annual Report of the Association for the Religious Instruction of the Negroes in Liberty County,

Georgia; Together with the Address to The Association By the President (Savannah, Ga.: Thomas Purse, 1843), p. 35.

[78]Jones, Third Annual Report for 1835, p. 6. M'Tyeire, Duties of Christian Masters, pp. 20, 138.

[79]Jones, Catechism of Scripture Doctrine and Practice, p. 128.

[80]Jones, Religious Instruction of the Negroes, pp. 240-41. Jones also argued that if the slaves had a little something of their own to care for they would identify more with the interests of the entire plantation.

[81]Smith, Lectures on the Philosophy and Practice of Slavery, pp. 294, 298.

[82]Frederick Law Olmsted, A Journey in the Back Country, 1853-1854, intro. by Clement Eaton (New York: Schocken Books, 1970), pp. 182-83.

[83]Proceedings of the Meeting in Charleston, p. 25.

[84]In Harrison, ed., Gospel Among the Slaves, pp. 272-73.

[85]Axson, Eighth Annual Report for 1842, pp. 19-20.

[86]Proceedings of the Meeting in Charleston, p. 55. Another planter testified along the same lines: "A near neighbor of mine, a prominent member of the Church to which he belonged, had contented himself with giving his people the usual religious privileges. They gave him a great deal of trouble, especially in their family relations. About six months ago he commenced giving them special religious instruction. He used Jones' Catechism, principally. His people soon became interested; the children were pleased with the catechism; and at this time, there is apparently an entire change in the views, feelings, principles and temper of all without a single exception. He states that he has now comparatively no trouble in their management." Ibid., p. 22.

[87]Cited by Myers, The Children of Pride, p. 15.

[88]Adger, Religious Instruction of the Colored Population, pp. 4-6.

[89]Jones, Religious Instruction of the Negroes, pp. 110-11.

[90]Letter, S. L. Graham to William S. Plumer, July 7, 1834, Presbyterian Historical Society, Plumer Letter File.

CHAPTER IV

[1]Frances Anne Kemble, Journal of a Residence on a Georgia Plantation in 1838-1839 (New York: Harper & Brothers, 1863), p. 85.

[2]Charles C. Jones, The Religious Instruction of the Negroes in the United States (Savannah, Ga.: Thomas Purse, 1842), p. 127. [William Capers], "Report of the Missionary Society of the South Carolina Conference, of the Methodist Episcopal Church, South; for the year ending January, 1847, " in The Quarterly Review of the Methodist Episcopal Church, South, I, 3 (July, 1847), 321. See also, William Andrew Smith, Lectures on the Philosophy and Practice of Slavery as Exhibited in the Institution of Domestic Slavery in the United States: with the Duties of Masters to Slaves (Nashville, Tenn.: Stevenson and Evans, 1856), pp. 207, 321.

[3]David Christy, Pulpit Politics: or, Ecclesiastical Legislation on Slavery, in Its Disturbing Influence on the American Union (Cincinnati: Faran & McLean, 1862), p. 41. Edward A. Pollard, Black Diamonds Gathered in the Darkey Homes of the South (New York: Pudney & Russell, 1859), pp. 83-84. See also, David Benedict, A General History of the Baptist Denomination in America, and other Parts of the World (2 vols.; Boston: Lincoln & Edmands, 1813), II, 189.

[4]Herman Hooker, The Planter: Or, Thirteen Years in the South (1853; rpt. Miami, Florida: Mnemosyne Publishing, 1969), p. 252.

[5]John S. Mbiti, African Religions & Philosophies (New York: Frederick A. Praeger, Inc., 1969), pp. 37-49, passim. Geoffrey Parrinder, African Traditional Religion (London: Hutchinson's University Library, 1954), pp. 39-46. James D. Tyms, "African Contributions to World Religion, " in The Negro Impact on Western Civilization, ed. by Joseph Roucek (New York: Philosophical Library, Inc., 1970), pp. 110-21. Various terms have been used to describe African traditional religion, among them being "animism, " "totemism, " "fetishism, " "ancestor worship, " "dynamism, " "voodooism, " and "primitivism. " Each of these is accurate only to a limited extent and the use of any one as an exclusive description of the tribal religions results in a serious distortion.

[6]Carter G. Woodson, The African Background Outlined or Handbook for the Study of the Negro (Washington, D.C.: Association for the Study of Negro Life and History, 1936), p. 172. Woodson speculated that the Christianization of the Negro was easier than that of the European pagans "because Christianity is an Oriental cult and the Negro has an Oriental mind. " See also, John W. Blassingame, The Slave Community (New York: Oxford University Press, 1972), p. 18.

[7]William Pope Harrison, ed., The Gospel Among the Slaves

(Nashville, Tenn.: Publishing House of the Methodist Episcopal Church, South, 1893), pp. 214-15.

[8]The case for a significant number of Africanisms in Negro religious life is made by Melville J. Herskovitts, The Myth of the Negro Past (Boston: Beacon Press, 1958), pp. 206-69. Also see his "On the Provenience of New World Negroes, " Social Forces, XII, 2 (December, 1933), 247-62. Woodson, a strong advocate of the importance of the African background to the American Negro, expressed the opinion that the first generation of slaves "had difficulty in abandoning immediately the customs and practices of their religion brought from Africa, and some of their descendants have not even done so today." African Background Outlined, p. 367. An opposing position was taken by E. Franklin Frazier, The Negro in the United States (Chicago: University of Chicago Press, 1939), pp. 30-31. Frazier, The Negro in the United States (New York: The Macmillan Company, 1949), pp. 2-6, 13. Frazier, The Negro Church in America (New York: Schocken Books, 1964), pp. 1-19. G. R. Wilson also took the position that in the United States the slave soon forgot his African background and "became a decidedly different person, having a new religion...." See "The Religion of the American Negro Slave: His Attitude Toward Life and Death, " The Journal of Negro History, VIII, 1 (January, 1923), 41. Herskovitts admitted that the United States was probably the "region where departure from African modes of life was greatest." Myth of the Negro Past, p. 122.

[9]A judicious treatment of the question can be found in Blassingame, Slave Community, pp. 18-40. African influences evident in the religious and secular slave songs are examined by Sterling Stuckey, "Through the Prism of Folklore: The Black Ethos in Slavery, " in Vol. I of The Underside of American History, edited by Thomas R. Frazier (2 vols.; New York: Harcourt, Brace, Jovanovich, Inc., 1971), pp. 229-46.

[10]Rawick's observations on the process of cultural interaction are most helpful. He writes: "The black slaves in North America utilized West African concepts in a new and totally different context. In so doing they transformed those West African forms into something which was neither African nor European-American but a syncretic blend of the two that produced a totality which must be looked at in its own terms. While it is true that all blends depend upon the elements being fused, it is also true that one cannot sift out 'African' traits or 'European-American' traits from the product which was qualitatively different from any of the influences that fed into its development." See From Sundown to Sunup: The Making of the Black Community, Vol. I of The American Slave: A Composite Autobiography, Series One (7 vols.; Westport, Conn.: Greenwood Publishing Company, 1972), pp. 37-38.

[11]Kenneth M. Stampp, The Peculiar Institution (New York: Vintage Books, 1956), p. 375. Robert E. Park, "The Conflict and Fusion of Culture, " The Journal of Negro History, IV, 2 (April, 1919), 116.

12Vassa recalled: "As to religion, the natives believe that
there is one Creator of all things, and that he lives in the sun, and
is girt round with a belt; that he may never eat or drink, but, according to some, he smokes a pipe, which is our own favorite
luxury. They believe he governs events, especially our deaths or
captivity; but, as for the doctrine of eternity, I do not remember
to have ever heard of it; some, however, believe in the transmi-
gration of souls in a certain degree. Those spirits which were not
transmigrated, such as their dear friends or relations, they believe
always attend them, and guard them from the bad spirits or their
foes." The Life of Olaudah Equiano, or Gustavus Vassa, the African in Great Slave Narratives, edited by Arna Bontemps (Boston:
Beacon Press, 1969), pp. 12-13.

13Frederick Law Olmsted, The Cotton Kingdom, ed. by.
Arthur M. Schlesinger (New York: Knopf Press, 1953), p. 349.
See also Peter Randolph, From Slave Cabin to the Pulpit: The
Autobiography of Rev. Peter Randolph (Boston: James H. Earle,
1893), p. 51.

14Herskovitts, Myth of the Negro Past, pp. 232-33.

15William E. Hatcher, John Jasper: The Unmatched Negro
Philosopher and Preacher (New York: Fleming H. Revell Company,
1908), pp. 24-29.

16As told by the Rev. H. H. Montgomery who heard Pompey
in 1832, quoted by Caleb Perry Patterson, The Negro in Tennessee,
1790-1865 (Austin, Texas: The University of Texas Press, 1922),
p. 119. Pompey had himself been converted at a revival while
traveling as the body servant of a Methodist itinerant. Timothy L.
Smith has perceptively applied the categories of forgiveness, awe
and ecstasy, followed by self-respect, ethical earnestness and hope
to the personal religious experience of the slaves. See his "Slavery
and Theology: The Emergence of Black Christian Consciousness in
Nineteenth-Century America," Church History, XLI, 4 (December,
1972), 497-512.

17Josiah Henson, Truth Stranger than Fiction, Father Henson's Story of His Own Life (Boston: John P. Jewett and Company,
1858), pp. 28-29, 86. Mrs. Stowe made specific reference to
Josiah Henson, a deeply religious slave who fled from Kentucky to
Canada in 1830, as the model for her extraordinary exemplar of the
Christian virtues in the person of Uncle Tom. She provided the
introduction for the narrative of his adventures which was published
in 1858. See A Key to Uncle Tom's Cabin: Presenting the Original
Facts and Documents Upon Which the Story is Founded (Boston:
John P. Jewett & Co., 1853), p. 25. John Thompson, The Life of
John Thompson, A Fugitive Slave: Containing His History of 25
Years in Bondage, and His Providential Escape (Worchester, Mass.:
By the Author, 1856), pp. 75-81.

18Charles T. Raymond, "The Religious Life of the Negro

Slave, " Second Paper, Harper's New Monthly Magazine, XXVII, No.
CLX (October, 1863), 681. Third Paper, XXVII, No. CLXI (November, 1863), 816-20. Raymond was a Northern correspondent who spent 14 years in the South.

19Jones, Religious Instruction of the Negroes in the United States, pp. 131-32.

20See Rawick, From Sundown to Sunup, pp. 45-48. Rawick suggests that the "little man," variously described, parallels Elegba, or, Legba, among the Yoruba people of West Africa. Elegba is a messenger for the other gods.

21Fisk University, Unwritten History of Slavery: Autobiographical Account of Negro Ex-Slaves, Social Science Document, No. 1 (1945; rpt. Washington, D.C.: Microcard Editions, 1968), p. 59. These interviews with ex-slaves, residing mostly in Tennessee and Kentucky, were conducted in 1929 and 1930 by Ophelia Settle Egypt. Moses Grandy, Narrative of the Life of Moses Grandy, Late a Slave in the United States of America (Boston: Oliver Johnson, 1844), pp. 35-36. Benjamin Drew, The Refugee: A North Side View of Slavery (Boston: John P. Jewett & Co., 1856), pp. 331-32. Drew was a school principal and part-time journalist from Boston. He interviewed the fugitive slaves living in Canada in order to get a more accurate picture of slavery than that offered by another Northerner, Nehemiah Adams, who published A South-Side View of Slavery in 1854. Henry Bibb, Narrative of the Life and Adventures of Henry Bibb, An American Slave. Written by Himself (1849), in Puttin' On Ole Massa, ed. by Gilbert Osofsky (New York: Harper & Row, 1969), pp. 104-05. The white mob also took from him a certificate which had been given to Bibb by his classleader "testifying to my worthiness as a member of that church. "

22Jacob Stroyer, My Life in the South (2nd ed.; Salem, Mass.: Newcomb & Glass, 1898), p. 44. Thompson, Life, pp. 19, 46. John Dixon Long, Pictures of Slavery in Church and State (Philadelphia: Published by the Author, 1857), pp. 70-71. Martyrdom was the fate of one Christian slave who died as the result of a severe flogging after he refused to deny his faith. The ultimate test was given when a fellow planter bet the slave's owner that "all profession of religion among slaves was mere hypocrisy. " The incident was related to Sarah M. Grimke and is cited in Theodore Dwight Weld's American Slavery As it Is (New York: American Anti-Slavery Society, 1839), p. 24. Harriet (Brent) Jacobs, Incidents in the Life of a Slave Girl, ed. by L. Maria Child (Boston: Published by the Author, 1861), p. 79. Drew, The Refugee, p. 95.

23Kemble, Residence on a Georgia Plantation, p. 153.

24Jacobs, Incidents in the Life of a Slave Girl, pp. 71-72.

25Norman P. Yetman, Life Under the "Peculiar Institution":

Selections from the Slave Narrative Collection (New York: Holt,
Rinehart and Winston, Inc., 1970), pp. 182-83.

[26]Long, Pictures of Slavery, p. 127.

[27]See Drew, The Refugee, p. 22; Isaac Mason, Life of
Isaac Mason, as a Slave (Worchester, Mass.: By the Author,
1893), p. 27, 31-32; Austin Steward, Twenty-two Years a Slave
and Forty Years a Freeman, Embracing a Correspondence of
Several Years While President of Wilberforce Colony (Rochester,
New York: W. Alling, 1857), pp. 60-61; Lunsford Lane, The Narrative of Lunsford Lane, Formerly of Raleigh, N.C. (Boston: Published by Himself, 1892), pp. 11-12; Moses Roper, A Narrative of
the Adventures and Escape of Moses Roper from American Slavery
(London: Darton, Harvey and Darton, 1838), p. 59; and Bibb, Life
and Adventures, p. 69.

[28]Jermain W. Loguen, The Rev. J. W. Loguen, as a Slave
and Freeman. A Narrative of Real Life (Syracuse, N.Y.:   Office
of the Daily Journal, 1859), p. 330. This narrative is very likely
the product of a ghostwriter, who says of the subject: "In after
life, when Mr. Loguen described the offices of religion in his lectures and speeches, he was often reminded of 'the good life,' or
'natural good,' of these Indians, and contrasted it with the religion
of the whites."

[29]Douglas C. Stange, "Document: Bishop Daniel Alexander
Payne's Protestation of American Slavery," The Journal of Negro
History, LII, 1 (January, 1967), 63.

[30]John D. Paxton, Letters on Slavery Addressed to the Cumberland Congregation, Virginia (Lexington, Ky.: A. T. Skillman),
pp. 9, 130-32.

[31]Frederick Douglass, Life and Times of Frederick Douglass.
Written By Himself (rev. ed. of 1892; rpt. London: The Crowell-
Collier Publishing Company, 1962), pp. 85, 108-09.

[32]Louis Hughes, Thirty Years a Slave: From Bondage to
Freedom (Milwaukee: South Side Printing Company, 1897), p. 90.
When James Redpath, a Northern abolitionist who called himself
"the roving editor," visited Richmond in 1854, he encountered a
Negro storekeeper who had some very forthright notions on Christianity and slavery. This man told him about a sermon in which the
minister had said "that God had given all this continent to the white
man, and that it was our duty to submit." Redpath inquired if
blacks generally believed such nonsense. "Oh, no, sir," the storekeeper replied, "one man whispered to me as the minister said
that, 'He be d--d! God am not such a fool!'" The Roving Editor:
or, Talks with Slaves in the Southern States (New York: A. B.
Burdick, 1859), p. 19.

[33]Philip S. Foner, ed., The Life and Writings of Frederick

Douglass (4 vols.: New York: International Publishers Co., Inc., 1950), I, 197; II, 273.

[34]William Craft, Running a Thousand Miles for Freedom or The Escape of William and Ellen Craft from Slavery, in Great Slave Narratives, edited by Arna Bontemps (Boston: Beacon Press, 1969), pp. 275-76. Originally published in 1860 by W. Tweedie, London. On this same theme, see Blassingame, Slave Community, pp. 62-64.

[35]William Wells Brown, My Southern Home: The South and Its People (Boston: A. G. Brown & Co., 1880), p. 3. Solomon Northup, Twelve Years a Slave, Narrative of Solomon Northup, A Citizen of New York, Kidnapped in Washington City in 1841 and Rescued in January, 1853, from a Cotton Plantation near Red River, in Louisiana, in Puttin' On Ole Massa, ed. by Gilbert Osofsky (New York: Harper & Row, 1969), pp. 270, 278. Originally published in 1853 by Derby, Orton, and Mulligan at Buffalo, New York. See also, Douglass, Life and Times, p. 110. Journal of Mrs. Mary S. Mallard, December 21, 1864, excerpted in Robert Manson Myers, The Children of Pride (New Haven, Conn.: Yale University Press, 1972), p. 1232.

[36]Harrison, ed., Gospel Among the Slaves, pp. 221, 291. Henry Clay Bruce, The New Man: Twenty-Nine Years a Slave, Twenty-Nine Years a Free Man (York, Pa.: P. Anstadt & Sons, 1895), pp. 71-72.

[37]Bibb, Narrative, pp. 169-70. William Wells Brown reported: "It was not uncommon in St. Louis to pass by an auction-stand, and behold a woman upon the auction-block, and hear the seller crying out, 'How much is offered for this woman? She is a good cook, good washer, a good obedient servant. She has got religion!' Why should this man tell the purchasers that she has religion? I answer, because in Missouri, and as far as I have any knowledge of slavery in the other states, the religious teaching consists in teaching the slave that he must never strike a white man; that God made him for a slave; and that, when whipped, he must not find fault, -- for the Bible says, 'He that knoweth his master's will, and doeth it not, shall be beaten with many stripes!' And slave-holders find such religion very profitable to them." Narrative of William Wells Brown, a Fugitive Slave, Written by Himself (1847), in Puttin' On Ole Massa, ed. by Gilbert Osofsky, p. 211. See also Loguen, The Rev. J. W. Loguen, p. 106.

[38]Brown, My Southern Home, pp. 28-29. See also, Stanley Feldstein, Once a Slave (New York: William Morrow and Company, Inc., 1970), pp. 166-70. Raymond A. Bauer and Alice H. Bauer, "Day to Day Resistance to Slavery," The Journal of Negro History, XXVII, 4 (October, 1942), 388-419. Stampp, The Peculiar Institution, pp. 87-88.

[39]James W. C. Pennington, The Fugitive Blacksmith or Events in the History of James W. C. Pennington, Pastor of a Presbyterian Church, New York, Formerly a Slave in the State of

Maryland, United States, in Great Slave Narratives, edited by Arna Bontemps, pp. 221-28. Originally published by Charles Gilpin, London, in 1849.

[40]Raymond, "Religious Life of the Slaves, " Third Paper, 820-22.

[41]Douglass, Life and Times, pp. 104-05. Booker T. Washington, The Story of My Life and Work (Toronto: J. L. Nichols & Co., 1900), pp. 30-32.

[42]Jacobs, Incidents in the Life of a Slave Girl, p. 290.

[43]Pennington, Fugitive Blacksmith, p. 228. Clarke, Narrative, pp. 119-20. Henson, Truth Stranger than Fiction. pp. 90-92.

[44]Yetman, Life Under the "Peculiar Institution, " p. 95.

[45]Robert Emory, History of the Discipline of the Methodist Episcopal Church (New York: G. Lane & P. P. Sanford, 1844), p. 279. Benjamin Franklin Riley, A History of the Baptists in the Southern States East of the Mississippi (Philadelphia: American Baptist Publication Society, 1898), p. 319. The Methodists were sometimes able to sidestep those police ordinances of the Southern States which prohibited preaching by blacks by licensing Negroes as "exhorters." See Donald G. Mathews, Slavery and Methodism (Princeton, N.J.: Princeton University Press, 1965), pp. 65-66, note 7.

[46]Frederick Law Olmsted, A Journey in the Back Country (1860), introduction by Clement Eaton (New York: Schocken Books, Inc., 1970), pp. 92-93. Henry Benjamin Whipple, Bishop Whipple's Southern Diary, 1843-1844, ed. by Lester B. Shippee (1937; rpt. New York: De Capo Press, 1968), p. 35. Parsons, Inside View of Slavery, p. 159.

[47]Quoted by William S. Plumer, Thoughts on the Religious Instruction of the Negroes of This Country (Savannah, Ga.: Edward J. Purse, 1848), p. 20.

[48]Charles Cotesworth Pinckney, An Address Delivered in Charleston, before the Agricultural Society of South Carolina at its Anniversary Meeting, on Tuesday, the 18th August, 1829 (Charleston, S.C.: Published by Order of the Society, 1829), note E.

[49]Walter Brownlow Posey, Frontier Mission: A History of Religion West of the Southern Appalachians to 1861 (Lexington: University of Kentucky Press, 1966), p. 196.

[50]Clifton H. Johnson, ed., God Struck Me Dead (Philadelphia: The United Church Press, 1969), pp. 75-76. This useful little volume contains accounts of the religious experiences of 50

ex-slaves who told their stories to A. P. Watson, a graduate student in anthropology at Fisk University, in the years 1927-29.

[51]Charles C. Jones, Suggestions on the Religious Instruction of the Negroes in the Southern States: Together with an Appendix Containing Forms of Church Registers, Form of a Constitution, and Plans of Different Denominations of Christians (Philadelphia: Presbyterian Board of Publication, 1847), p. 18. Holland Nimmons M'Tyeire, Duties of Christian Masters, ed. by Thomas O. Summers (Nashville, Tenn.: Southern Methodist Publishing House, 1859), p. 157.

[52]See, for example, John Harris, Voices from Slavery (New York: Tower Publications, Inc., 1971), p. 58. Harris, a black activist, is of the opinion that religion, which he calls "the heroin of slavery," has always been dysfunctional in the black community and has nothing to contribute to the current struggle against exploitation. Ibid., pp. 68-70. See also Earl E. Thorpe, The Mind of the Negro (Baton Rouge, La.: Ortlieb Press, 1961), p. 116.

[53]Joseph R. Washington, Jr., Black Religion (Boston: Beacon Press, 1969), pp. 33-34, 203-04. Vincent Harding, "Rebellion and Resistence Among Antebellum Negroes, 1800-1860," in The Making of Black America, Vol. I of The Origins of Black Americans, ed. by August Meier and Eliot Rudwick (New York: Atheneum Press, 1969), pp. 183, 188-190.

[54]Miles Mark Fisher, Negro Slave Songs (New York: Cornell University Press, 1953), pp. 32-33, 84, 88. W. E. Burghardt Du Bois, The Souls of Black Folk (New York: Fawcett World Library, 1961), p. 144.

[55]The evolutionary interpretation is employed, for example, by Howard H. Harlan in John Jasper--A Case History in Leadership (Richmond: University of Virginia Press, 1936), pp. 9-10.

[56]Carter G. Woodson, The History of the Negro Church (2nd ed., Washington, D.C.: The Associated Publishers, 1921), pp. 48-49. William M. Wightman, Life of William Capers, D.D., One of the Bishops of the Methodist Episcopal Church, South: Including an Autobiography (Nashville, Tenn.: Southern Methodist Publishing House, 1858), pp. 124, 127. William A. Pope, "Lott Carey: Man of Purchased Freedom," Church History, XXXIX, 1 (March, 1970), 49-61.

[57]George W. Williams, History of the Negro Race in America (2 vols; New York: G. P. Putnam's Sons, 1882), II, 466-67. See also, James Benson Sellers, Slavery in Alabama (University, Ala.: University Press, 1950), p. 307.

[58]Benedict, General History of the Baptists, II, 211-12. See also the high reputation which "Uncle Jack" the African preacher had

in William S. White, The African Preacher, An Authentic Narrative
(Philadelphia: Presbyterian Board of Publications, 1849, pp. 52-89.

59Quoted by Clement Eaton, The Mind of the Old South (rev.
ed.; Baton Rouge, La.: Louisiana State University Press, 1967),
p. 183.

60William Goodell, The American Slave Code in Theory and
Practice (New York: American and Foreign Anti-Slavery Society,
1853), pp. 303-10. John Codman Hurd, The Law of Freedom and
Bondage in the United States (2 vols.; Boston: Little, Brown Co.,
1862), II, 9, 80, 106, 147, 170. William White Spotswood, Rev.
William S. White, D.D., and His Times, ed. by H. M. White
(Richmond, Va.: Presbyterian Committee of Publication, 1891), p.
184. George M. Stroud, A Sketch of the Laws Relating to Slavery
in the Several States of the United States of America (2nd ed.;
Philadelphia: Henry Longstreth, 1856), pp. 149-52.

61Jones, Suggestions on Religious Instruction, p. 19. Susan
Markey Fickling, Slave-Conversion in South Carolina, 1830-1860,
Bulletin of the University of South Carolina, September, 1924 (Co-
lumbia, S.C.: University of South Carolina Press, 1924), pp. 22-23.

62Harrison, ed., The Gospel Among the Slaves, p. 290.

63William Henry Milburn, Ten Years of Preacher Life;
Chapters from an Autobiography (New York: Derby & Jackson,
1859), p. 337.

64Bruce, The New Man, pp. 72-73.

65Testimony of Pearl Randolph, Federal Writers' Project, as
excerpted in Harris, Voices from Slavery, p. 58.

66James Lindsay Smith, Autobiography of James Lindsay
Smith (Norwich, Conn.: Press of the Bulletin Company, 1881),
p. 28.

67Fisk University, Unwritten History of Slavery, pp. 131,
154. Hughes, Thirty Years a Slave, p. 54.

68Long, Pictures of Slavery in Church and State, p. 233.
See also, Bruce, The New Man, p. 73, and Fisk University,
Unwritten History of Slavery, p. 46.

69B. A. Botkin, ed., Lay My Burden Down: A Folk History
of Slavery (Chicago: University of Chicago Press, 1945), p. 26.

70Bruce, The New Man, p. 73.

71Quoted by Stiles B. Lines, "Slaves and Churchmen: The
Work of the Episcopal Church Among Southern Negroes, 1830-1860"
(unpublished Ph.D. dissertation, Columbia University, 1960), p. 97.

[72]Letter, Henry C. Ruffner to William S. Plumer, June 17, 1834, Presbyterian Historical Society, Plumer Letter File.

[73]Harding, "Religion and Resistance Among Antebellum Negroes," p. 188.

[74]Quoted by John W. Cromwell, "The Aftermath of Nat Turner's Insurrection," The Journal of Negro History, V, 2 (April, 1920), 218-19.

[75]Botkin, ed., Lay My Burden Down, pp. 29-33. Fisk University, Unwritten History of Slavery, p. 46.

[76]Jones, Religious Instruction of the Negroes, p. 128. Taylor, Negro Slavery in Louisiana, p. 134.

[77]Herskovitts, Myth of the Negro Past, pp. 245-51. Parrinder, African Traditional Religion, pp. 103-06. The persistence of both "good" and "bad" magic in modern African society is treated in Mbiti, African Religions and Philosophies, pp. 194-203. William C. Suttles, Jr., "African Religious Survivals as Factors in American Slave Revolts," The Journal of Negro History, LVI, 2 (April, 1971), 97-104. Blassingame, Slave Community, pp. 32-33.

[78]Feldstein, Once a Slave, pp. 178-82. Botkin, ed., Lay My Burden Down, pp. 29-38.

[79]Brown, My Southern Home, pp. 70-71. Botkin, ed., Lay My Burden Down, p. 30. Blassingame, Slave Community, pp. 45, 48-49.

[80]Douglass, Life and Times, pp. 137-39. Bibb, Life and Adventures, pp. 71-72. Hughes, Thirty Years a Slave, p. 108.

[81]Fisk University, Unwritten History of Slavery, p. 46.

[82]Hughes, Thirty Years a Slave, p. 108.

[83]Yetman, Life Under the "Peculiar Institution," pp. 63, 95.

[84]Brown, My Southern Home, p. 97. Fisk University, Unwritten History of Slavery, p. 112. Jacobs, Life of A Slave Girl, p. 103. Yetman, Life Under the "Peculiar Institution," pp. 13, 53, 166, 177, 266-67.

[85]Charles Emery Stevens, Anthony Burns: A History (Boston: John P. Jewett and Company, 1856), pp. 166-67.

[86]H. M. Henry, The Police Control of the Slave in South Carolina (1914); rpt. New York: Negro Universities Press, 1968), p. 141. Jones, Suggestions on Religious Instruction of Negroes, p. 32.

[87]Yetman, Life Under the "Peculiar Institution," p. 53.

[88]Fisk University, Unwritten History of Slavery, pp. 10, 45, 74, 98. Johnson, ed., God Struck Me Dead, p. 69. Thorpe, Mind of the Negro, p. 105. Yetman, Life Under the "Peculiar Institution," pp. 166, 229, 335. Fisher, Negro Slave Songs, p. 29. George Rawick suggests that the pot-washpot syndrome, derived from West Africa, indicates how the slaves continued a practice even though its original meaning and purpose was lost. Rawick, From Sundown to Sunup, pp. 39-44.

[89]Peter Randolph, From Slave Cabin to Pulpit: The Autobiography of Peter Randolph (Boston: James H. Earle, 1893), pp. 202-03.

[90]Smith, Autobiography, p. 27.

[91]Hughes, Thirty Years A Slave, pp. 53-54. See also, Robert Anderson, From Slavery to Affluence. Memoirs of Robert Anderson, Ex-Slave (Hemingsford, Neb.: Hemingsford Ledger, 1927), p. 29. Johnson, ed., God Struck Me Dead, p. 70.

[92]Olmsted, The Cotton Kingdom, pp. 201-02.

[93]Quoted by Bell Irvin Wiley, Southern Negroes, 1861-1865 (2nd ed.; New York: Rinehart & Co., 1953), p. 107.

[94]Long, Pictures of Slavery in Church and State, pp. 159-60. At a revival meeting, dances, raffles, cock-fights, foot-races, and other amusements might present themselves. There would be plenty of food, perhaps barbecued hog. Poor whites, blacks, slave and free, would rub shoulders with classy whites who had come out from town to witness the excitement. A nearby creek might be dammed up to provide the necessary water for the baptisms which climaxed the revival. All in all, a camp meeting was a holiday for the slaves. Brown, My Southern Home, p. 97. Yetman, Life Under the "Peculiar Institution," pp. 236, 266-67.

[95]Walter B. Posey, The Development of Methodism in the Old Southwest, 1793-1824 (Tuscaloosa, Ala.: Weatherford Printing Company, 1933), p. 98.

[96]The Methodists in South Carolina resolved: "At our camp-meetings let such accommodations be furnished at the back of the stand, or pulpit, as shall be convenient for the holding of prayer-meeting among the coloured people after preaching, as is usual with the whites, in front of the stand." Cited by Thomas L. Williams, "The Methodist Mission to the Slaves" (unpublished Ph.D. dissertation, Yale, 1943), p. 193. See also, Charles A. Johnson, The Frontier Camp Meeting (Dallas, Tex.: Southern Methodist University Press, 1955), pp. 46, 114-15. Smith, Autobiography, p. 31.

[97]Frances Trollope, Domestic Manners of the Americans (1832), ed. by Donald Smalley (New York: Alfred A. Knopf, Inc., 1949), pp. 170-73.

98Herskovitts, Myth of the Negro Past, pp. 224-32.

99James Weldon Johnson, "O Black and Unknown Bards, " in American Negro Poetry, ed. by Arna Bontemps (New York: Hill and Wang, 1963), p. 1.

100William Francis Allen, Charles Pickard Ware, and Lucy McKim Garrison, Slave Songs of the United States (New York: A. Sampson & Co., 1867). See excerpts from the introduction to this original edition in Bernard Katz, ed., The Social Implications of Early Negro Music in the United States (New York: Arno Press, Inc., 1969), pp. xxii-xxxiii. Yankee minstrels with burnt cork upon their faces had been entertaining Northerners with imitations of the spirituals long before the Civil War. But they were no match for authentic black singers. One of the most famous of the white minstrel groups was that formed by Edwin P. Christy. He claimed to be the "Originator of Ethiopian Minstrelsy and the First to Harmonize Negro Melodies." See his songbook, Christy's Plantation Melodies (Philadelphia: Fisher & Brother, 1853).

101Thomas Wentworth Higginson, Army Life in a Black Regiment (new ed.; Boston: Houghton, Mifflin and Company, 1900), pp. 270-96. Higginson, "Negro Spirituals, " The Atlantic Monthly, XIX, No. CXVI (June, 1867), 685-94.

102Higginson, Army Life in a Black Regiment, pp. 295-96.

103Jacobs, Incidents in the Life of a Slave Girl, pp. 107-08. Yetman, Life Under the "Peculiar Institution, " p. 112.

104Jones, Religious Instruction of the Negroes, p. 266.

105Newman I. White, American Negro Folk-Songs (1928; rpt. Hatboro, Pa.: Folklore Associates, Inc., 1965). George Pullen Jackson, White Spirituals in the Southern Uplands, The Story of the Fasola Folk, Their Songs, Singing, and "Buckwheat Notes" (Chapel Hill, N.C.: The University of North Carolina Press, 1933). See also his White and Negro Spirituals, Their Life Span and Kinship ... 116 Songs as Sung by Both Races (New York: J. J. Augustin, 1944).

106Woodson, African Background Outlined, p. 449. Du Bois, Souls of Black Folk, pp. 183-85.

107Fisher, Negro Slave Songs, pp. 1-26, 49, 63, 78, 86, 178-79, and passim. Almost all of the songs for which Fisher discovered specific historical circumstances seem to have come from the Port Royal Islands. One gets the impression that, of all the slave regions, here was the "Nashville" of black folksong. While valuable in focusing our attention upon the relation of the spirituals to the slaves' personal experiences, Fisher simply does not provide satisfactory evidence for his highly speculative conclusions. Internal evidence alone is insufficient in proving authorship, place of origin,

and historical circumstances. The thesis that the songs were elabo-
rate double entendres and not spirituals at all would surely have
seemed strange to the antebellum black Christians of whom we have
written.

[108]Higginson, "Negro Spirituals, " 692. Douglass, Life and
Times, p. 159. Blassingame, Slave Community, pp. 70-74.

[109]Benjamin E. Mays, The Negro's God as Reflected in His
Literature (1938; rpt. New York: Atheneum, 1968), pp. 19-28,
245-46. See also Howard Thurman, "Religious Ideas in Negro
Spirituals, " Christendom, IV, 4 (Autumn, 1939), 515-28, and James
Weldon Johnson, The Book of American Spirituals (New York:
Viking Press, 1925), pp. 20-21.

[110]As proof of this, one need only glance at some of the old
hymns. See selections from Benjamin Franklin Crawford, Our
Methodist Hymnody (Carnegie, Pa.: Carnegie Church Press, 1940)
and Henry Sweetser Burrage, Baptist Hymn Writers and Their
Hymns (Portland, Me.: Brown Thurston & Company, 1888).

[111]Drew, The Refugee, p. 108.

[112]Ibid., p. 269.

[113]Blassingame, Slave Community, pp. 74-75. Also see
Stuckey, "The Black Ethos in Slavery, " pp. 238-40.

[114]Arnold J. Toynbee, A Study of History, abridgement of
vols. I-VI by D. C. Somervill (New York and London: Oxford University Press, 1947), p. 129. Compare Smith, "Slavery and
Theology, " 497.

[115]Joseph R. Washington, The Politics of God (Boston:
Beacon Press, 1969), p. 151.

[116]Stroyer, My Life in the South, p. 85. Drew, The Refugee,
p. 22. Grandy, Narrative, p. 41.

[117]Yetman, Life Under the "Peculiar Institution, " p. 280.

[118](Mrs.) A. M. French, Slavery in South Carolina, and the
Ex-Slaves; or, The Port Royal Mission (1862; rpt. New York: Negro
Universities Press, 1969), p. 29.

[119]Stroyer, My Life in the South, p. 47.

[120]Kemble, Residence on a Georgia Plantation, p. 72.

CHAPTER V

[1]David Walker, Walker's Appeal in Four Articles, Together

With a Preamble to the Colored Citizens of the World, But in Particular and Very Expressly to Those of the United States of America
(2nd ed., 1930), in Henry Highland Garnet, Walker's Appeal with a
Brief Sketch of His Life. Also Garnet's Address to the Slaves of
the United States of America (New York: J. H. Tobitt, 1848), p.
69.

[2]Richard Allen, The Life Experience and Gospel Labors of
the Rt. Rev. Richard Allen, to which is annexed the Rise and Progress of the African Methodist Episcopal Church in the United States
of America, intro. by George A. Singleton (New York and Nashville: Abingdon Press, 1969), p. 17. Charles H. Wesley, Richard
Allen: Apostle of Freedom (Washington, D.C.: The Associated
Publishers, Inc., 1935), pp. 16-17.

[3]The chief contenders for the honor due the Silver Bluff
Church are two churches in Savannah, which actually are the result
of a split in the group formed under Andrew Bryan in 1788. The
story of the first Bryan church is told in James M. Simms, The
First Colored Baptist Church in North America (Philadelphia: J.
B. Lippincott Company, 1888). The claims of the other wing are
put forth by Emanuel K. Love, History of the First African Baptist
Church, from its Organization, January 20th, 1788, to July 1st,
1888 (Savannah, Ga.: Morning News Print, 1888), and Edgar Garfield Thomas, The First African Baptist Church of North America
(Savannah, Ga.: By the Author, 1925). Thomas would like to date
the origin of the Savannah church as far back as 1775, the probable
date of George Liele's ordination, but at this time Liele was doing
only occasional preaching in the western "suburbs" and no group was
officially constituted.

[4]"Letters Showing the Rise and Progress of the Early Negro
Churches of Georgia and the West Indies," The Journal of Negro
History, I, 1 (January, 1916), 69. These letters are from John
Rippon's Baptist Annual Register, 1790-1793. See Walter H. Brooks,
"The Priority of the Silver Bluff Church and its Promoters," The
Journal of Negro History, VII, 2 (April, 1922), 172-95.

[5]Letter, George Liele to John Rippon, Dec. 18, 1791, in
"Letters," p. 71.

[6]Letter, Abraham Marshall to John Rippon, May 1, 1793, in
"Letters," p. 86. Brooks, "Priority of the Silver Bluff Church,"
189-90.

[7]Letters, Jonathan Clarke to John Rippon, July 19, 1790;
Clarke to Rippon, December 22, 1792; and Marshall to Rippon,
May 1, 1793, in "Letters," pp. 77-80, 82-83, 85-86. In his The
History of the Negro Church, second edition (Washington, D.C.:
The Associated Publishers, 1945), pp. 42-45, Carter G. Woodson
told the Bryan story with an incorrect sequence of events. Of chief
importance is his error of placing the whipping and imprisonment
of Andrew and Sampson after the constitution of the church in 1788

rather than during the pre-Brampton period, as Clarke's letter of
July 19, 1790 clearly indicates. Perhaps Woodson followed the ac-
count of Simms, First Colored Baptist Church, pp. 1923. The
correct version is given by Thomas in his First African Baptist
Church, pp. 33-38, and by John W. Davis, "George Liele and
Andrew Bryan, Pioneer Negro Baptist Preachers," The Journal of
Negro History, III, 2 (April, 1918), 119-27.

[8]Letter, Andrew Bryan to Rippon, December 23, 1800, in
"Letters," pp. 86-87. Lorenzo Dow, Perambulations of Cosmo-
polite; or Travels and Labors of Lorenzo Dow, in Europe and
America (New York: Richard C. Valentine, 1855), pp. 93-95.

[9]Benjamin Franklin Riley, A History of the Baptists in the
Southern States East of the Mississippi (Philadelphia: American
Baptist Publication Society, 1898), p. 314.

[10]Simms, First Colored Baptist Church, p. 61.

[11]The special circumstances which fostered all-black churches
in the urban areas are well described by Richard C. Wade in
Slavery in the Cities (New York: Oxford University Press, 1964),
pp. 160-172.

[12]Walter H. Brooks, "The Evolution of the Negro Baptist
Church," The Journal of Negro History, VII, 1 (January, 1922), 14-
15. Lewis G. Jordan, Negro Baptist History, U.S.A., 1750-1930
(Nashville, Tenn.: The Sunday School Publishing Board, 1930), pp.
58-59. Garnett Ryland, The Baptists of Virginia, 1699-1926 (Richmond, Va.: Baptist Board of Mission and Education, 1955), pp.
284-85.

[13]Robert B. Semple, A History of the Rise and Progress of
the Baptists in Virginia, revised by C. W. Beale (Philadelphia:
American Baptist Publication Society, 1894), p. 148. Riley, History
of Baptists, p. 318.

[14]Luther P. Jackson, "Religious Development of the Negro
in Virginia from 1760 to 1860," The Journal of Negro History, XVI,
2 (April, 1931), 203.

[15]The natal dates of Baptist churches and organizations are
often difficult to ascertain. That of the Providence Missionary Association in Ohio has been variously given as anywhere from 1833
to 1836. I have accepted the date of 1836, as given by Woodson
and Jordan. See Woodson, Negro Church, p. 107, and Jordan,
Negro Baptist History, p. 63. The natal date of the Wood River
Baptist Association of Illinois was probably sometime during April
of 1839. See Miles Mark Fisher, "Negro Churches in Illinois,"
Journal of the Illinois Historical Society, LVI, (Autumn, 1963), 553.
I could not reconcile this date with the account which the Negro historian George W. Williams gave of the role that Duke William Anderson performed in bringing together several Negro Baptist churches in

the Alton, Illinois, area along the Wood River. Williams dated the
formation of the Wood River Association sometime after 1845. See
his History of the Negro Race in America From 1619 to 1880 (2
vols.; New York: G. P. Putnam's Sons, 1882), II, 476-97.

16Jackson, "Religious Development of the Negro in Virginia,"
205-08. W. Harrison Daniel, "Virginia Baptists and the Negro
in the Antebellum Era," The Journal of Negro History, LVI, 1
(January, 1971), 4. John W. Cromwell, "The Aftermath of Nat
Turner's Insurrection," The Journal of Negro History, V, 2 (April,
1920), 230-34.

17Simms, First Colored Baptist Church, pp. 94-99. Thomas,
First African Baptist Church, pp. 49-52. The group which remained
loyal to the Sunbury Association was enrolled as the Third African
Baptist Church but in 1866 received a favorable court ruling that it
could lay claim to the name of First Bryan Baptist Church.

18Benjamin Quarles, "Ante-Bellum Relationships Between the
First African Baptist Church of New Orleans and White Agencies,"
The Chronicle, XVIII, 1 (January, 1955), 28-29.

19Cited by Robert F. Durden, "The Establishment of Calvary
Protestant Episcopal Church for Negroes in Charleston," The South
Carolina Historical Magazine, LXV, 2 (April, 1964), 79.

20Daniel Alexander Payne, "Morris Brown," in Lives of
Methodist Bishops, ed. by Theodore L. Flood and John W. Hamilton
(New York: Phillips & Hart, 1882), pp. 669-74. Payne, History of
the African Methodist Episcopal Church, ed. by C. S. Smith (Nashville, Tenn.: Publishing House of the A.M.E. Sunday School Union,
1891), pp. 26, 32, 45.

21Allen, Life Experience, p. 24. Biographical studies of
Allen have been provided by Charles H. Wesley in his Richard Allen:
Apostle of Freedom (Washington, D.C.: The Associated Publishers,
Inc., 1935), and by Carol V. R. George in Segregated Sabbaths:
Richard Allen and the Emergence of Independent Black Churches,
1760-1840 (New York: Oxford University Press, 1973).

22Letter, Benjamin Rush to Granville Sharp, Philadelphia,
August, 1791, in Letters of Benjamin Rush, ed. by L. H. Butter-
field (Princeton, N.J.: Princeton University Press, 1951), p. 608.

23"The Articles of Association of the Free African Society"
have been reprinted in Black Nationalism in America, ed. by John
H. Bracey, Jr., August Meier, and Elliott Rudwick (Indianapolis
and New York: The Bobbs-Merrill Company, Inc., 1970), pp. 19-21.

24November, 1787, is the date given to the gallery incident
by George A. Singleton, in his introduction to The Life Experience
and Gospel Labors of the Rt. Rev. Richard Allen, p. 7. In his
The Romance of African Methodism (New York: Exposition Press,

1952) much is made of the fact "that in the same year that Richard
Allen and his associates decided to withdraw from Old St. George
and begin a chapel, the Founding Fathers of the Republic were in
session in the State House at Sixth and Chestnut Streets" (p. 19).
Daniel Alexander Payne, the first historian of the A.M.E. connection, simply says: "About three years after the organization of the
M.E. Church, the colored members of that body in the city of
Philadelphia, suffering from the 'unkind treatment of their white
brethren, who considered them a nuisance in the house of worship'
met for the purpose of canvassing their wrongs and devising means
to remedy the same. The result of this meeting was the determina-
tion to erect a house of worship wherein they could worship God
under their own 'vine and fig tree'." Payne does not mention the
gallery incident but does imply that in 1787 (three years after the
famous Baltimore Christmas Conference of the Methodists) Allen
and his fellow blacks were intent on going their separate way. See
Payne, History of the A.M.E. Church, p. 4.

In her otherwise excellent and reliable history of Allen and
the rise of the independent black churches, Carol V. R. George
has, unfortunately, not questioned the traditional dating. See Segregated Sabbaths, p. 55. Some historians have maintained that the
gallery incident was the cause not only of the founding of the First
African Church but also of the Free African Society, which we know
was established in April, 1787. This is entirely in error. The
mistake has been perpetuated, no doubt, because of Carter G. Woodson's account in The History of the Negro Church, pp. 64-65, and
E. Franklin Frazier's The Negro Church in America (New York:
Schocken Books, 1964), pp. 26-27. Leon Litwack has the correct
sequence but mistakenly dates the gallery incident in November,
1787. See North of Slavery (Chicago: University of Chicago Press,
1961), pp. 191-192.

25St. George's was without wooden floors until 1790, as
flooring was not given consideration until after the end of the Revolutionary conflict. During the British occupation of Philadelphia,
St. George's was used as a "rough ground floor" was laid in the east end,
Shortly thereafter a "rough ground floor" was laid in the east end,
but the rest remained dirt until 1790. The original estimate and
various bills from the firm of Mosley & Smith, the builders of the
galleries in 1792, can be found in a scrapbook entitled "A Book of
Antiquities" which was collected by Francis H. Tees, a longtime
pastor and historian of Old St. George's. It is in the vault of the
Methodist Historical Center which adjoins Old St. George's in Philadelphia. See also Francis H. Tees, Ancient Landmark of American
Methodism, or, Historic Old St. George's (Philadelphia: The Messenger Publishing Co., 1951), pp. 53, 92-94. Albert W. Cliffe has
some information on the problem in his Glory of Our Methodist Heritage (Philadelphia: n.p., 1957), pp. 65-69. Several older publications also indicate that the balconies could not have been in existence
in 1787. In 1859 John Lednum wrote: "About 1791, the galleries
were put in at St. George's, after the Methodists had owned it more
than twenty years." See Lednum, A History of the Rise of Methodism in America, Containing Sketches of Methodist Itinerant Preachers,

220   Black Religion

From 1736 to 1785, Numbering One Hundred and Sixty or Seventy,
Also a Short Account of Many Hundreds of the First Race of Lay
Members, Male and Female, From New York to South Carolina.
Together with an Account of Many of the First Societies and Chapels
(Philadelphia: Published for the Author, 1859), p. 47. Also see,
John F. Watson, Annals of Philadelphia and Pennsylvania in the
Olden Time, Being a Collection of Memoirs, Anecdotes and Inci-
dents of the City, and Its Inhabitants and of the Earliest Settlements
of the Inland Part of Pennsylvania, From the Days of the Founders
(2 vols.; Philadelphia: J. B. Lippincott & Co., 1870), II, 456.

[26]Allen, Life Experience, p. 26. Just prior to the incident,
Allen wrote, "the Rev. Mr. W____ took the charge, and the Rev.
L____ G____." Life Experience, p. 24. These men would be
Henry Willis, who was appointed to the St. George's station in 1791,
and Lemuel Green, who became presiding elder of the Chester-
Wilmington-Philadelphia circuit for the first time in 1791. No
where does Allen mention Samuel Dudley and William Thomas who
were the co-pastors of St. George's in 1787. It is evident that between the departure of "C____ B____," whom Allen says opposed
the erection of a separate place of worship for the Negroes, and the
mentioning of Willis and Green, there is a gap of five years in
Allen's memoirs. "C____ B____" is one Caleb Boyer who became
elder in Philadelphia in 1786 but was relieved of his duties because
of family responsibilities. It is also significant that Allen relates
that he and his associates made a complaint to John McClaskey, the
supervising elder, who opposed their subscription paper. McClaskey
became elder in 1792. Allen, Life Experiences, pp. 26-27. For
verification of the dates when the designated individuals were assigned, see the Minutes of the General Conference of the Methodist
Episcopal Church for the General Conference of the Methodist Episcopal Church for the years 1786 through 1792, in Minutes of the
Methodist Conferences 1773 to 1794 Under the Superintendence of
John Wesley, Bishops Asbury and Coke (Botetourt County, Va.: n.p.,
1794).

[27]Letter, Benjamin Rush to Julia Rush, July 16, 1791,
Letters of Benjamin Rush, pp. 599-600. Rush and Robert Ralston
subsequently met with a dozen free blacks at the home of William
Wilcher, one of Allen's close associates. Rush recorded in his
commonplace book for July 25, 1791, that the blacks "appeared
well satisfied" with the "sundry articles of faith and a plan of church
government which I had composed for them." See The Autobiography
of Benjamin Rush, ed. by George W. Corner (Princeton, N.J.:
Princeton University Press, 1948), p. 202. Letter, Rush to Granville Sharp, August, 1791, Letters of Benjamin Rush, pp. 608-09.
Letter, Rush to Julia Rush, August 12, 1791, Letters of Benjamin
Rush, pp. 602-23. Allen, Life Experience, p. 28.

[28]Letter of Rush to Julia Rush, August 12, 1791, Letters of
Benjamin Rush, pp. 602-03.

[29]Allen, Life Experience, pp. 26-31. Wesley, Richard Allen,

pp. 70-78. The subsequent history of Absalom Jones and his church is told by William Douglass in Annals of the First African Church in the United States of America, Now Styled the African Episcopal Church of St. Thomas, Philadelphia (Philadelphia: King & Baird, 1862). After 22 years of service Jones died in 1818. For a number of years thereafter the pulpit of St. Thomas was filled by white preachers. In 1834, William Douglass took the charge and served his fellow blacks until his death in 1862. The African Church of St. Thomas' contended for representation in the Diocesan Convention unsuccessfully until the 1795 regulation barring them was rescinded during the Civil War. See George Freeman Bragg, History of the Episcopal Afro-American Group of the Episcopal Church (Baltimore: Church Advocate Press, 1922), pp. 59-68.

30Allen, Life Experience, pp. 28-31.

31James A. Handy, Scraps of African Methodist Episcopal History (Philadelphia: A.M.E. Book Concern, n.d.), pp. 13-14, 22-26, 35-36.

32Christopher Rush, A Short Account of the Rise and Progress of the African Methodist Episcopal Church in America (New York: Published by the Author, 1843), p. 10. J. B. Wakely, Lost Chapters Recovered from the Early History of American Methodism (New York: Published for the Author, 1858), pp. 429-70.

33John Jamison Moore, History of the A.M.E. Zion Church in America (York, Pa.: Teacher's Journal Office, 1884), p. 15. David Henry Bradley, Sr., A History of the A.M.E. Zion Church, Part I, 1796-1872 (Nashville, Tenn.: The Parthenon Press, 1956), p. 54.

34Jay Harris, "State was Birthplace of the Negro Church," The Morning News (Wilmington, Delaware) CLXXI, 43 (February 19, 1971), p. 2. Wesley, Richard Allen, pp. 133-34.

35George H. Hansell, Reminiscences of Baptist Churches and Baptist Leaders in New York City and Vicinity, (Philadelphia: American Baptist Society, 1899), p. 25. Jordan, Negro Baptist History, p. 58. Woodson, Negro Church, pp. 74-78. Woodson has all three congregations being constituted in 1809 while Jordan lists them in the following order: Boston, 1805, New York, 1808, and Philadelphia, 1809. George, Segregated Sabbaths, pp. 145-46.

36Allen, Life Experience, pp. 30-32. The "Articles of Association" are reprinted in Bradley, History of the A.M.E. Zion Church, pp. 51-54. Wesley, Richard Allen, pp. 85-86, 98.

37Allen, Life Experience, p. 32. Wesley, Richard Allen, pp. 135-36. The "African Supplement" is reprinted in the Singleton edition of Allen's Life Experience and Gospel Labors, pp. 37-41. Benjamin Tucker Tanner, An Outline of Our History and Government for African Methodist Episcopal Churchmen, Ministerial and Lay (Philadelphia: A.M.E. Book Concern, 1884), p. 151.

222

38Allen, Life Experience, pp. 32-34. Wesley, Richard Allen, pp. 138-40. George, Segregated Sabbaths, pp. 65-71, 80-85.

39Wesley, Richard Allen, pp. 152-53. Singleton, Romance of African Methodism, p. 22.

40Daniel Alexander Payne, Recollections of Seventy Years (Nashville, Tenn.: Publishing House of the A.M.E. Sunday School Union, 1883), pp. 100-01. In his history Payne simply says that Coker was first nominated and "resigned, or rather, declined" the office the next day and Allen was then chosen. See Payne, History of the African Methodist Episcopal Church (Nashville, Tenn.: Publishing House of the A.M.E. Sunday School Union, 1891), p. 14.

41Rush, Short Account, pp. 28-29. Bradley, History of the A.M.E. Zion Church, p. 62.

42Rush, Short Account, pp. 37-38. Bradley, History of the A.M.E. Zion Church, pp. 73-79.

43Rush, Short Account, pp. 34, 35.

44Bradley, History of the A.M.E. Zion Church, p. 91. James Walker Hood, One Hundred Years of the African Methodist Episcopal Church; or, The Centennial of African Methodism (New York: A.M.E. Zion Book Company, 1895), pp. 15-28.

45Rush, Short Account, pp. 83-85. According to James Walker Hood, the office of bishop for which Varick and later Rush were chosen was in reality an "elective superintendency" and therefore more democratic in nature than the lifetime office which Richard Allen held as bishop of the A.M.E. Church. Hood, One Hundred Years, p. 63. As it turned out, however, the bishops in the Zion connection usually remained in the episcopal chair until their deaths.

46See, for example, Bracey, Meier, and Rudwick, editors, Black Nationalism in America, introduction, pp. xxxi, lvii; James H. Cone, Black Theology and Black Power (New York: The Seabury Press, 1969), p. 94; and George, Segregated Sabbaths, p. 5.

47Cited from Tanner, Outline of Our History, Appendix, p. 145.

48The memorial of the A.M.E. Church trustees to the Philadelphia Conference and a reply by Francis Asbury are reprinted in The Journal and Letters of Francis Asbury, ed. by J. Manning Potts, Elmer T. Clark, and Jacob S. Payton (London and Nashville: Epworth Press and Abingdon Press, 1958), III, 367.

49The address is reprinted in Hood, One Hundred Years, pp. 8-9. It was signed by Abraham Thompson, James Varick, and William Miller.

[50]Payne, History of the A.M.E. Church, pp. 16, 21, 68, 128-31, and passim.

[51]Allen's will, dated December 9, 1830, is reprinted in the Appendix to Wesley, Richard Allen, pp. 270-74. Payne, History of the A.M.E. Church, pp. 69, 81, 84-85. George, Segregated Sabbaths, pp. 75-76.

[52]Rush, The Autobiography of Benjamin Rush, pp. 239, 250.

[53]Payne, History of the A.M.E. Church, p. 69. The epitaph was originally for Henry Fox, who died on August 9, 1830, at the age of ninety after many years as an "acceptable deacon" in Frenchton, Maryland.

[54]Payne, History of the A.M.E. Church, pp. 111, 113, 125. Payne at the last two places cited gives different figures for the total membership: p. 113 - 17,594 and p. 125 - 27,250.

[55]Bradley, History of the A.M.E. Zion Church, pp. 104, 120-23. An A.M.E. Zion Church in Rochester, New York, was often a place of refuge for Harriet Tubman and those whom she was seeking to get to Canada. In 1903 she deeded her home and 25 acres to the A.M.E. Zion Church. Earl Conrad, Harriet Tubman, Negro Soldier and Abolitionist (New York: International Publishers, 1942), pp. 61, 211. Frederick Douglass, My Bondage and My Freedom (New York: Miller, Orton, and Mulligan, 1855), p. 23. Jermain Loguen was first licensed to preach by the A.M.E. Zion Church in Syracuse, New York, in 1841. In 1854, although still technically a fugitive slave, he was named as one of the superintendents of the Zion connection. His story, which was probably ghost-written, is told in The Reverend Jermain W. Loguen, As A Slave And As A Freeman: A Narrative of Real Life (Syracuse, N.Y.: Office of the Daily Journal, 1859). Sojourner Truth withdrew from St. John's in New York to join the Zionites. See Francis W. Titus, Narrative of Sojourner Truth; A Bondswoman of Olden Time (Battle Creek, Mich.: Published for the Author, 1878), p. 79.

[56]Payne, History of the A.M.E. Church, pp. 58, 94. Daniel A. Payne, "Morris Brown," in Flood, Lives of Methodist Bishops, pp. 669-74.

[57]Hood, One Hundred Years, pp. 68-72. Bradley, History of the A.M.E. Zion Church, pp. 134-35. Tees, Landmark of American Methodism, p. 106. Rush, Short Account, p. 92.

[58]Bradley, History of the A.M.E. Zion Church, pp. 146, 159. James Beverly Ford Shaw, The Negro in the History of Methodism (Nashville, Tenn.: The Parthenon Press, 1954), p. 78.

[59]Douglass, My Bondage and My Freedom, pp. 350-54.

[60]Frederick Douglass, "What are the Colored People Doing

224   Black Religion

for Themselves," The Life and Writings of Frederick Douglass, ed.
by Philip S. Foner (4 vols.; New York: International Publishers
Co., Inc., 1950), I, 317-18.

[61]Shelton M. Bishop, "A History of St. Philip's Church,
New York City," Historical Magazine of the Protestant Episcopal
Church, XV, 4 (December, 1946), 302-06. Bragg, Afro-American
Group of the Episcopal Church, p. 68.

[62]Robin W. Winks, The Blacks in Canada (New Haven, Conn.:
Yale University Press, 1971), pp. 341-44.

[63]Payne, Recollections of Seventy Years, pp. 11-17, 19, 27-
28, 35.

[64]Ibid., pp. 44-45, 58, 61-65, 68-75. See also, John W.
Cromwell, "The First Negro Churches in the District of Columbia,"
The Journal of Negro History, VII, 1 (January, 1922), 68.

[65]Payne, History of the A.M.E. Church, pp. 171-72. John
M. Brown, "William Paul Quinn," in Lives of Methodist Bishops,
pp. 659-66.

[66]Tanner, Outline of Our History, pp. 45-46. Payne, History
of the A.M.E. Church, pp. 361-91. In the Maritime Provinces some
of the A.M.E. churches remained in connection with the American-
based church. In 1884 the A.M.E. and B.M.E. reunited but not all
the former B.M.E. churches went along with the merger. Winks,
The Blacks in Canada, pp. 355-58.

[67]Payne, Recollections of Seventy Years, pp. 109-10. This
still is the best source for information on this most important figure
in Negro religious history. There are two biographies on the life
and work of Daniel Alexander Payne, but I did not find them to be
very useful. See Charles Spencer Smith, The Life of Daniel Alexander Payne, D.D., LL.D. (Nashville, Tenn.: Publishing House of
the A.M.E. Church Sunday School Union, 1894); and Josephus R.
Coan, Daniel Alexander Payne (Philadelphia: A.M.E. Book Concern,
1935).

[68]Payne, History of the A.M.E. Church, p. 141.

[69]Ibid., p. 467.

[70]The story of this region and the social upheavals that took
place in the transition from Confederate to Union control is well told
in Willie Lee Rose's Rehearsal for Reconstruction: The Port Royal
Experiment (New York: Vintage Books, 1967). While much is said
of the white Evangelicals in "Gideon's Band," no mention is made of
the black Methodists who also went south to minister to the ex-slaves.

[71]Payne, History of the A.M.E. Church, pp. 467-68. Smith,
African Methodist Episcopal Church, pp. 51-52.

72Payne, Recollections of Seventy Years, pp. 161-62, 469, 472.

73Booker T. Washington, The Story of the Negro (2 vols.; New York: Doubleday, Page & Co., 1909), I, 278.

74W. E. B. Du Bois, The Souls of Black Folk, introduction by Saunders Redding (New York: Fawcett World Library, 1961), pp. 142-43.

CHAPTER VI

1Quoted by Herbert Aptheker, The Negro in the Abolitionist Movement (New York: International Publishers, 1941), p. 18.

2The Coloured American, I, 14 (June 13, 1840), 2; I, 15 (June 20, 1840), 2; and I, 19 (July 11, 1840), 2. Minutes of the General and Annual Conferences of the African Methodist Episcopal Church, 1839-1840 (Brooklyn: George Hogarth, 1840), pp. 33, 39-42.

3George A. Singleton, The Romance of African Methodism (New York: Exposition Press, 1952), pp. 10-11. Charles Spencer Smith, The Catechism of the A.M.E. Church, Formerly "The Turner Catechism," Revised and Improved (Bloomington, Ill.: Connectional Sunday School Union of the A.M.E. Church, 1885), p. 41.

4Levi Jenkins Coppin, Unwritten History (Philadelphia: A.M.E. Book Concern, 1919), pp. 144-47, 153-54. Also see the "Editorial" on the Rev. James F. Sisson in the A.M.E. Church Review, LXXVI, 203 (January-March, 1960), 3-4. Sisson was an ex-pharmicist in his early sixties when he entered the A.M.E. ministry. After the Civil War he labored mostly in Georgia among the Freedmen. Coppin, later to be a bishop of the A.M.E. Church, knew Sisson from his early travels.

5Jupiter Hammon, An Address to Negroes in the State of New York (New York: Carroll & Patterson, 1787), p. 3.

6Richard Allen, "To the People of Color," reprinted in The Life Experience and Gospel Labors of the Rt. Rev. Richard Allen, introduction by George A. Singleton (New York and Nashville: Abingdon Press, 1960), p. 73. This address was prefaced to the first published conference minutes of the A.M.E. Church in 1818.

7Absalom Jones and Richard Allen, A Narrative of the Proceedings of the Black People During the Late Awful Calamity in Philadelphia in the Year 1793; and a Refutation of Some Censures Thrown Upon Them in Some Late Publications (Philadelphia: Printed for the Authors, 1794), p. 3. The full story is told in the Narrative by Jones and Allen and in J. H. Powell's Bring Out Your Dead: The Great Plague of Yellow Fever in Philadelphia in 1793 (Philadelphia: University of Pennsylvania Press, 1949), pp. 91-101.

[8]Richard Allen, Confession of John Joyce, alias Davis, who
was executed on Monday, the 14th of March, 1808, for the Murder
of Mrs. Sarah Cross, with an Address to the Public and People of
Colour, Together with the Substance of the Trial and Chief Justice
Tilgham on His Condemnation (Philadelphia: Printed for the Benefit
of Bethel Church, 1808), p. 5. Allen published a similar pamphlet
with the confessions of Peter Matthias, alias Mathews.

[9]Daniel Alexander Payne, The Semi-Centenary and the Retrospection of the African Methodist Episcopal Church in the United
States of America (Baltimore, Md.: Sherwood & Co., 1866), pp.
27, 37. Carol V. R. George, Segregated Sabbaths (New York:
Oxford University Press, 1973), pp. 125-27.

[10]Christian Recorder, I, 18 (August 17, 1854), 69. Minutes
of the General and Annual Conferences of the African Methodist
Episcopal Church (Brooklyn, N.Y.: George Hogarth, 1849), pp. 4,
21. Payne, Semi-Centenary of the A.M.E. Church, pp. 30, 36, 44.
George, Segregated Sabbaths, p. 127. Negro Baptists also remon-
strated against alcohol. See The Articles of Faith, Church Discipline, and By-Laws of the Abyssinian Baptist Church of New York,
April 3, 1833 (New York: From J. Post's Office, 1833), p. 17.

[11]Christian Recorder, I, 33 (August, 18, 1855), 130; and I,
34 (October 20, 1855), 136. Essays against smoking by Hiram K.
Revels are reproduced in Payne, Semi-Centenary of the A.M.E.
Church, pp. 154-57.

[12]Christian Recorder, I, 29 (March 19, 1855), 113. C. M.
Tanner, Reprint of the First Edition of the Discipline of the African
Methodist Episcopal Church with Historical Preface and Notes (At-
lanta, Ga.: n.p., 1916), p. 66. Payne, Semi-Centenary of the
A.M.E. Church, pp. 36-37.

[13]Frederick Douglass, "What are the Colored People Doing
for Themselves," in The Life and Writings of Frederick Douglass,
ed. by Philip S. Foner (4 vols.; New York: International Publishers,
Inc., 1950), I, 317.

[14]Carter G. Woodson, The Education of the Negro Prior to
1861 (2nd. ed.; Washington, D.C.: The Associated Publishers, Inc.,
1919), chapters VI, X, and XIII. See also Leon Litwack, North of
Slavery (Chicago: University of Chicago Press, 1961), chapter IV.

[15]"Articles of Association of the African Methodist Church of
the City of Philadelphia, in the Commonwealth of Pennsylvania." A
photostatic copy from the Commonwealth's archives is found among
the Carter G. Woodson papers in the Library of Congress, Washington, D.C. Daniel Alexander Payne, "Morris Brown," in Theodore
L. Flood and James W. Hamilton, editors, Lives of Methodist
Bishops (New York: Phillips & Hart, 1882), p. 670. Daniel Alexander Payne, History of the African Methodist Episcopal Church, ed.
by C. S. Smith (Nashville, Tenn.: Publishing House of the A.M.E.

Sunday School Union, 1891), p. 16.   John Jamison Moore, History of the A.M.E. Zion Church in America (York, Pa.:   Teacher's Journal Office, 1884), p. 25.

16Daniel Alexander Payne, Recollections of Seventy Years (Nashville, Tenn.:   Publishing House of the A.M.E. Sunday School Union, 1888), p. 64.

17See the excellent study by William Pipes, Say Amen Brother! Old-Time Negro Preaching: a Study in American Frustration (New York: William Frederick Press, 1951).

18Martin Robinson Delany, The Condition, Elevation, Emigration, and Destiny of the Coloured People of the United States (Philadelphia: Published by the Author, 1852), pp. 112-28.   Carter G. Woodson, The History of the Negro Church (2nd. ed.; Washington, D.C.:   The Associated Publishers, 1945), pp. 153-58.   The encounter of 14 black boys, including Garnet and Crummell, with the segregationist interests of the Granite State is told in Litwack, North of Slavery, pp. 117-20.   W. E. Burghardt Du Bois gave an unforgettable portrait of Alexander Crummell in The Souls of Black Folk, introduction by Saunders Redding (Greenwish, Conn.:   Fawcett Publications, Inc., 1961), pp. 157-65.

19Josephus Roosevelt Coan, Daniel Alexander Payne: Christian Educator (Philadelphia: A.M.E. Book Concern, 1935), passim.

20Daniel Alexander Payne, History of the African Methodist Episcopal Church (Nashville, Tenn.:   Publishing House of the A.M.E. Sunday School Union, 1891), p. 155.   Payne, Recollections of Seventy Years, p. 76.

21Payne, History of the A.M.E. Church, pp. 169-70, 395. Payne, Semi-Centenary of the A.M.E. Church, pp. 60-61.

22Payne, "Essay on the Education of the Ministry," in History of the A.M.E. Church, pp. 195-96.

23Minutes of the Fortieth Annual Conference of the African Methodist Episcopal Church for the Baltimore District, April 24, 1857 (Baltimore: James Young, 1857), p. 18.

24Minutes of the Genesee Annual Conference of the African M.E. Zion Church in America, Convened at Montrose, Pa., September 1st, 1858 (Ithaca, N.Y.:   Published by Rev. John Thomas and Rev. William Sanford for the Conference, 1858), p. 7.

25Payne, History of the A.M.E. Church, pp. 456-58.   Payne, Semi-Centenary of the A.M.E. Church, p. 45.

26Payne, Recollections of Seventy Years, pp. 92-94.

27Payne, History of the A.M.E. Church, pp. 135, 176-77.

[28]Ibid., pp. 185-88, 357, 399, 423-28.

[29]Payne, Recollections of Seventy Years, pp. 149-52, 226.
Payne, Semi-Centenary of the A.M.E. Church, pp. 105-06.

[30]Payne, History of the A.M.E. Church, p. 428.   Payne,
Recollections of Seventy Years, pp. 152-53, 229-30.

[31]John M. Brown, "Richard Allen and His Co-adjutors,"
Repository of Religion and Literature, III, 1 (January, 1861), 1.
David Henry Bradley, Sr., A History of the A.M.E. Zion Church,
Part II, 1872-1968 (Nashville, Tenn.: The Parthenon Press, 1970),
p. 15. James Beverly Ford Shaw, The Negro in the History of
Methodism (Nashville, Tenn.: The Parthenon Press, 1954), pp. 79-
80.

[32]Samuel Ringgold Ward, Autobiography of A Fugitive Negro
(London: John Snow, 1855), p. 206.

[33]P. J. Staudenraus, The African Colonization Movement,
1816-1865 (New York: Columbia University Press, 1961), pp. 16-
25. Phil Samuel Sigler, "The Attitudes of Free Blacks Towards
Emancipation" (unpublished Ph.D. dissertation, Boston University,
1969), pp. 14-15.

[34]Letter, James Forten to Paul Cuffe, January 25, 1817, reprinted in John H. Bracey, Jr., August Meier, and Elliot Rudwick,
editors, Black Nationalism in America (Indianapolis and New York:
The Bobbs-Merrill Co., Inc., 1970), pp. 45-46. Cuffe was a
wealthy black merchant of Massachusetts who sought to establish
free blacks in Sierra Leone. James Forten owned a sailloft in
Philadelphia. Although sympathetic with Cuffe's plans, he was
deeply opposed to the colonization ideas of the whites. Benjamin
Quarles, Black Abolitionists (New York: Oxford University Press,
1969), pp. 3-6. Quarles has a good account of the 1817 meeting
and its consequences. George, Segregated Sabbaths, pp. 136-40.

[35]This letter, from the November 27, 1827, issue of Free-
dom's Journal, is reprinted in Charles Wesley, Richard Allen:
Apostle of Freedom (Washington, D.C.: The Associated Publishers,
Inc., 1935), pp. 219-20. See also Richard Allen, "The Colonization
Movement," A.M.E. Church Review, LXXXII, 223 (January-March,
1965), 23-24.

[36]Delany, Colored People of the United States, p. 30.

[37]Christian Recorder, I, 29 (April 4, 1855), 115. Africa's
"isolation, dryness, heat, barrenness and unhealthiness" are depicted in two essays opposing colonization by the Rev. L. Woodson.
See Payne, Semi-Centenary of the A.M.E. Church, pp. 85-90.

[38]Peter Williams, "Slavery and Colonization," in Woodson,
editor, Negro Orators, pp. 79, 83. For other examples of opposition

by black clergy towards the colonization enterprise see Levin Tilmon, A Brief Miscellaneous Narrative of the More Early Part of
the Life of L. Tilmon, Pastor of A Colored Methodist Congregational Church in the City of New York (Jersey City, N.J.: Pratt,
1835), pp. 52-53, and the Rev. Samuel E. Cornish, "Rights of All, "
in Henry Highland Garnet, Walker's Appeal with a Brief Sketch of
His Life. Also Garnet's Address to the Slaves of the United States
of America (New York: J. H. Tobitt, 1848), p. 77. In 1851 the
Philadelphia Annual Conference of the A.M.E. Church officially condemned the Liberian scheme of the American Colonization Society.
It is interesting to note that Charles Spencer Smith, a black clergyman who served in the Reconstruction legislature of Alabama, considered the 1851 condemnation unwise when he updated Payne's
history of the A.M.E. Church in 1922. Marcus Garvey's "Back to
Africa" slogan appealed to many blacks and the idea of a refuge
beneath the Liberian flag was highly attractive. Smith felt that it
was "better that the bodies of these should fatten Africa's prolific
soil than that they should be incinerated in bonfires in America. "
See A History of the African Methodist Episcopal Church, Being A
Volume Supplemental to a History of the African Methodist Episcopal
Church, By Daniel Alexander Payne, D.D., LL.D., Late One of Its
Bishops, Chronicling the Principal Events in the Advance of the
African Methodist Episcopal Church From 1856 to 1922 (Philadelphia:
Book Concern of the A.M.E. Church, 1922), p. 21.

[39]This series of letters, to which there never was a reply,
is reprinted in Carter G. Woodson, editor, The Mind of the Negro
As Reflected in Letters Written During the Crisis, 1800-1860 (Washington, D.C.: The Association for the Study of Negro Life and
History, Inc., 1926), pp. 15-17. For similar pleas see also the
letters by John Jones, Peter Butler, and Isaiah Wilson, Ibid., pp.
9-10, 93, 106.

[40]Cited by Miles M. Fisher, "Lott Cary, The Colonizing
Missionary, " The Journal of Negro History, VII, 4 (October, 1922),
389.

[41]The mixed missionary motives of free blacks are examined
by Sigler, "Attitudes of Free Blacks Towards Emigration to Liberia, "
pp. 47-62.

[42]Daniel Coker, Journal of Daniel Coker (Baltimore, Md.:
Press of Edward J. Coate, 1820), pp. 43-44.

[43]Singleton, Romance of African Methodism, pp. 68-70.
Smith, History of the African Methodist Episcopal Church, pp. 174-
75. Payne, History of the A.M.E. Church, p. 357. L. L. Berry,
A Century of Missions of the African Methodist Episcopal Church,
1840-1940 (New York: Gutenberg Printery, 1942), p. 41. The full
impact of the A.M.E. Church was not felt until 1891 when Bishop
Henry M. Turner, a leading black nationalist of his day, went to
Africa and organized the Sierra Leone Annual Conference. See
Mungo M. Ponton, Life and Times of Henry M. Turner (Atlanta,
Ga.: A. B. Caldwell Publishing Co., 1917), p. 77.

[44]Letter, Richard Allen to President Boyer, August 24, 1824, cited by Frederick D. Maser, "Through Service to Greatness; the story of Richard Allen," A.M.E. Church Review, LXXVI, 203 (January-March, 1960), 30.

[45]Berry, Century of Missions, pp. 43-44. Payne, History of the A.M.E. Church, pp. 55, 64-69. Payne, Semi-Centenary of the A.M.E. Church, pp. 28, 41. Woodson, Negro Church, pp. 78-79.

[46]Minutes of the Twelfth General Conference of the African Methodist Episcopal Church, Assembled in Pittsburgh, Pa., May 7th, 1860, reprinted by Smith, History of the African Methodist Episcopal Church, p. 444. In 1856 a mission station was opened in Central America composed "partly of English persons, and partly of colored persons." Singleton, Romance of African Methodism, p. 75. Payne, History of the A.M.E. Church, p. 390.

[47]Williams, "Slavery and Colonization," p. 84.

[48]Payne, History of the A.M.E. Church, pp. 128-29. Payne, Semi-Centenary of the A.M.E. Church, pp. 28, 106-07. The Ohio story is told by Litwack, North of Slavery, pp. 72-73.

[49]Payne, Semi-Centenary of the A.M.E. Church, pp. 106-07.

[50]Christian Recorder, I, 29 (April 4, 1855), 114.

[51]Allen, "To the People of Color," pp. 72-73.

[52]Allen, "An Address to Those Who Keep Slaves and Approve the Practice," in Singleton, editor, Life Experience and Gospel Labors, p. 71.

[53]Benjamin Quarles, Black Abolitionists (New York: Oxford University Press, 1969), p. 191.

[54]Absalom Jones, A Thanksgiving Sermon, Preached January 1, 1808, in St. Thomas's, or the African Episcopal Church, Philadelphia: On Account of the Abolition of the African Slave Trade, On that Day By the Congress of the United States (Philadelphia: Printed for the use of the Congregation. Fry and Kammerer, Printers, 1808), pp. 12-13, 16, 18.

[55]David Walker, Walker's Appeal in Four Articles in Henry Highland Garnet, Walker's Appeal ... Also Garnet's Address, pp. 67-69.

[56]Ibid., pp. 22-23, 25-26. See also Herbert Aptheker, "One Continual Cry," David Walker's Appeal to the Colored Citizens of the World, 1829-1830 (New York: Humanities Press, 1965), pp. 46-59.

[57]Garnet, Address to the Slaves of the United States of

America, published together with Walker's Appeal, pp. 93-96. The high point of Garnet's career as abolitionist and orator came in 1865 when he preached before the House of Representatives on the occasion of the passage of the Thirteenth Amendment. After a number of years as president of Avery College, Garnet was appointed ambassador to Liberia. He died and was buried there in 1882.

58Tanner, Reprint of the First Edition of the Discipline, p. 105. Shaw, Negro in the History of Methodism, p. 81.

59Robert Emory, History of the Discipline of the Methodist Episcopal Church (New York: G. Lane & P. P. Sandford, 1844), pp. 278-79.

60Payne, History of the A.M.E. Church, p. 336.

61Ibid., pp. 337-45. At the 1860 General Conference the Committee on Slavery, not wanting to rake over dead coals, simply took note of what the Discipline then said on slavery and no further discussion seems to have taken place on the matter. But it is most interesting that the "due notice" clause is missing. See Smith, History of the African Methodist Episcopal Church, p. 445.

62Douglas C. Stange, "Document: Bishop Daniel Alexander Payne's Protestation of American Slavery," The Journal of Negro History, LII, 1 (January, 1967), 60-64. Payne, Recollections of Seventy Years, p. 65.

63Douglas C. Stange, Radicalism for Humanity: A Study of Lutheran Abolitionism (St. Louis, Mo.: O. Slave, 1970), passim.

64Daniel Coker, A Dialogue Between A Virginian and an African Methodist Minister (Baltimore: Joseph James, 1810), pp. 5, 15-28, 33-34, 37.

65Berry, Century of Missions, p. 54.

66Peter Williams, "An Oration on the Abolition of the Slave Trade, delivered in the African Church in the City of New York, January 1, 1808," in Woodson, editor, Negro Orators, pp. 32-41.

67Letter, Bishop Onderdonk to the Rev. Peter Williams, July 12, 1834, in Woodson, editor, Mind of the Negro, pp. 629-30.

68"Rev. Mr. Williams to the Citizens of New York," in Woodson, editor, Mind of the Negro, pp. 632-34. The Coloured American, I, 4 (March 28, 1840), 2.

69Litwack, North of Slavery, pp. 72-74, 211. John Malvin, North Into Freedom, The Autobiography of John Malvin, Free Negro, 1795-1880, ed. by Allan Peskin (Cleveland: The Press of Western Reserve University, 1966), pp. 43-44.

[70]Austin Steward, Twenty-two Years a Slave and Forty Years a Freeman, in Four Fugitive Slave Narratives, intro. by Jane H. Pease and William H. Pease (Reading, Mass.: Addison-Wesley Publishing Co., 1969), p. 101.

[71]Wesley, Richard Allen, pp. 234-38, 241. George, Segregated Sabbaths, pp. 235-38.

[72]Litwack, North of Slavery, pp. 235-36. See also Howard H. Bell, "National Negro Conventions of the Middle 1840's: Moral Suasion vs. Political Action," The Journal of Negro History, XLII, 4 (October, 1957), 247-60.

[73]Payne, Recollections of Seventy Years, pp. 67-68.

[74]Ibid., pp. 146-48.

[75]Quarles, Black Abolitionists, p. 68. Aptheker, The Negro in the Abolitionist Movement (New York: International Publishers, 1941), p. 42.

[76]One can do no better than to start with Benjamin Quarles' Black Abolitionists.

[77]Payne, History of the A.M.E. Church, p. 338. Particular reference was made to Louisiana, where we find the anomaly of an A.M.E. congregation in New Orleans which was organized under an antislavery Discipline. See Singleton, Romance of African Methodism, pp. 37, 75.

[78]Quarles, Black Abolitionists, p. 82.

[79]Harriet (Brent) Jacobs, Incidents in the Life of A Slave Girl, ed. by L. Maria Child (Boston: Published for the Author, 1861), p. 243.

[80]Payne, History of the A.M.E. Church, p. 81. Wesley, Richard Allen, p. 96. The speculator was arrested and thrown into prison for inability to pay $800 bail. After three months Allen went to the authorities and asked for his release.

[81]John Thompson, The Life of John Thompson; A Fugitive Slave: Containing His History of 25 Years in Bondage, and His Providential Escape (Worcester, Mass.: By the Author, 1856), pp. 101-02.

[82]Bradley, History of the A.M.E. Zion Church, I, 116-21. Conrad, Harriet Tubman, p. 61. Miles Mark Fisher, "Negro Churches in Illinois," Illinois Historical Society Journal, LVI, 3 (Autumn, 1963), 554.

[83]Douglass, Life and Times, p. 279.

[84]Ibid.

[85]Jermain Wesley Loguen, The Rev. J. W. Loguen, as A
Slave and As a Freeman, A Narrative of Real Life (Syracuse,
N.Y.: Office of the Daily Journal, 1859), pp. 379, 391-94, 401-09.

[86]Ward, Autobiography, pp. 124-28. Ward, "Speech on the
Fugitive Slave Bill," in Woodson, ed., Negro Orators, p. 195.
This speech first appeared in the Liberator, April 5, 1850.

[87]Christian Recorder, I, 16 (July 13, 1854), 64.

[88]Alexander Walker Wayman, My Recollections of African
M.E. Ministers, or Forty Years' Experience in the African Methodist Episcopal Church (Philadelphia: A.M.E. Book Rooms, 1881),
p. 73.

[89]Coppin, Unwritten History, pp. 73-74. Ironically, the
passage from Daniel refers to the overthrow of the Persians by the
Greeks and the consequent end of the relative autonomy the Persians
had allowed the Israelites. In this case, it was "the king of the
North," Alexander the Great, who came up against the "chosen
people of God."

[90]Payne, Semi-Centenary of the A.M.E. Church, p. 130.

[91]Minutes of the New York Annual Conference of the African
Methodist Episcopal Church: Held in the Bridge Street A.M.E.
Church, Brooklyn, From June 8th to June 19th, 1865 (Brooklyn,
N.Y.: Published by Order of the Conference, 1865), p. 15.

[92]Christian Recorder, I, 33 (August 18, 1855), 130.

[93]Daniel Alexander Payne, "Thoughts About the Past, the
Present, and the Future of the African M.E. Church," The A.M.E.
Church Review, I, 1 (July, 1884), 1.

CHAPTER VII

[1]David Hackett Fischer, Historians' Fallacies (New York:
Harper & Row, 1970), p. 141.

[2]William G. Brownlow and Abram Pryne, Ought American
Slavery to Be Perpetuated? A Debate Between Rev. W. G. Brown-
low and Rev. A. Pryne. Held at Philadelphia, 1858 (Philadelphia:
J. B. Lippincott & Co., 1858), pp. 40, 99, 126, 165, 295. Brown-
low was a Methodist cleric from Knoxville. Pryne hailed from New
York state and was editor of the antislavery Central Reformer.

[3]Quoted by Daniel G. Mathews, Slavery and Methodism
(Princeton, N.J.: Princeton University Press, 1965), p. 85.

[4]Brownlow and Pryne, Ought American Slavery to be Perpetuated?, p. 138. Thomas Wentworth Higginson, Does Slavery Christianize the Negro? Anti-Slavery Tract, No. 4 (New York: American Anti-Slavery Society, 1855), pp. 2, 4, 7. Harvey Newcomb, The "Negro Pew": Being An Inquiry Concerning the Propriety of Distinctions in the House of God, on Account of Color (Boston: Isaac Knapp, 1837), passim.

[5]Douglass' Monthly, III, 5 (October, 1860), 340.

[6]In 1861 the Methodist Episcopal Church, South, claimed in excess of 200,000 Negro members. By 1866 there were only 78,742 left, and of this number a mere 8000 remained with the white Methodists when the C.M.E. Church was organized. Elmer T. Clark, The Negro and His Religion (Nashville, Tenn.: The Cokesbury Press, 1924), pp. 35-36. Joseph Crane Hartzell, Methodism and the Negro in the United States (New York: Hunt & Eaton, 1894), p. 9. Charles Henry Phillips, The History of the Colored Methodist Episcopal Church in America; Comprising Its Organization, Subsequent Development, And Present Status (Jackson, Tenn.: Publishing House of the C.M.E. Church, 1898), pp. 23, 25, and passim. Negro Methodists who comprised the C.M.E. Church, although "set off" as a distinct organization, remained in a kind of poor cousin relationship with the white Methodists.

[7]Clark, The Negro and His Religion, p. 35. James H. McNeilly, Religion and Slavery: A Vindication of the Southern Churches (Nashville, Tenn.: Publishing House of the M.E. Church, South, 1911), p. 21. Joseph B. Earnest, The Religious Development of the Negro in Virginia (Charlottesville, Va.: The Michie Co., 1914), p. 104. For a dozen years after the Civil War, according to Atticus G. Haygood, well-meaning Southerners were disqualified by the new conditions that came with emancipation and the Freedmen did not welcome Southern cooperation--"excepting always money." Thus the door was left open to "cranks," "busybodies" and other "difficult people" from the North. Haygood, Our Brother in Black: His Freedom and His Future (1866, rpt.; Miami, Fla.: Mnemosyne Publishing Inc., 1969), pp. 238, 304-05.

[8]W. E. Burghardt Du Bois, The Souls of Black Folk (Greenwich, Conn.: Fawcett Publications, Inc., 1961), pp. 149-50. First published in hardcover in 1903 by A. C. McClurg & Co., Chicago.

[9]Earnest, Religious Development of the Negro, p. 8. Richard Clark Reed, "A Sketch of the Religious History of the Negroes in the South," in Papers of the American Society of Church History, Second Series, IV (1914), 178. Charles M. Melden, "Religion and the Negro," in Progress of a Race, under the general authorship of William H. Crogman and J. L. Nichols (Naperville, Ill.: J. L. Nichols & Co., 1920), pp. 310, 313. Clark, The Negro and His Religion, pp. 17-18. Haygood, Our Brother in Black, p. 300.

[10]James Battle Avirett, The Old Plantation: How We Lived in Great House and Cabin Before the War (New York: F. Tennyson Neely Co., 1901), p. 122. A longing for the pious old-time Negro was also expressed by Haygood, Our Brother in Black, pp. 221, 223, 313; Victoria V. Clayton, White and Black Under the Old Regime (Milwaukee, Wis.: The Young Churchman Co., 1899), pp. 58-59, and McNeilly, Religion and Slavery, pp. 29, 76-78, 88. Those Negro preachers whose most important role, according to Howard H. Harlan, was to lead their race "toward a satisfactory accommodation to a social structure dominated by the white group" were fondly remembered. Harlan, John Jasper--A Case History in Leadership (Richmond: University of Virginia Press, 1930), pp. 4-5. See also, Earnest, Religious Development of the Negro, pp. 61, 67-68; Meldon, "Religion and the Negro," p. 316; and William Pope Harrison, The Gospel Among the Slaves (Nashville, Tenn.: Publishing House of the M.E. Church, South, 1911), p. 115.

[11]Melden, "Religion and the Negro," p. 314. William T. Alexander, History of the Colored Race in America (New Orleans: Palmetto Publishing Co., 1887), p. 527. Winthrop Jordan, White Over Black (Baltimore, Md.: Penguin Books, Inc., 1968), pp. 179-90, 435-61.

[12]Southern churchmen not only refused to abandon the notion that slavery had been ordained by God, but they continued to provide grist for the racists' mill in the post-Reconstruction era. See H. Shelton Smith, In His Image, But ... Racism in Southern Religion, 1780-1910 (Durham, N.C.: Duke University Press, 1972), pp. 258-305. The triumph of racial orthodoxy during the early part of the twentieth century and the contributions made by religious spokesmen are examined in I. A. Newby, Jim Crow's Defense: Anti-Negro Thought in America 1900-1930 (Baton Rouge, La.: Louisiana State University Press, 1965), pp. 83-109.

[13]J. Sella Martin, "A Speech Before the Paris Anti-slavery Conference, August 27, 1867," in Negro Orators and Their Orations, ed. by Carter G. Woodson (Washington, D.C.: The Associated Publishers, Inc., 1925), p. 260.

[14]Timothy L. Smith, "Slavery and Theology: The Emergence of Black Christian Consciousness in Nineteenth-Century America," Church History, XLI, 4 (December, 1972), 512.

[15]George Freeman Bragg, History of the Afro-American Group of the Episcopal Church (Baltimore: Church Advocate Press, 1922), pp. 31-32, 38. George Arnett Singleton, "Religious Instruction of the Negro Under the Slave Regime" (unpublished M.A. dissertation, University of Chicago, 1929), pp. 1-2, 57-58. Singleton, "The Effect of Slavery Upon the Religion of the Negro" (unpublished B.D. thesis, University of Chicago Divinity School, 1930), pp. 45, 58. G[old] R[efined] Wilson, "The Religion of the American Negro Slave: His Attitude Toward Life and Death," The Journal of Negro History, VIII, 1 (January, 1923), 41, 43, 65, 71. Benjamin

E. Mays, The Negro's God as Reflected in His Literature, with a
preface by Vincent Harding (New York: Atheneum, 1968), pp. 22-
23, 25-26. Originally published in 1938 by Chapman & Grimes,
Inc., Boston. See also, William R. Rigell, "Negro Religious
Leadership on the Southern Seaboard: Maryland, Virginia, North
Carolina, South Carolina, and Georgia, 1830-1861" (unpublished
M.A. dissertation, University of Chicago Divinity School, 1916),
p. 7. Rigell maintained that the Negro antebellum preacher spiritually lived in the future and that his messages were "dominated
by otherworldliness."

16Du Bois, Souls of Black Folk, pp. 140-46. Elsewhere
DuBois had written that the Black Church was "the only social institution among the Negroes which started in the African forest and
survived slavery" and under the leadership of the priest and the
medicine man preserved African tribal life. Quoted from DuBois'
Some Efforts of the American Negroes for Their Own Betterment
(Atlanta, Ga.: 1898) by E. Franklin Frazier, The Negro Church
in America (New York: Schocken Books, Inc., 1964), pp. 5-6.

17Carter G. Woodson, The African Background Outlined or
Handbook for the Study of the Negro (Washington, D.C.: Association for the Study of Negro Life and History, 1936), pp. 171-73,
358-59, 365-67.

18E. Franklin Frazier, The Negro in the United States (New
York: The Macmillan Company, 1949), pp. 7-10, 14-15. Frazier,
Negro Church, pp. 1-19.

19Frazier, Negro Church, pp. 13-16. Du Bois, Souls of
Black Folk, pp. 146-47. Woodson, African Background Outlined,
pp. 361, 449.

20Miles Mark Fisher, Negro Slave Songs in the United States
(New York: Cornell University Press, 1953), passim. Fisher
began to rethink the meaning of the spirituals when he was studying
the Hebrew Psalms at the University of Chicago Divinity School.
Yet the Psalms, as well as the spirituals, are essentially religious
in character with, of course, strong social overtones. This does
not deny the possibility that the slaves attached double meanings to
"Swing Low, Sweet Chariot," "Steal Away, Steal Away to Jesus,"
or to "Go Down, Moses."

21See Gary T. Marx, "Religion: Opiate or Inspiration of
Civil Rights Militancy Among Negroes?" American Sociological Review, XXXII, 1 (February, 1967), 64-65, 71.

22Vincent Harding, "Religion and Resistance Among Ante-
bellum Negroes, 1800-1869," in The Making of Black America,
Vol. I of The Origins of Black Americans, ed. by August Meier
and Elliott Rudwick (New York: Atheneum, 1969), pp. 179-97.
George M. Frederickson and Christopher Lasch, "Resistance to
Slavery," Civil War History, XIII, 4 (December, 1967), 317-18.

William C. Suttles, Jr., "African Religious Survivals as Factors in American Slave Revolts," The Journal of Negro History, LVI, 2 (April, 1971), 97-104.

23James H. Cone, Black Theology & Black Power (New York: The Seabury Press, 1969), pp. 94, 137. Cone, "Black Consciousness and the Black Church," Christianity and Crisis, XXX, 18 (November 2 & 16, 1970), 244-50. John H. Bracey, Jr., August Meier, and Elliott Rudwick, editors, Black Nationalism in America (Indianapolis, Ind.: The Bobbs-Merrill Co., Inc., 1970), pp. 4-10, and passim.

24Lawrence N. Jones, "They Sought a City: The Black Church and Churchmen in the Nineteenth Century," Union Seminary Quarterly Review, XXVI, 3 (Spring, 1971), 262. Jones, "Black Churches in Historical Perspective," Christianity and Crisis, XXX, 18 (November 2 & 16, 1970), 228. Lerone Bennett, Jr., "The Black Pioneer Period," Part IV of "The Making of Black America," Ebony, XXV, 12 (October, 1970), 54.

25This has been the continual refrain of their spiritual descendants. See Horace Talbert, The Sons of Allen (Xenia, Ohio: The Aldine Press, 1906), p. 24; V. M. Townsend, Fifty-four Years of African Methodism (New York: Exposition Press, 1953), p. 104; and Richard R. Wright, The Bishops of the African Methodist Episcopal Church (Nashville, Tenn.: The A.M.E. Sunday School Union, 1963), p. 19.

26Quoted by Leon F. Litwack, North of Slavery (Chicago: The University of Chicago Press, 1961), p. 212.

27A provocative yet helpful discussion on some of these points can be found in Joseph R. Washington, Jr., Black Sects and Cults (Garden City, N.Y.: Doubleday & Company, Inc., 1972), pp. 48-57. "Allen's movement," writes Washington, "was not a movement for a new religion. It was not a return to an old religion. It was the beginning of a tradition. The tradition has as its central thrust the affirmation that blacks should be Christians with the opportunity to develop separately from whites." Ibid., p. 48. A similar perspective is taken by Gayraud S. Wilmore, Black Religion and Black Radicalism (Garden City, N.Y.: Doubleday & Company, Inc., 1972), pp. 132-35.

28Daniel Alexander Payne, The Semi-Centenary and the Retrospection of the African Methodist Episcopal Church in the United States of America (Baltimore, Md.: Sherwood & Co., 1866), pp. 5, 22. Compare J. W. Cromwell, "Our Colored Churches," The A.M.E. Church Review, I, 2 (October, 1884), 90.

29A thorough systematic study of Black Theology, portraying the meaning, validity, and implications of the concept, is badly needed. William R. Jones has examined the writings of Joseph Washington, James Cone, Albert Cleage, Major Jones and J. Deotis

Roberts, from the perspective of the question "What meaneth black suffering?" See Is God a White Racist? (Garden City, N.Y.: Anchor Press/Doubleday, Inc., 1973). A concise overview of various themes in Black Theology is available in Wilmore, Black Religion and Black Radicalism, pp. 288-306. Two books by James Cone, a prominent advocate of Black Theology, are essential reading. See Black Theology and Black Power (New York: Seabury Press, 1969) and A Black Theology of Liberation (Philadelphia: J. B. Lippincott Co., 1970).

[30]Washington, Black Sects and Cults, p. 146.

[31]Carol V. R. George's recent biographical portrait of Allen concludes with suggestions in this direction. She argues that a single frame of reference which combines militant and otherworldly aspects fits Allen better than the category of "doubleness" or one that would pit religion against social concern. Segregated Sabbaths (New York: Oxford University Press, Inc., 1973), pp. 182-83. Wilmore, Black Religion and Black Radicalism, pp. 132-35.

[32]Major J. Jones, Black Awareness: A Theology of Hope (Nashville, Tenn.: Abingdon Press, 1971), p. 46.

[33]Smith, "Slavery and Theology," p. 503.

[34]Kyle Haselden, The Racial Problem in Christian Perspective (New York: Harper & Brothers, 1959), pp. 42-43.

[35]Howard Thurman, Deep Is the Hunger: Meditations for Apostles of Sensitiveness (New York: Harper & Brothers, Publishers, 1951), pp. 13-14.

POSTSCRIPT

[1]James W. C. Pennington, The Fugitive Blacksmith: or, Events in the History of James W. C. Pennington, Pastor of a Presbyterian Church, New York, Formerly a Slave in the State of Maryland, United States (3rd ed.; 1850), as reprinted in Great Slave Narratives, edited by Arna Bontemps (Boston: Beacon Press, 1969), pp. 260-67.

[2]Ibid., p. 261.

[3]Ibid., pp. 254-55.

[4]Ibid., pp. 265-66.

[5]Ibid., p. 261.

BIBLIOGRAPHY

Author's note: Of the hundreds of sources consulted, those most germane to the content of this study have been listed. Many an item which found its way into the footnotes, because of an incidental fact or an opinion that seemed pertinent, does not appear here. A truly Herculean task needs to be done to gather together and preserve materials relating to the early history of the independent black churches, which, except for the printed items I have made use of, are exceedingly difficult to obtain. Had not Bishop Payne almost singlehandedly documented the history of the A.M.E. Church, our story would have had several missing chapters. It is unfortunate that the other Negro churches did not have equally farsighted and painstaking historians.

The chapters dealing with American Evangelicalism and the plantation missions, methods and message, were largely based on contemporary histories, catechisms, church minutes, reports of missionary societies, accounts by observers and participants, sermons, correspondence, and other sources more easily attainable. Whites have always been more visible in the printed record. Yet because of the large number of slave and ex-slave narratives which have recently been reprinted or republished, the story of black religion on the plantation no longer needs to be dressed in the castoff clothes of the master and mistress. Finally, there are a large number of secondary sources, of varying quality, from which I gleaned supplementary data to help carry the narrative forward.

CONTEMPORARY SOURCES

I. MISCELLANEOUS UNPUBLISHED MATERIALS

Plumer Letter File. Presbyterian Historical Society, Philadelphia.

239

240   Black Religion

Preston-Davis Manuscripts. University of Virginia Library,
    Charlottesville. Selected items supplied to me by Ann
    Stauffenberg, Manuscripts Cataloguer.

Carter G. Woodson Papers. Library of Congress, Washing-
    ton, D.C.

II. NEWSPAPERS
    (Some issues of these newspapers are missing.)

Christian Recorder (Philadelphia), 1854-62.

The Coloured American (New York), 1837-42.

Douglass' Monthly (Rochester, N.Y.), 1858-63.

Frederick Douglass' Paper (Rochester, N.Y.), 1852-58.

North Star (Rochester, N.Y.), 1847-51.

III. CHURCH MINUTES

Minutes of the Annual Conferences of the Methodist Church,
    1773-1828. 2 vols. New York: T. Mason & G. Lane,
    1840.

Minutes of the Fortieth Annual Conference of the African
    Methodist Episcopal Church for the Baltimore District,
    April 24, 1857. Baltimore: James Young, 1857.

Minutes of the General and Annual Conferences of the African
    Methodist Episcopal Church, 1839-1840. Brooklyn:
    George Hogarth, 1840.

Minutes of the Genesee Annual Conference of the African
    M.E. Zion Church in America, Convened at Montrose,
    Pa., September 1st, 1858. Ithaca, N.Y.: Published
    by Rev. John Thomas and Rev. William Sanford for
    the Conference, 1858.

Minutes of the Methodist Conferences 1773 to 1794 Under the
    Superintendence of John Wesley, Bishops Asbury and
    Coke. Botetourt County, Va.: n.p., 1794.

Minutes of the Methodist Conferences Annually Held in America,

From 1773 to 1813, Inclusive.   Vol I.   New York:
Daniel Hitt and Thomas Ware, 1813.

Minutes of the New York Annual Conference of the African
Methodist Episcopal Church: Held in the Bridge Street
A.M.E. Church, Brooklyn, From June 8th to June
19th, 1865.   Brooklyn: Published by Order of the
Conference, 1865.

Minutes of the Third Presbyterian and Congregational Convention, Together with the Organization of the Evangelical Association of Clergymen of Color in the United
States.   Brooklyn: F. A. Brockway, Book & Job
Printer, 1858.

IV.   CATECHISMS AND SERMONS USED AMONG THE
SLAVES

Bacon, Thomas.   Sermons Addressed to Masters and Servants and Published in the Year 1743.   Winchester,
Va.:   John Heiskell, 1813.

Capers, William D.   A Catechism for Little Children (and
for use on) The Missions to the Slaves in South-Carolina.   Charleston, S.C.:   Printed by J. S. Barges,
1833.

_____.   A Short Catechism for the Use of the Colored
Members on Trial of the Methodist Episcopal Church
in South Carolina.   Charleston, S.C.:   Observer Office
Press, 1833.

Castleman, T. T.   Plain Sermons for Servants.   New York:
Stanford & Delisser, 1858.

Dickson, Andrew Flinn.   Lessons About Salvation, From the
Life and Words of the Lord Jesus.   Being a Second
Series of Plantation Sermons.   Philadelphia: Presby-
terian Board of Publication, 1860.

_____.   Plantation Sermons or Plain and Familiar Dis-
courses for the Instruction of the Unlearned.   Philadelphia: Presbyterian Board of Publication, 1856.

Glennie, Alexander.   Sermons Preached on Plantations to
Congregations of Negroes.   Charleston, S.C.:   A. E.
Miller, 1844.

242

Black Religion

Hoff, John F. A Manual of Religious Instruction Specially
Intended for the Oral Teaching of Colored Persons, But
Adapted to General Use in Families and Schools. Rev.
ed. Richmond: P. B. Price, 1857.

Jones, Charles Colcock. A Catechism of Scripture Doctrine
and Practice for Families and Sabbath-Schools Designed
Also For the Oral Instruction of Colored Persons.
Philadelphia: Presbyterian Board of Publication, 1852.

Meade, William. A Catechism to be Taught Orally to Those
Who Cannot Read; Designed Especially for the Instruction of the Slaves in the Protestant Episcopal Church
in the Confederate States. Raleigh, N.C.: Office of
the Church Intelligencer, 1862.

_____. Sermons, Dialogues and Narratives for Servants
to be Read to Them in Families; Abridged, Altered,
and Adapted to Their Conditions. Richmond: James
C. Walker, 1836.

Mines, John. The Evangelical Catechism, of a Plain and
Easy System of the Principal Doctrines and Duties of
the Christian Religion, Adapted to the Use of Sabbath
Schools and Families, with a New Method of Instructing
Those Who Cannot Read. Richmond:: N. Pollard,
1821.

Palmer, Benjamin Morgan. A Plain and Easy Catechism ...
Designed Chiefly for the Benefit of Colored Persons to
Which are Annexed Suitable Prayers and Hymns.
Charleston, S.C.: Observer Office Press, 1828.

Ryland, Robert. A Scripture Catechism for the Instruction
of Children and Servants. Richmond: Harrold and
Murray, 1848.

Watts, Isaac. The First Sett of Catechisms and Prayers:
or, The Religion of Little Children Under Seven or
Eight Years of Age. Collected Out of the Larger Books
of Prayer and Catechism for Children and Youth. 7th
ed. Boston: Rogers and Fowle, 1748.

V. EX-SLAVE NARRATIVES

Anderson, Robert. From Slavery to Affluence, Memoirs of

Robert Anderson, Ex-Slave. Hemingsford, Neb.:
Hemingsford Ledger, 1927.

Asher, Jeremiah. Incidents in the Life of the Rev. J.
   Asher, Pastor of Shiloh (Coloured) Baptist Church,
   Philadelphia, United States, and a Concluding Chapter
   of Facts Illustrating the Unrighteous Prejudice Existing
   in the Minds of American Citizens Toward Their
   Coloured Brethren. London: C. Gilpin, 1850.

Ball, Charles. Fifty Years in Chains, or, The Life of an
   American Slave. New York: H. Dayton, 1859.

Brown, Henry. Narrative of the Life of Henry Box Brown,
   Written by Himself. Boston: Samuel Webb, Bilston,
   1852.

Brown, William Wells. My Southern Home: or, The South
   and Its People. Boston: A. G. Brown & Co., 1880.

_____. Narrative of William Wells Brown, A Fugitive
   Slave, Written by Himself. Boston: Anti-Slavery
   Office, 1847.

Bruce, Henry Clay. The New Man, Twenty-nine Years a
   Slave, Twenty-nine years a Free Man. York, Pa.:
   P. Anstadt & Sons, 1895.

Burton, Annie L. Memories of Childhood's Slavery Days.
   Boston: Ross Pub. Co., 1919.

Clarke, Lewis. Narrative of the Sufferings of Lewis Clarke,
   during a Captivity of More than Twenty-Five Years
   among the Algerines of Kentucky. Boston: D. H. Eli,
   1845.

Coppin, Levi Jenkins. Unwritten History. Philadelphia:
   A.M.E. Book Concern, 1919.

Davis, Noah. A Narrative of the Life of Reverend Noah
   Davis, a Colored Man, Written by Himself. Baltimore: J. F. Weishampel, Jr., 1859.

Douglass, Frederick. Life and Times of Frederick Douglass.
   Rev. ed. of 1892. Rpt. London: Crowell-Collier, 1962.

_____. My Bondage and My Freedom. New York: Miller,
   Orton, & Mulligan, 1855.

Drayton, Daniel. Personal Memoir of Daniel Drayton.
    Boston: Bela Marsh, 1855.

Fedric, Francis. Slave Life in Virginia and Kentucky; or
    Fifty Years of Slavery in the Southern States of Ameri-
    ca, By Francis Fedric, An Escaped Slave, With Preface
    by the Reverend Charles Lee. London: Wertheim,
    Macintosh, and Hunt, 1863.

Frederick, Reverend Francis. Autobiography of Reverend
    Francis Frederick, of Virginia. Baltimore: J. W.
    Woods, 1869.

Grandy, Moses. Narrative of the Life of Moses Grandy,
    Late a Slave in the United States of America. Boston:
    Oliver Johnson, 1844.

Heard, William H. From Slavery to the Bishopric in the
    A.M.E. Church. Philadelphia: A.M.E. Publishing
    House, 1924.

Henson, Josiah. Truth Stranger Than Fiction, Father Hen-
    son's Story of His Own Life. Boston: John P. Jewett
    and Co., 1858.

Hughes, Louis B. Thirty Years a Slave; from Bondage to
    Freedom, the Institution of Slavery as Seen on the
    Plantation and in the Home of the Planters. Milwaukee,
    Wis.: South Side Printing Co., 1897.

Jacobs, Harriet (nee Brent). Incidents in the Life of a
    Slave Girl. Edited by L. Maria Child. Boston: By
    the Author, 1861.

Jones, Thomas H. The Experience of Thomas H. Jones
    Who Was a Slave for Forty Three Years, Written by
    a Friend As Told to Him By Brother Jones. Worces-
    ter, Mass.: Henry J. Howland, 1857.

Lane, Lunsford. The Narrative of Lunsford Lane, Formerly
    of Raleigh, N.C. Boston: Published by Himself, 1842.

Latta, M. L. The History of My Life and Work. Raleigh,
    N.C.: By the Author, 1903.

Loguen, Jermain Wesley. The Reverend J. W. Loguen, As
    a Slave And As A Freeman, A Narrative of Real Life.
    Syracuse, N.Y.: Office of the Daily Journal, 1859.

Bibliography: Sources 245

Malvin, John. North Into Freedom, The Autobiography of
John Malvin, Free Negro, 1795-1880. Edited by Alan
Peskin. Cleveland: The Press of Western Reserve
University, 1966.

Mason, Isaac. Life of Isaac Mason, as a Slave. Worcester,
Mass.: By the Author, 1893.

Offley, Reverend G. W. Narrative of the Life and Labors
of the Reverend G. W. Offley, a Coloured Man and Local Preacher, Written by Himself. Hartford: Published by the Author, 1860.

Pennington, James W. C. The Fugitive Blacksmith, or,
Events in the History of James W. C. Pennington,
Pastor of a Presbyterian Church New York, Formerly
a Slave in the State of Maryland, United States. 2nd
ed. London: Charles Gilpin, 1849.

Peterson, Daniel H. The Looking Glass: Being a True
Narrative of the Life of the Reverend D. H. Peterson.
New York: Printed by Wright, 1854.

Randolph, Peter. From Slave Cabin to Pulpit: The Auto-
biography of Peter Randolph: The Southern Question
Illustrated and Sketches of Slave Life. Boston: James
H. Earle, 1893.

_____. Sketches of Slave Life; or, Illustrations of the
"Peculiar Institution." By Peter Randolph, an Emanci-
pated Slave. Boston: By the Author, 1855.

Roper, Moses. A Narrative of the Adventures and Escape
of Moses Roper from American Slavery with a Preface
by the Reverend T. Price, D.D. London: Darton,
Harvey, and Darton, 1838.

Smith, Henry. Fifty Years of Slavery in the United States
of America. Grand Rapids, Mich.: West Michigan
Printing Co., 1891.

Smith, James Lindsay. Autobiography of James Lindsay
Smith. Norwich, Conn.: Press of the Bulletin Co.,
1881.

Stevens, Charles Emery. Anthony Burns: a History.
Boston: John P. Jewett and Co., 1856.

Steward, Austin. Twenty-two Years a Slave and Forty Years
    a Freeman, Embracing a Correspondence of Several
    Years While President of Wilberforce Colony. Roches-
    ter, N.Y.: W. Alling, 1857.

Stroyer, Jacob. My Life in the South. 2nd ed. Salem,
    Mass.: Newcomb & Glass, 1898.

Thompson, John. The Life of John Thompson, a Fugitive
    Slave: Containing His History of 25 Years in Bondage,
    and His Providential Escape. Worcester, Mass.: By
    the Author, 1856.

Tilmon, Levin. A Brief Miscellaneous Narrative of the
    More Early Part of the Life of L. Tilmon, Pastor of
    a Coloured Methodist Congregational Church in the
    City of New York. Jersey City, N.J.: Pratt, 1853.

Ward, Samuel Ringgold. The Autobiography of a Fugitive
    Negro: His Anti-Slavery Labours in the United States,
    Canada, and England. London: John Snow, 1855.

Washington, Booker T. The Story of My Life and Work.
    Toronto: J. L. Nichols & Co., 1900.

_____. Up From Slavery: an Autobiography. New York:
    A. L. Burt Co., 1900.

Watson, Henry. Narrative of Henry Watson, A Fugitive
    Slave, Written by Himself. Boston: B. Marsh, 1848.

White, William S. The African Preacher, an Authentic
    Narrative. Philadelphia: Presbyterian Board of Pub-
    lication, 1849.

Williams, James. The Life and Adventures of James
    Williams, a Fugitive Slave, with a Full Description
    of the Underground Railroad. San Francisco: Women's
    Union Print, 1873.

VI.   COLLECTIONS OF EX-SLAVE NARRATIVES
      AND SHORT REMINISCENCES

Armstrong, Orland Kay. Old Massa's People: The Old
    Slaves Tell Their Story. Indianapolis: Bobbs-Merrill,
    1939.

Bontemps, Arna, ed. Great Slave Narratives. Boston:
    Beacon Press, 1969.

Botkin, Benjamin A., ed. Lay My Burden Down: A Folk
    History of Slavery. Chicago: University of Chicago
    Press, 1945.

Drew, Benjamin. The Refugee: A North-Side View of
    Slavery. Boston: John P. Jewett and Co., 1856.

Fisk University. Unwritten History of Slavery: Autobio-
    graphical Account of Negro Ex-Slaves. Social Science
    Document, No. 1. 1945. Rpt. Washington, D.C.:
    Microcard Editions, 1968.

Harris, John. Voices from Slavery. New York: Tower
    Publications, 1971.

Johnson, Clifton H., ed. God Struck Me Dead: Religious
    Conversion Experiences and Autobiographies of Ex-
    Slaves. Philadelphia: United Church Press, 1969.

Mott, Abigail F. Biographical Sketches and Interesting
    Anecdotes of Persons of Color. New York: M. Day,
    1839.

Osofsky, Gilbert, ed. Puttin' On Ole Massa. New York:
    Harper & Row, 1969.

Pease, Jane H., and Pease, William H., eds. Four Fugi-
    tive Slave Narratives. Reading, Mass.: Addison-
    Wesley, 1969.

Redpath, James. The Roving Editor; or, Talks with Slaves
    in the Southern States. New York: A. B. Burdick,
    1859.

Yetman, Norman P. Life Under the "Peculiar Institution":
    Selections from the Slave Narrative Collection. New
    York: Holt, Rinehart and Winston, 1970.

VII. COLLECTIONS AND ANTHOLOGIES OF OTHER
    PRIMARY MATERIALS

Ahlstrom, Sydney, ed. Theology in America. New York:
    Bobbs-Merrill, 1967.

Aptheker, Herbert, ed. Documentary History of the American Negro. New York: Citadel Press, 1951.

Bracey, John H., Jr.; Meier, August; and Rudwick, Elliott,
eds. Black Nationalism in America. Indianapolis:
Bobbs-Merrill, 1970.

Dunbar, Alice Moore. Masterpieces of Negro Eloquence.
New York: The Bookery Pub. Co., 1914.

Essays and Pamphlets on Antislavery. Westport, Conn.:
Negro Universities Press, 1970.

Harrison, William Pope, ed. The Gospel Among the Slaves:
A Short Account of Missionary Operations Among the
African Slaves of the Southern States. Nashville,
Tenn.: Publishing House of the M.E. Church, South,
1893.

Johnson, James Weldon. The Book of American Spirituals.
New York: Viking Press, 1925.

McLoughlin, William G., ed. The American Evangelicals,
1800-1900, An Anthology. New York: Harper & Row,
1968.

Powell, Milton, ed. The Voluntary Church: American Religious Life, 1740-1865. New York: Macmillan, 1967.

Smith, H. Shelton; Handy, Robert T.; and Loetscher, Lefferts A. American Christianity: An Historical Interpretation with Representative Documents. 2 vols.
New York: Scribner's, 1966.

Woodson, Carter G., ed. The Mind of the Negro as Reflected in Letters Written During the Crisis, 1800-1860.
Washington, D.C.: Associated Publishers, 1926.

_____, ed. Negro Orators and Their Orations. Washing-
ton, D.C.: Associated Publishers, 1925.

VIII. PERIODICALS

Allen, Richard. "The Colonization Movement." Reprinted
in the A.M.E. Church Review, LXXXII, 203 (January-
March 1965), 23-24, 46.

_____. "First Conference Minutes of A.M.E. Convention As Composed by Bishop Richard Allen in the City of Baltimore, 1818." Reprinted in the A.M.E. Church Review, LXXXIV, 225 (July-September 1965), 3-4.

[Capers, William?] "Report of the Missionary Society of the South Carolina Conference, of the Methodist Episcopal Church, South; for the year ending January, 1847." The Quarterly Review of the Methodist Episcopal Church, South, I, 3 (July 1847), 319-38.

Higginson, Thomas Wentworth. "Negro Spirituals." The Atlantic Monthly, XIX, No. CXVI (June 1867), 685-94.

"Letters Showing the Rise and Progress of the Early Negro Churches of Georgia and the West Indies." The Journal of Negro History, I, 1 (January 1916), 69-92.

"Notices of Recent Publications." (Review of J. H. Thornwell's The Rights and the Duties of Masters.) The Christian Examiner and Religious Miscellany, XLIX, 3 (November 1850), 482-87.

Payne, Daniel Alexander. "Thoughts About the Past, the Present, and the Future of the African M.E. Church." The A.M.E. Church Review, I, 1 (July 1884), 1-2.

Raymond, Charles T. "The Religious Life of the Negro Slave." Harper's New Monthly Magazine, XXVII, First Paper, No. CLX (September 1863), 479-85; Second Paper, No. CLXI (October 1863), 676-82; Third Paper, No. CLXII (November 1863), 816-24.

Stange, Douglass C. "Document: Bishop Daniel Alexander Payne's Protestation of American Slavery." The Journal of Negro History, LII, 1 (January 1967), 60-64.

Watson, Richard. "Benefits of Affording Religious Instruction to the People of Colour." African Repository, I, 1 (January 1826), 327-34.

IX.   BOOKS AND PAMPHLETS

A Call Upon the Church for Progressive Action to Elevate the Colored American People. Fall River, Mass.: n.p., 1848.

Adams, Nehemiah. A South-Side View of Slavery, or,
    Three Months at the South, in 1854. 2nd ed. Boston:
    T. R. Martin and Sanborn, Carter and Bazin, 1855.

Address to the Presbyterians of Kentucky, Proposing a Plan
    for the Instruction and Emancipation of Their Slaves.
    Cincinnati: Taylor & Tracy, 1835.

Adger, John B. The Religious Instruction of the Coloured
    Population, A Sermon, May 9, 1847. Charleston,
    S. C.: T. W. Haynes, 1847.

Allen, Richard. Confession of John Joyce, alias Davis, who
    was Executed on Monday, the 14th of March, 1808, for
    the Murder of Mrs. Sarah Cross; with an Address to
    the Public and People of Colour, Together with the Sub-
    stance of the Trial and Chief Justice Tilgham on His
    Condemnation. Philadelphia: Printed for the Benefit
    of Bethel Church, 1808.

_____. The Life Experience and Gospel Labors of the Rt.
    Rev. Richard Allen. Introduction by George A. Single-
    ton. New York; Nashville, Tenn.: Abingdon Press,
    1960.

Armstrong, George D. The Christian Doctrine of Slavery.
    New York: Scribner's, 1857.

The Articles of Faith, Church Discipline, and By-Laws of
    the Abyssinian Baptist Church in the City of New York,
    April 3, 1833. New York: From J. Post's Office,
    1833.

Asbury, Francis. Journal and Letters. Edited by Elmer E.
    Clark, J. Manning Potts, and Jacob S. Payton. 3 vols.
    London: Epworth Press; Nashville, Tenn.: Abingdon
    Press, 1958.

Avirett, James Battle. The Old Plantation: How We Lived
    in Great House and Cabin Before the War. New York:
    F. Tennyson Neely Co., 1901.

Axson, Isaac S. K. Eighth Annual Report of the Association
    for the Religious Instruction of the Negroes In Liberty
    County, Georgia; Together with the Address to The
    Association By the President. Savannah, Ga.: Thomas
    Purse, 1843.

Baird, Robert. Religion in America [1856]. Edited by
    Henry Warner Bowden. New York: Harper & Row,
    1970.

Baird, Samuel J. A Collection of the Acts, Deliverances,
    and Testimonies of the Supreme Judicatory of the
    Presbyterian Church. Philadelphia: Presbyterian
    Board of Publication, 1855.

Baldwin, Joseph G. Flush Times in Alabama and Missis-
    sippi. San Francisco: S. Whitney and Co., 1853.

Ball, Charles. Slavery in the United States. New York:
    J. S. Taylor, 1837.

Bangs, Nathan. A History of the Methodist Episcopal Church.
    3rd ed. 2 vols. New York: Mason and Lane, 1840.

Barnes, Albert. An Inquiry into the Scriptural Views of
    Slavery. Philadelphia: Parry and McMillan, 1846.

_____. The Church and Slavery. Philadelphia: Parry
    and McMillan, 1857.

Beecher, Lyman. The Practicality of Suppressing Vice by
    Means of Societies for that Purpose. New London,
    Conn.: Samuel Green, 1804.

Benedict, David. A General History of the Baptist Denomina-
    tion in America, and Other Parts of the World. 2 vols.
    Boston: Lincoln & Edmands, 1813.

Birney, James Gillespie. The American Churches, the Bul-
    warks of Slavery. Newburyport, Mass.: Charles
    Whipple, 1842.

Blanchard, Jonathan, and Rice, N. L. A Debate on Slavery.
    Cincinnati: W. H. Moore & Co., 1846.

Brooke, Samuel. Slavery and the Slaveholder's Religion, as
    Opposed to Christianity. Cincinnati: The Author, 1846.

Brownlow, William G., and Pryne, Abram. Ought American
    Slavery to Be Perpetuated? A Debate Between Rev.
    W. G. Brownlow and Rev. A. Pryne Held at Philadel-
    phia, September, 1858. Philadelphia: J. B. Lippincott
    & Co., 1858.

Bourne, George. Picture of Slavery in the United States of
    America. Middletown, Conn.: E. Hunt, 1834.

Burwell, Letitia M. A Girl's Life in Virginia Before the
    War. 2nd ed. New York: Frederick A. Stober Co.,
    1895.

[Carleton, George Washington.] The Suppressed Book About
    Slavery. New York: Published by the Author, 1864.

Catto, William T. A Semi-Centenary Discourse, Delivered
    in the First African Presbyterian Church, Philadel-
    phia, On the Fourth Sabbath of May, 1857. Phila-
    delphia: Joseph M. Wilson, 1857.

Channing, William E. Slavery and Emancipation. 3rd ed.
    1836, 1841; rpt. New York: Negro Universities
    Press, 1968.

Christy, David. Pulpit Politics; or Ecclesiastical Legisla-
    tion on Slavery, in Its Disturbing Influences on the
    American Union. Cincinnati: Faran & McLean, 1862.

Christy, Edwin P. Christy's Plantation Melodies. Phila-
    delphia: Fisher & Brother, 1853.

Clayton, Victoria Virginia. White and Black Under the Old
    Regime. Milwaukee, Wis.: The Young Churchman
    Company, 1899.

Coker, Daniel. A Dialogue Between a Virginian and an
    African Methodist Minister. Baltimore: Joseph James,
    1810.

_____. Journal of Daniel Coker. Baltimore: Press of
    Edward J. Coate, 1820.

Crothers, Samuel. The Gospel of Typical Servitude. Hamil-
    ton, Ohio: Gradner and Gibbon, 1835.

Dalcho, Frederick. Practical Considerations Founded on the
    Scriptures Relative to the Slave Population of South
    Carolina. Charleston, S.C.: A. E. Miller, 1823.

Delany, Martin Robinson. The Condition, Elevation, Emi-
    gration, and Destiny of the Colored People of the United
    States. Philadelphia: By the Author, 1852.

The Doctrines and Discipline of the African Methodist Epis-
    copal Church in America; Established in the City of
    N.Y., Oct. 25, 1820. New York: Christopher Rush
    and George Collins, 1820.

Douglass, Frederick. The Life and Writings of Frederick
    Douglass. Edited by Philip S. Foner. 4 vols. New
    York: International Publishers, 1950.

Douglass, Margaret. Educational Laws of Virginia; The
    Personal Narrative of Mrs. Margaret Douglass. A
    Southern Woman, Who Was Imprisoned for One Month
    in the Common Jail of Norfolk, Under the Laws of
    Virginia, For the Crime of Teaching Free Coloured
    Children to Read. Reprinted in Legal and Moral As-
    pects of Slavery: Selected Essays. New York: Negro
    Universities Press, 1969.

Douglass, William. Annals of the First African Church in
    the United States of America, Now Styled the African
    Episcopal Church of St. Thomas'. Philadelphia: King
    & Baird, 1862.

_____. Sermons Preached in the African Protestant
    Church of St. Thomas', Philadelphia. Philadelphia:
    King & Baird, 1854.

Dwight, Timothy. A Discourse on Some Events of the Last
    Century, delivered in the Brick Church in New Haven,
    on Wednesday, January 7, 1801. New Haven, Conn.:
    Printed by Ezra Read, 1801.

Easton, Hosea H. A Treatise on the Intellectual Character,
    and Civil and Political Condition of the Colored People
    of the U. States; and the Prejudice Exercised Towards
    Them. Boston: Isaac Knapp, 1837.

French, A. M. (Mrs.). Slavery in South Carolina, and the
    Ex-Slaves; or, The Port Royal Mission. 1862; rpt.
    New York: Negro Universities Press, 1969.

Furman, Richard. Exposition of the Views of the Baptists
    Relative to the Colored Population of the United States
    in a Communication to the Governor of South Carolina.
    Charleston, S.C.: A. E. Miller, 1823.

Garnet, Henry Highland. Walker's Appeal, With a Brief

Sketch of His Life. Also Garnet's Address to the
Slaves of the United States of America. New York:
J. H. Tobitt, 1848.

Goodell, William. Slavery and Anti-Slavery; A History of
the Great Struggle in Both Hemispheres; With a View
of the Slavery Question in the United States. New
York: W. Harned, 1852.

Hamilton, William Thomas. Duties of Masters and Slaves
Respectively; or, Domestic Slavery as Sanctioned by
the Bible: A Discourse. Mobile, Ala.: F. H.
Brooks, 1844.

Hammon, Jupiter. An Address to Negroes in the State of
New York. New York: Carroll & Patterson, 1787.

Handy, James A. Scraps of African Methodist Episcopal
History. Philadelphia: A.M.E. Book Concern, n.d.

Hawkins, William G. Lunsford Lane; or Another Helper
from North Carolina. Boston: Crosby & Nichols,
1863.

Haygood, Atticus G. Our Brother in Black: His Freedom
and His Future. New York: Phillips & Hunt, 1881.

Higginson, Thomas Wentworth. Army Life in a Black Regiment. New ed. Boston: Houghton, Mifflin and
Company, 1900.

_____. Does Slavery Christianize the Negro? Anti-
Slavery Tracts No. 4. New York: American Anti-
Slavery Society, 1855.

Holcombe, Hosea. A History of the Rise and Progress of
the Baptists in Alabama. Philadelphia: Riny, 1840.

Holland, Edwin C. A Refutation of the Calumnies Circulated
Against the Southern and Western States, Respecting the
Institution and Existence of Slavery Among Them.
Charleston, S.C.: A. E. Miller, 1822.

Hooker, Herman. The Planter; or, Thirteen Years in the
South, By a Northern Man. 1853; rpt. Miami, Fla.:
Mnemosyne Pub. Co., 1969.

Hundley, Daniel Robinson. Social Relations in Our Southern
    States. New York: Henry B. Price, 1860.

Ingraham, Joseph Holt. The Sunny South; or, the Southerner
    at Home, Embracing Five Years' Experience of a
    Northern Governess in the Land of The Sugar and The
    Cotton. Philadelphia: G. G. Evans, 1860.

James, Horace. Our Duties to the Slave, A Sermon.
    Boston: Richardson and Filmer, 1847.

Jones, Absalom. A Thanksgiving Sermon, Preached January
    1, 1808, In St. Thomas's, or the African Episcopal
    Church, Philadelphia: On Account of The Abolition of
    the African Slave Trade, On that Day By the Congress
    of the United States. Philadelphia: Fry and Kamnerer,
    Printers, 1808.

_____, and Allen, Richard. A Narrative of the Proceed-
    ings of the Black People, During the Late Awful
    Calamity in Philadelphia, In the Year, 1793; And a
    Refutation of Some Censures, Thrown Upon Them in
    Some Late Publications. Philadelphia: By the Authors,
    1794.

Jones, Charles Colcock. Annual Report of the Missionary
    to the Negroes in Liberty Co., Georgia. Charleston,
    S.C.: Observer Office Press, 1833. [The 13 annual
    reports which Jones made from 1833 to 1848 are cited
    by number in this study.]

_____. The Religious Instruction of the Negroes. A
    Sermon, Delivered Before Associations of Planters in
    Liberty and M'Intosh Counties, Georgia. 4th ed.
    Princeton, N.J.: D'Hart & Connolly, 1832.

_____. The Religious Instruction of the Negroes in the
    United States. Savannah, Ga.: Thomas Purse, 1842.

_____. Report of the Committee to Whom Was Referred
    the Subject of the Religious Instruction of the Colored
    Population of the Synod of South Carolina, December
    5th-9th, 1833. Charleston, S.C.: Observer Office
    Press, 1834.

_____. Suggestions on the Religious Instruction of the
    Negroes in the Southern States; Together with An

Appendix Containing Forms of Church Registers, Form
of a Constitution, and Plans of Different Denominations
of Christians. Philadelphia: Presbyterian Board of
Publication, 1847.

Kemble, Frances Anne. Journal of a Residence on a Georgia
Plantation in 1838-1839. New York: Harper & Brothers, 1863.

Killens, John Oliver, ed. The Trial Record of Denmark
Vesey. Boston: Beacon Press, 1970.

Lednum, John. A History of the Rise of Methodism in
America, Containing Sketches of Methodist Itinerant
Preachers, From 1736 to 1785, Numbering One Hun-
dred and Sixty or Seventy, Also A Short Account of
Many Hundreds of the First Race of Lay Members,
Male and Female, From New York to South Carolina,
Together with an Account of Many of the First Societies
and Chapels. Philadelphia: Published for the Author,
1859.

Long, John Dixon. Pictures of Slavery in Church and State.
Philadelphia: By the Author, 1857.

Longstreet, Augustus Baldwin. Letters on the Epistle of
Paul to Philemon, or the Connection of Apostolical
Christianity with Slavery. Charleston, S.C.: B.
Jenkins, 1845.

Lowery, Irving E. Life on the Old Plantation in Ante-Bellum
Days or A Story Based on Facts. Columbia, S.C.:
The State Company, 1911.

M'Tyeire, Holland Nimmons. Duties of Christian Masters.
Edited by Thomas O. Summers. Nashville, Tenn.:
Southern Methodist Publishing House, 1859.

_____ ; Sturgiss, C. F.; and Holmes, A. T. Duties of
Masters to Servants: Three Premium Essays.
Charleston, S.C.: Southern Baptist Publication So-
ciety, 1851.

Mallard, Ralph Quarterman. Montevideo - Maybank: Some
Memoirs of a Southern Christian Household in the
Olden Time, or, The Family Life of the Reverend
Charles Colcock Jones, D.D. of Liberty County, Georgia.
Richmond: Presbyterian Committee of Publication, 1898.

_____. Plantation Life Before Emancipation. Richmond: Whittet & Shepperson, 1892.

Martineau, Harriet. Society in America. Paris: Baudry's European Library, 1837.

May, Samuel J. Some Recollections of Our Antislavery Conflict. Boston: Fields, Osgood, & Co., 1869.

Meade, William. Pastoral Letter to the Ministers, Members, and Families of the Protestant Episcopal Church on the Duty of Affording Religious Instruction to Those in Bondage, Delivered in the Year 1834. Richmond: H. K. Ellyson, 1853.

_____. Scriptural Duties of Masters Comprising a Pastoral Address of the Right Reverend William Meade, D.D. New York: American Tract Society, 1858.

Milburn, William Henry. Ten Years of Preacher-Life: Chapters from an Autobiography. New York: Derby & Jackson, 1859.

Murat, Achille. A Moral and Political Sketch of the United States of North America. London: Effingham Wilson, 1833.

[Necomb, Harvey.] The "Negro Pew": Being An Inquiry Concerning the Propriety of Distinctions in the House of God, On Account of Color. Boston: Isaac Knapp, 1837.

Nisbit, Richard. The Capacity of Negroes for Religious and Moral Improvement Considered: With Cursory Hints, To Proprietors and To Government for the Immediate Melioration of the Condition of Slaves in the Sugar Colonies: To Which Are Subjoined Short and Practical Discourses to Negroes, on the Plain and Obvious Principles of Religion and Morality. London: James Phillips, 1789.

Olmsted, Frederick Law. The Cotton Kingdom; A Traveller's Observations on Cotton and Slavery in the American Slave States. Edited by Arthur M. Schlesinger. New York: Knopf, 1953.

_____. A Journey in the Back Country, 1853-1854.

Introduction by Clement Eaton. New York: Schocken
Books, 1970.

Ozanne, T. D. The South as It Is; or, Twenty-one Years'
    Experience in the Southern States of America. London:
    Saunders, Otley and Co., 1863.

Page, William. An Address, Delivered by the Rev. William
    Page, of Boston, At the Laying of the Corner Stone of
    the African Methodist Episcopal Church of the Village
    of Canadaigua, N.Y., April, 1833. Canadaigua, N.Y.:
    Morse & Harvey, 1833.

Palmer, Benjamin Morgan. Letter to the Synods of South
    Carolina and Georgia, at Their Sessions in Augusta in
    November, 1840. Charleston, S.C.: B. Jenkins, 1843.

_____. The Life and Letters of James Henry Thornwell.
    Richmond: Whittet & Shepperson, 1875.

_____. Religion Profitable: with a Special Reference to
    the Case of Servants, Sermon Preached September 22,
    1822. Charleston, S.C.: J. R. Schenck, 1822.

Parsons, Charles Grandison. Inside View of Slavery: or a
    Tour Among the Planters. Boston: John P. Jewett
    and Co., 1855.

Paul, Nathaniel. An Address, Delivered on the Celebration
    of the Abolition of Slavery, in the State of New York,
    July 5, 1827. Albany, N.Y.: John B. Van Steenbergh,
    1827.

Payne, Daniel Alexander. History of the African Methodist
    Episcopal Church. Nashville, Tenn.: Publishing
    House of the A.M.E. Sunday School Union, 1891.

_____. Recollections of Seventy Years. Nashville, Tenn.:
    Publishing House of the A.M.E. Sunday School Union,
    1888.

_____. The Semi-Centenary and the Retrospection of the
    A.M.E. Church in the U.S. in America. Baltimore:
    Sherwood & Co., 1866.

_____. Welcome to the Ransomed; or, Duties of the
    Colored Inhabitants of the District of Columbia. Balti-
    more: Bull & Tuttle, 1862.

Peck, George. Slavery and the Episcopacy: Being an
    Examination of Dr. Bascom's Review of the Reply of
    the Majority to the Protest of the Minority of the Late
    General Conference of the M.E. Church, in the Case
    of Bishop Andrew. New York: G. Lane & C. B.
    Tippett, 1845.

Phoebus, George A. Beams of Light on Early Methodism
    in America, Chiefly Drawn From the Diary, Letters,
    Manuscripts, Documents, and Original Tracts of Rev.
    Ezekial Cooper. New York: Phillips & Hart, 1887.

Pierce, George F. A Sermon Delivered Before the General
    Assembly at Milledgeville, Georgia, on Fast Day,
    March 27, 1863. Milledgeville, Ga.: Boughton, Nis-
    bet, and Barnes, 1863.

Pinckney, Charles Cotesworth. An Address Delivered in
    Charleston, before the Agricultural Society of South
    Carolina at its Anniversary Meeting, on Tuesday, the
    18th August, 1829. Charleston, S.C.: Published by
    Order of the Society, 1829.

Plumer, William S. Thoughts on the Religious Instruction of
    the Negroes of this Country. Savannah, Ga.: Edward
    J. Purse, 1848.

Pollard, Edward Alfred. Black Diamonds Gathered in the
    Darkey Homes of the South. New York: Pudney &
    Russell, 1859.

Proceedings of the Meeting in Charleston, S.C., May 13-15,
    1845, on The Religious Instruction of The Negroes, To-
    gether With The Report of The Committee And The
    Address To The Public. Charleston, S.C.: B. Jen-
    kins, 1845.

Ramsay, James. An Essay on the Treatment and Conversion
    of African Slaves in the British Sugar Colonies. London:
    J. Phillips, 1784.

Robinson, John. The Testimony and Practice of the Presby-
    terian Church in Reference to American Slavery.
    Philadelphia: Presbyterian Historical Library, 1852.

Ross, Frederick Augustus. Slavery Ordained of God. Phila-
    delphia: J. B. Lippincott & Co., 1857.

260   Black Religion

Rush, Benjamin. The Autobiography of Benjamin Rush.
    Edited by George W. Corner. Princeton, N.J.:
    Princeton University Press, 1948.

_____. Letters of Benjamin Rush. Edited by L. H.
    Butterfield. Princeton, N.J.: Princeton University
    Press, 1951.

Rush, Christopher. A Short Account of the Rise and Prog-
    ress of the African Methodist Episcopal Church in
    America. New York: By the Author, 1843.

Seabrook, Benjamin Whitemarsh. A Concise View of the
    Critical Situation and Future Prospects of the Slave-
    holding States, in Relation to Their Coloured Popula-
    tion. Charleston, S.C.: A. E. Miller, 1825.

_____. Emancipation, By a South Carolinian. New York:
    J. A. Fraetas, 1843.

_____. An Essay on the Management of Slaves, and Es-
    pecially on Their Religious Instruction. Charleston,
    S.C.: A. E. Miller, 1834.

Smith, Charles Spencer. The Catechism of the A.M.E.
    Church, Formerly -- "The Turner Catechism," Re-
    vised and Improved. Bloomington, Ill.: Connectional
    Sunday School Union of the A.M.E. Church, 1885.

Smith, William Andrew. Lectures on the Philosophy and
    Practice of Slavery, as Exhibited in the Institution of
    Domestic Slavery in the United States; with the Duties
    of Masters to Slaves. Nashville, Tenn.: Stevenson
    and Evans, 1856.

_____. Letters on the Epistle of Paul to Philemon, or
    the Connection of Apostolical Christianity with Slavery.
    Charleston, S.C.: B. Jenkins, 1845.

Srygley, F. D. Seventy Years in Dixie: Recollections,
    Sermons, and Sayings of T. W. Caskey and Others.
    Nashville, Tenn.: Gospel Advocate Pub. Co., 1891.

Stowe, Harriet Beecher. A Key to Uncle Tom's Cabin:
    Presenting the Original Facts and Documents Upon
    Which the Story is Founded. Boston: John P. Jewett
    and Co., 1853.

Summers, Thomas O. , ed. Catechisms of the Wesleyan
  Methodists. Rev. ed. Nashville, Tenn.: Publishing
  House of the Methodist Episcopal Church, South, 1860.

Sunderland, LaRoy. Anti-Slavery Manual, Containing A Collection of Facts and Arguments on American Slavery.
  2nd ed. New York: S. W. Benedict, 1837.

_____. The Testimony of God Against Slavery, Or A
  Collection of Passages From the Bible, Which Show
  The Sin of Holding Property in Man, with Notes.
  Boston: Webster & Southard, 1835.

Tanner, Benjamin T. Apology for African Methodism.
  Baltimore: n.p., 1867.

Tanner, C. M. Reprint of the First Edition of the Discipline of the African Methodist Episcopal, with Historical
  Preface and Notes. Atlanta: n.p., 1916.

Taylor, James Barnett. Lives of Virginia Baptist Ministers.
  Richmond: Yale & Wyall, 1837.

Taylor, Stephen. Relation of Master and Servant, as Exhibited in the New Testament; Together with a Review
  of Dr. Wayland's Elements of Moral Science on the
  Subject of Slavery. Richmond: n.p., 1836.

Thornwell, James H. The Rights and Duties of Masters. A
  Sermon Preached at the Dedication of A Church Erected
  in Charleston, S.C., for the Benefit and Instruction of
  the Coloured Population. Charleston, S.C.: Walker &
  James, 1850.

Trollope, Frances. Domestic Manners of the Americans
  (1832). Edited by Donald Smalley. New York: Knopf,
  1949.

Van Evrie, John H. Negroes and Negro "Slavery": the
  First, an Inferior Race--the Latter, its Normal Condition. New York: Van Evrie, Horton & Co., 1861.

Wakely, J. B. Lost Chapters Recovered from the Early
  History of American Methodism. New York: Published
  for the Author, 1858.

Wayman, Alexander Walker. My Recollections of African M.

262   Black Religion

E. Ministers, or Forty Years' Experience in the
African Methodist Episcopal Church. Philadelphia:
A.M.E. Book Rooms, 1881.

[Weld, Theodore Dwight.] American Slavery As It Is:
Testimony of a Thousand Witnesses. New York:
American Anti-Slavery Society, 1839.

Whipple, Charles King. The Family Relation, as Affected
by Slavery. Cincinnati: American Reform Tract and
Book Society, 1858.

Whipple, Henry Benjamin. Bishop Whipple's Southern
Diary, 1843-1844. Edited by Lester B. Shippee.
1937; rpt. New York: Da Capo Press, 1968.

White, William S. Reverend William S. White, D.D., and
His Times: An Autobiography. Edited by H. M.
White. Richmond: Presbyterian Committee of Pub-
lication, 1891.

Wightman, William May. Life of William Capers, D.D.,
One of the Bishops of the Methodist Episcopal Church,
South, Including an Autobiography. Nashville, Tenn.:
Southern Methodist Pub. House, 1858.

Williams, John G. De Ole Plantation. Charleston, S.C.:
Walker, Evans & Cogwell Co., 1895.

Wilson, Joshua Lacy. The Relations and Duties of Servants
and Masters. Cincinnati: Hefley, 1839.

Wolher, William. John Bachman: Letters and Memories of
His Life. Charleston, S.C.: Evans & Cogwell, 1888.

                    SECONDARY WORKS

I. ARTICLES

Ahlstrom, Sydney E. "The Scottish Philosophy and American
Theology." Church History, XXIV, 3 (September 1955),
257-72.

Aptheker, Herbert. "The Quakers and Negro Slavery." The
Journal of Negro History, XXV, 3 (July 1940), 331-62.

Bardolph, Richard. "Social Origins of Distinguished Negroes, 1770-1865." The Journal of Negro History, XL,
3 (July 1955), 211-49.

Batten, J. Milton. "Henry M. Turner, Negro Bishop Extraordinary." Church History, VII, 3 (September 1938),
231-46.

Bauer, Raymond A., and Bauer, Alice H. "Day to Day
Resistance to Slavery." The Journal of Negro History,
XXVII, 4 (October 1942), 388-419.

Bell, Howard H. "National Negro Conventions of the Middle
1840's: Moral Suasion vs. Political Action." The
Journal of Negro History, XLIII, 4 (October 1957),
247-60.

Bennett, Lerone, Jr. "The Black Pioneer Period." Part
IV of "The Making of Black America," Ebony, XXV,
12 (October 1970), 46-55.

Berger, Max. "American Slavery as Seen by British
Visitors, 1836-1860." The Journal of Negro History,
XXX, 1 (January 1945), 181-202.

Bishop, Shelton M. "A History of St. Philip's Church,
New York City." Historical Magazine of the Protestant Episcopal Church, XV, 4 (December 1946), 302-06.

Blanks, W. D. "Corrective Church Discipline in the Presbyterian Churches of the Nineteenth-Century South."
The Journal of Presbyterian History, XLIV, 2 (June
1966), 89-105.

Brewer, William M. "Henry Highland Garnet." The Journal
of Negro History, XII, 1 (January 1928), 36-52.

Brooks, Walter H. "The Evolution of the Negro Baptist
Church." The Journal of Negro History, VII, 1 (January 1922), 11-22.

_____. "The Priority of the Silver Bluff Church and Its
Promoters." The Journal of Negro History, VII, 2
(April 1922), 172-96.

Brown, John M. "Richard Allen and His Co-adjutors."
Repository of Religion and Literature, III, 1 (January
1861), 1-4.

264   Black Religion

Burger, Nash. "A Side-Light on an Ante-Bellum Plantation
    Chapel." Historical Magazine of the Protestant Epis-
    copal Church, XII, 1 (March 1943), 69-73.

Cadbury, Henry J. "Negro Membership in the Society of
    Friends." The Journal of Negro History, XXI, 2
    (April 1936), 151-213.

Carroll, Kenneth L. "Religious Influences on Manumission
    of Slaves in Caroline, Dorchester, and Talbot Coun-
    ties." Maryland Historical Magazine, LVI, 4 (June
    1961), 176-97.

Cone, James H. "Black Consciousness and the Black
    Church." Christianity and Crisis, XXV, 18 (November
    2 & 16, 1970), 244-50.

Cromwell, John W. "The Aftermath of Nat Turner's Insur-
    rection." The Journal of Negro History, V, 2 (April
    1920), 208-34.

_____. "First Negro Churches in the District of Colum-
    bia." The Journal of Negro History, VII, 1 (January
    1922), 64-106.

Daniel, W. Harrison. "Southern Protestantism and the
    Negro, 1860-1865." The North Carolina Historical
    Review, XLI, 3 (July 1964), 338-59.

_____. "Virginia Baptists and the Negro in the Antebel-
    lum Era." The Journal of Negro History, LVI, 1
    (January 1971), 1-16.

Davis, John W. "George Liele and Andrew Bryan, Pioneer
    Negro Baptist Preachers." The Journal of Negro
    History, III, 2 (April 1918), 119-27.

Durden, Robert F. "The Establishment of Calvary Protes-
    tant Episcopal Church for Negroes in Charleston."
    South Carolina Historical Magazine, LXV, 2 (April
    1964), 63-86.

Fisher, Miles Mark. "Lott Cary, the Colonizing Missionary."
    The Journal of Negro History, VII, 4 (October 1922),
    380-418.

_____. "Negro Churches in Illinois." Illinois Historical
    Society Journal, LVI, 3 (Autumn 1963), 552-69.

Franklin, John Hope. "Negro Episcopalians in Ante-bellum North Carolina." Historical Magazine of the Protestant Episcopal Church, XIII (September 1944), 216-34.

Frederickson, George, and Lasch, Christopher. "Resistance to Slavery." Civil War History, XIII, 4 (December 1967), 315-29.

Gabriel, Ralph. "Evangelical Religion and Popular Romanticism in Early Nineteenth-Century America." Church History, XIX, 1 (March 1950), 34-47.

Green, Fletcher M. "Northern Missionary Activities in the South, 1846-1861." The Journal of Southern History, XXI, 2 (May 1955), 147-72.

Griffin, Clifford S. "Cooperation and Conflict: The Schism in the American Home Missionary Society, 1837-1861." The Journal of the Presbyterian Historical Society, XXXVIII, 4 (December 1960), 213-33.

Harris, Jay. "State was Birthplace of the Negro Church." The Morning News (Wilmington, Delaware), CLXXIX, No. 43 (February 19, 1971), 2.

Hartgrove, W. B. "The Story of Josiah Henson." The Journal of Negro History, III, 1 (January 1918), 1-21.

Herskovitts, Melville J. "On the Provenience of New World Negroes." Social Forces, XII, 2 (December 1933), 247-62.

Jackson, Luther P. "Religious Development of the Negro in Virginia from 1760 to 1860." The Journal of Negro History, XVI, 2 (April 1931), 168-239.

_____. "Religious Instruction of Negroes, 1830-1860, With Special Reference to South Carolina." The Journal of Negro History, XV, 1 (January 1930), 72-114.

Jernegan, Marcus W. "Slavery and Conversion in the American Colonies." The American Historical Review, XXI, 33 (April 1916), 504-27.

Jones, Lawrence N. "Black Churches in Historical Perspective." Christianity and Crisis, XXX, 18 (November 2 & 16, 1970), 226-28.

266   Black Religion

_____. "They Sought a City: The Black Church and
Churchmen in the Nineteenth Century." Union Seminary Quarterly Review, XXVI, 3 (Spring 1971), 253-72.

Klein, Herbert S. "Anglicanism, Catholicism, and the Negro Slave." Comparative Studies in Society and
History, VIII, 3 (April 1966), 295-327.

Lofton, John M., Jr. "Denmark Vesey's Call to Arms."
The Journal of Negro History, XXXIII, 4 (October
1948), 395-417.

_____. "The Enslavement of the Southern Mind: 1775-
1825." The Journal of Negro History, XVIII, 2 (April
1958), 132-39.

Marx, Gary T. "Religion: Opiate or Inspiration of Civil
Rights Militancy Among Negroes?" American Sociological Review, XXXII, 1 (February 1967), 64-72.

Maser, Frederick D. "Through Service to Greatness: The
Story of Richard Allen." A.M.E. Church Review,
LXXVI, 203 (January-March 1960), 22-30.

Mathews, Donald G. "The Methodist Schism of 1844 and
the Popularization of Antislavery Sentiment." Mid-
America, LI, 1 (January 1968), 3-23.

_____. "The Second Great Awakening as an Organizing
Process, 1780-1830: An Hypothesis." American
Quarterly, XXI, 1 (Spring 1969), 23-43.

Mead, Sidney E. "The 'Nation with the Soul of a Church'."
Church History, XXXVI, 3 (September 1967), 262-83.

_____. "Neither Church nor State: Reflections of James
Madison's 'Line of Separation'." The Journal of
Church and State, X, 3 (Autumn 1968), 349-63.

Moore, Le Roy, Jr. "The Spiritual: Soul of Black Religion." American Quarterly, XXIII, 5 (December
1971), 658-76.

Moore, Margaret D. "Religion in Mississippi in 1860."
The Journal of Mississippi History, XXII, 4 (October
1960), 223-38.

Morse, W. H. "Lemuel Hanyes." The Journal of Negro
    History, IV, 1 (January 1919), 22-32.

Park, Robert E. "The Conflict and Fusion of Culture."
    The Journal of Negro History, IV, 2 (April 1969), 111-
    33.

Pennington, Edgar Legare. "Thomas Bray's Associates and
    Their Work Among the Negroes." Proceedings of the
    American Antiquarian Society, New Series, XLVIII
    (1938), 311-418.

Perkins, Haven P. "Religion for Slaves: Difficulties and
    Methods." Church History, X, 3 (September 1941),
    228-45.

Pierre, C. E. "The Work of the Society for the Propagation
    of the Gospel in Foreign Parts among the Negroes of
    the Colonies." The Journal of Negro History, I, 4
    (October 1916), 347-58.

Pope, Liston. "The Negro and Religion in America." Re-
    view of Religious Research, V, 3 (Spring 1964), 152-56.

Pope, William A. "Lott Carey: Man of Purchased Freedom."
    Church History, XXXIX, 1 (March 1970), 49-61.

Posey, Walter B. "The Baptists and Slavery in the Lower
    Mississippi Valley." The Journal of Negro History,
    XLI, 2 (April 1956), 117-30.

Powdermaker, Hortense. "Channeling the Negro's Aggres-
    sions." American Journal of Sociology, XLVIII, 6
    (May 1943), 750-58.

Powell, Adam Clayton. "A Tribute to the Bicentennial of
    Richard Allen, A Great American." A.M.E. Church
    Review, LXXVIII, 206 (October-December 1960), 3-4.

Puckett, Newell N. "Religious Folk Beliefs of Whites and
    Negroes." The Journal of Negro History, XVI, 1
    (January 1931), 9-35.

Quarles, Benjamin. "Ante-Bellum Relationships Between the
    First African Baptist Church of New Orleans and White
    Agencies." The Chronicle, XVIII, 1 (January 1955),
    26-36.

Reed, Richard Clark. "A Sketch of the Religious History of
    the Negroes in the South." Papers of the American
    Society of Church History, Second Series, IV (1914),
    175-204.

Shanks, Caroline L. "The Biblical Anti-Slavery Argument
    of the Decade 1830-1840." The Journal of Negro His-
    tory, XVI, 2 (April 1931), 132-57.

Sheares, Reuben A., II. "Beyond White Theology." Chris-
    tianity and Crisis, XXX, 18 (November 2 & 16, 1970),
    229-35.

Smith, Elwyn A. "The Role of the South in the Presbyterian
    Schism of 1837-38." Church History, XXIX, 1 (March
    1960), 44-63.

Smith, H. Shelton. "The Church and the Social Order in the
    Old South as Interpreted by James H. Thornwell."
    Church History, VII, 2 (June 1938), 115-24.

Smith, Timothy L. "Slavery and Theology: The Emergence
    of Black Christian Consciousness in Nineteenth Century
    America." Church History, XLI, 4 (December 1972),
    497-512.

Southall, Eugene Portlette. "The Attitude of the Methodist
    Episcopal Church, South, Toward the Negro from 1844
    to 1870." The Journal of Negro History, XVI, 4
    (October 1931), 359-70.

Staiger, C. Bruce. "Abolitionism and the Presbyterian
    Schism of 1837-38." The Mississippi Valley Historical
    Review, XXXVI, 3 (December 1949), 391-414.

Stampp, Kenneth M. "The Fate of the Southern Anti-Slavery
    Movement." The Journal of Negro History, XXVIII, 1
    (January 1943), 10-22.

Stuckey, Sterling. "Through the Prism of Folklore: The
    Black Ethos in Slavery." The Underside of American
    History. Volume 1: to 1877. Edited by Thomas R.
    Frazier. New York: Harcourt Brace Jovanovich, 1971.

Suttles, William., Jr. "African Religious Survivals as
    Factors in American Slave Revolts." The Journal of
    Negro History, LVI, 2 (April 1971), 97-104.

Sweet, William Warren. "The Churches As Moral Courts of
    the Frontier." Church History, II, 1 (March 1933),
    3-21.

Thurman, Howard. "Religious Ideas in Negro Spirituals."
    Christendom, IV, 4 (Autumn 1939), 515-28.

Trueblood, Roy W. "Union Negotiations Between Black
    Methodists in America." Methodist History, XIII, 3
    (July 1970), 18-29.

Vibert, Faith. "The Society for the Propagation of the
    Gospel in Foreign Parts: Its Work for the Negroes
    in North America before 1783." The Journal of Negro
    History, XVIII, 2 (April 1933), 171-212.

Welter, Rush. "The Frontier West as Image of American
    Society: Conservative Attitudes before the Civil War."
    The Mississippi Valley Historical Review, XLVI, 4
    (March 1960), 593-614.

Wilson, G[old] R[efined]. "The Religion of the American
    Negro Slave: His Attitude toward Life and Death."
    The Journal of Negro History, VIII, 1 (January 1923),
    41-71.

Wish, Harvey. "American Slave Insurrections before 1861."
    The Journal of Negro History, XXII, 3 (July 1937),
    299-320.

Wolf, Richard. "The Middle Period, 1800-1870: The Matrix
    of Modern Christianity." Religion in Life, XXII (1953),
    72-84.

[Woodson, Carter G.]. "Suggestions for Improving the
    Negro Church." The Negro History Bulletin, III, 1
    (October 1939), 9-10.

II. BOOKS

Ahlstrom, Sydney E. A Religious History of the American
    People. New Haven, Conn.: Yale University Press,
    1972.

Alexander, Gross. History of the Methodist Episcopal
    Church, South. The American Church History Series,
    Vol. XI. New York: Christian Literature Co., 1894.

Alexander, William T. History of the Colored Race in
    America. 2nd rev. ed. New Orleans: Palmetto Pub.
    Co., 1887.

Allen, William Francis; Ware, Charles Pickard; and Garri-
    son, Lucy McKim. Slave Songs of the United States.
    New York: A. Sampson & Co., 1867.

Aptheker, Herbert. American Negro Slave Revolts. New
    York: Columbia University Press, 1943.

_____. Nat Turner's Slave Rebellion. New York: Hu-
    manities Press, 1966.

_____. The Negro in the Abolitionist Movement. New
    York: International Publishers, 1941.

_____. "One Continual Cry": David Walker's Appeal to
    the Colored Citizens of the World, 1829-1830. New
    York: Humanities Press, 1965.

Bachman, Catherine L. John Bachman, D.D., LL.D.,
    Ph.D., the Pastor of St. John's Lutheran Church.
    Charleston, S.C.: Walker, 1888.

Bacon, Leonard Woolsey. A History of American Chris-
    tianity. The American Church History Series, Vol.
    XIII. New York: Christian Literature Co., 1897.

Ballagh, James Curtis. A History of Slavery in Virginia.
    Johns Hopkins University Studies in Historical and
    Political Science, Vol. XXIV. Baltimore: Johns
    Hopkins University Press, 1902.

Barber, Jesse Belmont. Climbing Jacob's Ladder. New
    York: Presbyterian Church, U.S.A., 1952.

Barclay, Wade Crawford. Early American Methodism, 1769-
    1844. 2 vols. New York: Board of Missions and Ex-
    pansion of the Methodist Church, 1949-50.

Bardolph, Richard. The Negro Vanguard. New York: Vin-
    tage Books, 1959.

Barnes, Albert. The Antislavery Impulse, 1830-1844. New
    York: D. Appleton-Century Co., 1933.

Bassatt, John Spencer. Slavery in the State of North Carolina. The Johns Hopkins University Studies in Historical and Political Science. Vol. XVIII. Baltimore:
Johns Hopkins University Press, 1899.

Bennent, William W. Memorials of Methodism in Virginia,
From Its Introduction into the State in the Year 1772,
to the Year 1829. Richmond: By the Author, 1871.

Berry, L. L. A Century of Missions of the African Methodist Episcopal Church, 1840-1940. New York: Gutten-
berg Printery, 1942.

Betts, Albert Deems. History of South Carolina Methodism.
Columbia, S.C.: Advocate Press, 1952.

Blassingame, John W. The Slave Community. New York:
Oxford University Press, 1972.

Boone, Theodore Sylvester. A Social History of Negro
Baptists. Detroit: Historical Commission, National
Baptist Convention, U.S.A., 1952.

Boyd, Jesse Laney. A History of Baptists in America Prior
to 1845. New York: American Press, 1957.

Bradley, David Henry, Sr. A History of the A.M.E. Zion
Church, Part I, 1796-1872. Nashville, Tenn.: Parthenon Press, 1956.

_____. A History of the A.M.E. Zion Church, Part II,
1872-1968. Nashville, Tenn.: Parthenon Press, 1970.

Bragg, George Freeman. History of the Afro-American
Group of the Episcopal Church. Baltimore: Church
Advocate Press, 1922.

Bullock, Henry Allen. A History of Negro Education in the
South from 1619 to the Present. Cambridge, Mass.:
Harvard University Press, 1967.

Cannon, James, III. History of Southern Methodist Missions.
Nashville, Tenn.: Cokesbury Press, 1926.

Carter, Edward R. Biographical Sketches of Our Pulpit.
1888: rpt., Chicago: Afro-American Press, 1966.

Cash, W. J.   The Mind of the South.   New York: Vintage
    Books, 1941.

Christian, John Tyler.   A History of the Baptists of the
    United States, from the First Settlement of the Country
    to the Year 1845.   Nashville, Tenn.:   Sunday School
    Board of the Southern Baptist Convention, 1926.

Christie, John W., and Dumond, Dwight L.   George Bourne
    and The Book and Slavery Irreconcilable.   Wilmington:
    Historical Society of Delaware, 1969.

Clark, Elmer Talmadge.   The Negro and His Religion.
    Nashville, Tenn.:   Cokesbury Press, 1924.

Clark, Joseph B.   Leavening the Nation, The Story of Ameri-
    can Home Missions.   New York: Baker & Taylor Co.,
    1903.

Cleveland, Catherine C.   The Great Revival in the West,
    1797-1805.   Chicago: University of Chicago Press,
    1916.

Cliffe, Albert W.   The Glory of Our Methodist Heritage.
    Philadelphia: n.p., 1957.

Coan, Josephus R.   Daniel Alexander Payne: Christian Edu-
    cator.   Philadelphia: A.M.E. Book Concern, 1935.

Cole, Charles C., Jr.   The Social Ideas of the Northern
    Evangelists, 1826-1860.   New York: Columbia Uni-
    versity Press, 1954.

Cone, James H.   Black Theology and Black Power.   New
    York: Seabury Press, 1969.

_____.   A Black Theology of Liberation.   Philadelphia:
    J. B. Lippincott Co., 1970.

Conrad, Earl.   Harriet Tubman, Negro Soldier and Aboli-
    tionist.   New York: International Publishers, 1942.

Courlander, Harold.   Negro Folk Music, U.S.A.   New York:
    Columbia University Press, 1963.

Crogman, William H., and Nichols, J. L.   Progress of a
    Race.   Naperville, Ill.:   J. L. Nichols & Co., 1920.

Cromwell, John W. The Negro in American History. Washington, D.C.: American Negro Academy, 1914.

Cross, Whitney R. The Burned-over District. New York: Harper & Row, 1965.

_____. The Negro in the Methodist Church. New York: Board of Missions and Church Extension, Methodist Church, 1951.

Crum, Mason. Gullah: Negro Life in the Carolina Sea Islands. Durham, N.C.: Duke University Press, 1940.

Culver, Dwight W. Negro Segregation in the Methodist Church. New Haven, Conn.: Yale University Press, 1953.

Davis, David Brion. The Problem of Slavery in Western Culture. Ithaca, N.Y.: Cornell University Press, 1966.

Davis, M. H. The Dogmas and Precepts of the Fathers. Nashville, Tenn.: A.M.E. Sunday School Union, 1948.

Department of the Commerce, Bureau of the Census. Negro Population, 1790-1915. Washington, D.C.: Government Printing Office, 1918.

Du Bois, W. E. Burghardt. The Negro Church. Atlanta: 'Atlanta University Press, 1903.

_____. The Souls of Black Folk. Greenwich, Conn.: Fawcett Publications, 1961.

Dumond, Dwight Lowell. Antislavery: the Crusade for Freedom in America. New York: W. W. Norton, 1966.

Earnest, Joseph B. The Religious Development of the Negro in Virginia. Charlottesville, Va.: Michie Co., 1914.

Eaton, Clement. The Mind of the Old South. Rev. ed. Baton Rouge: Louisiana State University Press, 1967.

Elkins, Stanley M. Slavery. New York: Grosset & Dunlap, 1963.

274   Black Religion

Emory, Robert. History of the Discipline of the Methodist
    Episcopal Church. New York: G. Lane & P. P.
    Sandford, 1844.

Feldstein, Stanley. Once a Slave. New York: William
    Morrow, 1970.

Ferguson, Charles W. Organizing to Beat the Devil: Metho-
    dists and the Making of America. Garden City, N.Y.:
    Doubleday, 1971.

Fickling, Susan Markey. Slave-Conversion in South Caro-
    lina. Published as the Bulletin of the University of
    South Carolina. September, 1924. Columbia: Uni-
    versity of South Carolina, 1924.

Fisher, Miles Mark. Negro Slave Songs. Ithaca, N.Y.:
    Cornell University Press, 1953.

Flood, Theodore L., and Hamilton, John W., eds. Lives
    of Methodist Bishops. New York: Phillips and Hunt,
    1882.

Foster, Charles I. An Errand of Mercy: The Evangelical
    United Front. Chapel Hill: University of North Caro-
    lina Press, 1960.

Franklin, John Hope. From Slavery to Freedom. New
    York: Knopf, 1956.

Frazier, E. Franklin. The Negro Church in America.
    New York: Schocken Books, 1964.

_____. The Negro Family in the United States. Chicago:
    University of Chicago Press, 1939.

_____. The Negro in the United States. New York:
    Macmillan, 1949.

Fuller, Thomas Oscar. History of the Negro Baptists of
    Tennessee. Memphis: Haskins Print, 1936.

Gardinar, James J., and Roberts, J. Deotis, Sr., editors.
    Quest for a Black Theology. Philadelphia: United
    Church Press, 1971.

Gaustad, Edwin Scott. Historical Atlas of Religion in Ameri-
    ca. New York: Harper & Row, 1962.

George, Carol V. R. Segregated Sabbaths: Richard Allen
    and the Emergence of Independent Black Churches;
    1760-1840. New York: Oxford University Press, 1973.

Gewehr, Wesley M. The Great Awakening in Virginia, 1740-
    1790. Durham, N.C.: Duke University Press, 1930.

Gillet, E. H. History of the Presbyterian Church in the
    United States of America. Philadelphia: Presbyterian
    Board of Publication, 1864.

Goodell, William. The American Slave Code in Theory and
    Practice; Its Distinctive Features Shown by its Statutes,
    Judicial Decisions, and Illustrative Facts. New York:
    American and Foreign Anti-Slavery Society, 1853.

Goodykoontz, Colin Brumitt. Home Missions on the Ameri-
    can Frontier, with Particular Reference to the Ameri-
    can Home Missionary Society. Caldwell, Idaho: Caxton
    Printers, Ltd., 1939.

Gray, Joe Taylor. Negro Slavery in Louisiana. Baton
    Rouge, La.: Louisiana Historical Assoc., 1963.

Greene, Lorenzo Johnston. The Negro in Colonial New Eng-
    land, 1620-1776. New York: Columbia University
    Press, 1942.

Griffin, Clifford S. Their Brothers' Keepers: Moral
    Stewardship in the United States, 1800-1865. New
    Brunswick, N.J.: Rutgers University Press, 1960.

Grimke, Francis J. The Afro-American Pulpit in Relation
    to Race Elevation. Washington, D.C.: n.p., 1893.

Gullins, William R. The Heroes of the Virginia Annual Con-
    ference of the A.M.E. Church. Norfolk, Va.: n.p.,
    1899.

Hagood, Lewis Marshall. The Colored Man in the Methodist
    Episcopal Church. Cincinnati: Cranston & Stowe, 1890.

Hamilton, Charles V. The Black Preacher in America. New
    York: William Morrow, 1972.

Handy, Robert T. "Negro Christianity and American Church
    Historiography." Reinterpretation in American Church

History. Edited by Jerald C. Brauer. Chicago: University of Chicago Press, 1968.

Hansell, George H. Reminiscences of Baptist Churches and Baptist Leaders in New York City and Vicinity. Philadelphia: American Baptist Society, 1899.

Harlan, Howard Harper. John Jasper--A Case History in Leadership. Charlottesville: University of Virginia Press, 1936.

Hartzell, Joseph Crane. Methodism and the Negro in the United States. New York: Hunt & Eaton, 1894.

Hatcher, William E. John Jasper: The Unmatched Negro Philosopher and Preacher. New York: Fleming H. Revell Company, 1880.

Haynes, Leonard L. The Negro Community within American Protestantism, 1619-1844. Boston: Christopher Publishing House, 1954.

Henry, Howell M. The Police Control of the Slave in South Carolina. 1914; rpt. New York: Negro Universities Press, 1968.

Herskovits, Melville J. The Myth of the Negro Past. Boston: Beacon Press, 1958.

Hood, James Walker. One Hundred Years of the African Methodist Episcopal Church: or, The Centennial of African Methodism. New York: A.M.E. Zion Book Company, 1895.

_____. Sketch of the Early History of the African Methodist Episcopal Zion Church with Jubilee Souvenir and Appendix. Charlotte, N.C.: A.M.E. Zion Publication House, 1914.

Hudson, Winthrop S. Religion in America. New York: Scribner's, 1965.

Hurd, John Codman. The Law of Freedom and Bondage in the United States. 2 vols. Boston: Little, Brown, Co.; New York: D. Van Nostrand, 1862.

Jackson, George Pullen. White and Negro Spirituals, Their

Life Span and Kinship ... 116 Songs as Sung by Both Races. New York: J. J. Augustin, 1943.

Jackson, Joseph Julius. A Compendium of Historical Facts of Early African Baptist Churches. Bellefontaine, Ohio: n. p., 1922.

Jenkins, William Sumner. Pro-Slavery Thought in the Old South. Chapel Hill: University of North Carolina Press, 1935.

Johnson, Charles A. The Frontier Camp Meeting. Dallas: Southern Methodist University Press, 1955.

Johnson, Guy B. Folk Culture on St. Helena Island, South Carolina. Chapel Hill: University of North Carolina Press, 1930.

Johnston, Ruby F. The Development of Negro Religion. New York: Philosophical Library, 1956.

Jones, Major J. Black Awareness: A Theology of Hope. Nashville, Tenn.: Abingdon Press, 1971.

Jones, William R. Is God a White Racist? Garden City, N.Y.: Doubleday, 1973.

Jordan, Lewis Garnett. Negro Baptist History, U.S.A., 1750-1930. Nashville, Tenn.: Sunday School Publishing Board, 1930.

Jordan, Winthrop D. White Over Black. Baltimore: Pelican Books, 1969.

Love, Emanuel King. History of the First African Baptist Church, from Its Organization January 20, 1788 to July 1, 1888. Savannah, Ga.: Morning News Print, 1888.

Katz, Bernard, ed. The Social Implications of Early Negro Music in the United States. New York: Arno Press, 1969.

Keller, Charles Roy. The Second Great Awakening in Connecticut. New Haven, Conn.: Yale University Press, 1942.

Koch, Adolf. Religion of the American Enlightenment. New
    York: Thomas Y. Crowell, 1968.

Latourette, Kenneth Scott. A History of the Expansion of
    Christianity. Vol. IV: The Great Century in Europe
    and the United States of America, A.D. 1800-A.D.
    1914. New York and London: Harper & Brothers,
    1946.

Littell, Franklin Hamlin. From State Church to Pluralism.
    Garden City, N.Y.: Anchor Books, 1962.

Litwack, Leon. North of Slavery: The Negro in the Free
    States, 1790-1860. Chicago: University of Chicago
    Press, 1961.

McCall, Emmanuel L., ed. The Black Christian Experience.
    Nashville, Tenn.: Broadman Press, 1972.

McLoughlin, William G. and Bellah, Robert N., eds. Reli-
    gion in America. Boston: Beacon Press, 1968.

M'Tyeire, Holland Nimmons. History of Methodism: Com-
    prising a View of the Rise of This Revival. Nashville,
    Tenn.: Southern Methodist Publishing House, 1887.

Manross, William Wilson. The Episcopal Church in the
    United States, 1800-1840. New York: Columbia Uni-
    versity Press, 1938.

Marty, Martin E. The Infidel. New York: World Pub. Co.,
    1961.

Mathews, Donald G. Slavery and Methodism. Princeton,
    N.J.: Princeton University Press, 1965.

Matlack, Lucius C. The Antislavery Struggle and Triumph
    in the Methodist Episcopal Church. New York: Phil-
    lips & Hunt, 1881.

Mays, Benjamin Elijah. The Negro's God as Reflected in
    His Literature. 1938; rpt. New York: Atheneum,
    1968.

_____, and Nicholson, Joseph William. The Negro's
    Church. New York: Institute of Social and Religious
    Research, 1933.

Mbiti, John S. African Religions and Philosophies. New
    York: Praeger, 1969.

Mead, Sidney E. The Lively Experiment. New York:
    Harper & Row, 1963.

Meier, August, and Rudwick, Elliott, eds. The Origins of
    Black Americans. Vol. I: The Making of Black
    America. New York: Atheneum, 1969.

Miller, Perry. The Life of the Mind in America. New
    York: Harcourt, Brace & World, 1965.

Mitchell, Henry H. Black Preaching. Philadelphia: J. B.
    Lippincott, 1970.

Moore, John Jamison. History of the A.M.E. Zion Church
    in America. York, Pa.: Teacher's Journal Office,
    1884.

Moorehouse, Henry L. Baptist Home Missions in America.
    New York: Temple Court, 1883.

Moss, Lemuel. The Baptists and the National Centenary.
    Philadelphia: American Baptist Publishing Society,
    1876.

Murray, Andrew E. Presbyterians and the Negro--A History.
    Philadelphia: Presbyterian Historical Society, 1966.

Myers, Robert Manson. The Children of Pride: A True
    Story of Georgia and the Civil War. New Haven, Conn.:
    Yale University Press, 1972.

Nelsen, Hart M., Yokley, Raytha L., and Nelsen, Anne K.,
    eds. The Black Church in America. New York: Basic
    Books, Inc., 1971.

Newman, Albert H., ed. A Century of Baptist Achievement.
    Philadelphia: American Baptist Publication Society,
    1901.

_____. A History of the Baptist Churches in the United
    States. 6th ed. New York: Charles Scribner & Sons,
    1915.

Nichols, Charles H. Many Thousands Gone: The Ex-Slaves'

Account of Their Freedom and Bondage.   Leiden,
Netherlands: E. J. Brill, 1963.

Niebuhr, H. Richard. The Kingdom of God in America.
New York: Harper & Row, 1937.

Noble, William Francis Pringle. A Century of Gospel Work;
A History of the Growth of Evangelical Religion in the
United States. Philadelphia: H. C. Watts & Company,
1877.

Norwood, John Nelson. The Schism in the Methodist Episcopal Church in 1844; A Study of Slavery and Ecclesiastical Politics. New York: Alfred University Press,
1923.

Odum, Howard W., and Johnson, Guy B. The Negro and
His Songs. Chapel Hill: University of North Carolina
Press, 1925.

Parrinder, Geoffrey. African Traditional Religion. London:
Hutchinson's University Library, 1954.

Patterson, Caleb Perry. The Negro in Tennessee, 1790-
1865. Austin: University of Texas Press, 1922.

Pelt, Owen D., and Smith, Ralph Lee. The Story of the
National Baptists. New York: Vantage Press, 1960.

Phillips, Charles Henry. The History of the Colored Metho-
dist Episcopal Church in America: Comprising its
Organization, Subsequent Development, and Present
Status. Jackson, Tenn.: Publishing House of the
C. M. E. Church, 1898.

Pipes, William Harrison. Say Amen, Brother! Old-Time
Negro Preaching: a Study in American Frustration.
New York: William Frederick Press, 1951.

Ponton, Mungo M. Life and Times of Henry M. Turner.
Atlanta: A. B. Caldwell Pub. Co., 1917.

Posey, Walter Brownlow. The Baptist Church in the Lower
Mississippi Valley. Lexington: University of Kentucky
Press, 1957.

_____. The Development of Methodism in the Old South-

west, 1783-1824. Tuscaloosa, Ala.: Weatherford
Printing Co., 1933.

_____. Frontier Mission: A History of Religion West
of the Southern Appalachians to 1861. Lexington: University of Kentucky Press, 1966.

Powell, J. H. Bring Out Your Dead: The Great Plague of
Yellow Fever in Philadelphia in 1793. Philadelphia:
University of Pennsylvania Press, 1949.

Quarles, Benjamin. Black Abolitionists. New York: Oxford University Press, 1969.

Rawick, George D. From Sundown to Sunup. Vol. I of
The American Slave: A Composite Autobiography.
Series One, 7 vols. Westport Conn.: Greenwood Pub.
Co., 1972.

Redford, A. H. History of the Organization of the Methodist Episcopal Church, South. Nashville, Tenn.: Publishing House of the M.E. Church, South, 1871.

Reimers, David M. White Protestantism and the Negro.
New York: Oxford University Press, 1965.

Riley, Benjamin F. History of the Baptists of Alabama:
From the Time of Their First Occupation of Alabama
in 1808, until 1894. Birmingham, Ala.: Roberts &
Son, 1895.

_____. A History of the Baptists in the Southern States
East of the Mississippi. Philadelphia: American Baptist Publication Society, 1898.

Rose, Willie Lee. Rehearsal for Reconstruction: The Port
Royal Experiment. New York: Vintage Books, 1967.

Roucek, Joseph, ed. The Negro Impact on Western Civilization. New York: Philosophical Library, Inc., 1970.

Ryland, Garnett. The Baptists of Virginia, 1699-1926.
Richmond: Virginia Board of Missions and Education,
1955.

Sellers, James Benson. Slavery in Alabama. University:
University of Alabama Press, 1950.

Semple, Robert Baylor. A History of the Rise and Prog-
    ress of the Baptists in Virginia. Revised by G. W.
    Beale. Philadelphia: American Baptist Publication
    Society, 1894.

Shaw, James Beverly Ford. The Negro in the History of
    Methodism. Nashville, Tenn.: Parthenon Press, 1954.

Shipp, Albert M. The History of Methodism in South Caro-
    lina. Nashville, Tenn.: Southern Methodist Pub-
    lishing House, 1887.

Simms, James M. The First Colored Baptist Church in
    North America. Philadelphia: J. B. Lippincott Co.,
    1888.

Singleton, George A. The Romance of African Methodism.
    New York: Exposition Press, 1952.

Smith, Charles Spencer. A History of the African Methodist
    Church: Being a Volume Supplemental to a History of
    the African Methodist Episcopal Church, by Daniel
    Alexander Payne, D.D., LL.D., Late One of Its Bis-
    hops, Chronicling the Principal Events in the Advance
    of the African Methodist Episcopal Church From 1856
    to 1922. Philadelphia: Book Concern of the A.M.E.
    Church, 1922.

_____. The Life of Daniel Alexander Payne, D.D.,
    LL.D. Nashville, Tenn.: A.M.E. Church Sunday
    School Union, 1894.

Smith, Timothy L. Revivalism and Social Reform. New
    York: Harper & Row, 1965.

Spotswood, William White. Rev. William S. White, D.D.,
    and His Times. Edited by H. M. White. Richmond:
    Presbyterian Committee of Publication, 1891.

Stampp, Kenneth M. The Peculiar Institution. New York:
    Vintage Books, 1956.

Stange, Douglas C. Radicalism for Humanity: A Study of
    Lutheran Abolitionism. St. Louis: O. Slave, 1970.

Staudenraus, P. J. The African Colonization Movement,
    1816-1865. New York: Columbia University Press,
    1961.

Stevens, Abel. History of the Methodist Episcopal Church.
    Vol. IV. New York: Carlton & Porter, 1867.

Stroud, George M. A Sketch of the Laws Relating to Slavery
    in the Several States of the United States of America.
    2nd ed. Philadelphia: Henry Longstreth, 1856.

Sweet, William Warren. Religion on the American Frontier:
    The Baptists, 1783-1830. New York: Henry Holt &
    Co., 1931.

_____. Religion in the Development of American Culture,
    1765-1840. New York: Scribner's, 1952.

_____. The Story of Religion in America. New York:
    Harper & Brothers, 1930.

Sydnor, Charles S. The Development of Southern Sectional-
    ism, 1819-1848. Vol. V. of A History of the South.
    Edited by Wendell Holmes Stephenson and E. Merton
    Coulter. 10 vols. Baton Rouge: Louisiana State Uni-
    versity Press, 1948.

_____. Slavery in Mississippi. Baton Rouge: Louisiana
    State University Press, 1966.

Talbert, Horace. The Sons of Allen. Xenia, Ohio: Aldine
    Press, 1906.

Tannenbaum, Frank. Slave and Citizen. New York: Knopf,
    1946.

Tanner, Benjamin Tucker. An Outline of Our History and
    Government for African Methodist Episcopal Churchmen,
    Ministerial and Lay. Philadelphia: A.M.E. Book Con-
    cern, 1884.

Taylor, Joe Gray. Negro Slavery in Louisiana. Baton Rouge:
    Louisiana Historical Assoc., 1963.

Tees, Francis H. The Ancient Landmark of American Metho-
    dism, or Historic Old St. George's. Philadelphia:
    Message Pub. Co., 1951.

Thomas, Edgar Garfield. The First African Baptist Church
    of North America. Savannah, Ga.: By the Author,
    1925.

284   Black Religion

Thompson, Charles L. Times of Refreshing: A History of
    American Revivals from 1740 to 1877, With Their
    Philosophy and Methods. Chicago: L. T. Palmer &
    Co., 1877.

Thompson, Ernest Trice. Presbyterians in the South. Vol.
    I. Richmond: John Knox Press, 1963.

Thorpe, Earl E. Black Historians. New York: William
    Morrow, 1971.

_____. The Mind of the Negro: An Intellectual History
    of Afro-Americans. Baton Rouge, La.: Ortlieb Press,
    1961.

Tillinghast, Joseph Alexander. The Negro in Africa and
    America. New York: Published for the American
    Economic Assoc. by the Macmillan Co., 1902.

Tipple, Ezra S. Francis Asbury, the Prophet of the Long
    Road. New York: Methodist Book Concern, 1916.

Titus, Francis W. Narrative of Sojourner Truth; A Bonds-
    woman of Olden Time. Battle Creek, Mich.: Pub-
    lished for the Author, 1878.

Townsend, Vince. Fifty-four Years of African Methodism.
    New York: Exposition Press, 1953.

Turner, Edward Raymond. The Negro in Pennsylvania:
    Slavery-Servitude-Freedom, 1639-1861. Washington,
    D.C.: American Historical Assoc., 1911.

Tyms, James Daniel. The Rise of Religious Education
    Among Negro Baptists. New York: Exposition Press,
    1965.

Vickers, John. Thomas Coke. Nashville, Tenn., and New
    York: Abingdon Press, 1969.

Wade, Richard C. Slavery in the Cities. New York: Oxford
    University Press, 1964.

Washington, Booker T. The Story of the Negro. 2 vols.
    New York: Doubleday, Page & Co., 1909.

Washington, Joseph R., Jr. Black Religion. Boston: Beacon
    Press, 1964.

_____. Black Sects and Cults. Garden City, N.Y.: Doubleday, 1972.

_____. The Politics of God. Boston: Beacon Press, 1967.

Weatherford, Willis Duke. American Churches and the Negro: An Historical Study from Early Slave Days to the Present. Boston: Christopher Pub. House, 1957.

_____. The Negro from Africa to America. New York: George H. Doran Co., 1924.

Weeks, Stephen B. Southern Quakers and Slavery. Baltimore: Johns Hopkins University Press, 1896.

Weisberger, Bernard A. They Gathered at the River. Chicago: Quadrangle Books, Inc., 1966.

Wells, John Miller. Southern Presbyterian Worthies. Richmond: Presbyterian Committee of Publication, 1936.

Wesley, Charles H. Richard Allen: Apostle of Freedom. Washington, D.C.: Associated Publishers, 1935.

Wheeler, Benjamin F. The Varick Family. Mobile, Ala.: n.p., 1906.

White, Charles L. A Century of Faith ... Centenary Volume Published for the American Baptist Home Missionary Society. Philadelphia: Pub. for American Baptist Home Mission Society by the Judson Press, 1932.

White, Henry Alexander. Southern Presbyterian Leaders. Harrisburg, Pa.: Neal Pub. Co., 1911.

White, Newman I. American Negro Folk-Songs. 1928; rpt. Hatboro, Pa.: Folklore Associates, 1965.

Wiley, Bell Irvin. Southern Negroes, 1861-1865. 2nd ed. New York: Rinehart & Co., 1953.

Williams, George W. History of the Negro Race in America From 1619 to 1880. New York: G. P. Putnam's Sons, 1882.

Wilmore, Gayrand S. Black Religion and Black Radicalism.
    Garden City, N.Y.: Doubleday, 1972.

Winks, Robin W. The Blacks in Canada. New Haven, Conn.:
    Yale University Press, 1971.

Woodson, Carter G. The African Background Outlined, or
    Handbook for the Study of Negro. Washington, D.C.:
    Association for the Study of Negro Life and History,
    1936.

_____. The Education of the Negro Prior to 1861. 2nd
    ed. Washington, D.C.: Associated Publishers, 1919.

_____. The History of the Negro Church. 2nd ed.
    Washington, D.C.: Associated Publishers, 1945.

Wright, James M. The Free Negro in Maryland, 1634-1860.
    New York: Columbia University Press, 1921.

Wright, Louis B. Culture on the Moving Frontier. New
    York: Harper & Row, 1961.

Wright, Richard Robert. Centennial Encyclopedia of the
    African Methodist Episcopal Church. Philadelphia:
    Book Concern of the A.M.E. Church, 1916.

III.   UNPUBLISHED DISSERTATIONS AND THESES

Baker, Robert A. "The American Baptist Home Mission So-
    ciety and the South, 1832-1894." Unpublished Ph.D.
    dissertation, Yale, 1947.

Bruner, Clarence V. "Religious Instruction of the Slaves in
    the Antebellum South." Unpublished Ph.D. dissertation,
    George Peabody College for Teachers, 1933.

Des Champs, Margaret B. "The Presbyterian Church in the
    South Atlantic States, 1801-1861." Unpublished Ph.D.
    dissertation, Emory University, 1952.

Johnson, Clifton H. "The American Missionary Association,
    1846-1861: A Study of Christian Abolitionism." Un-
    published Ph.D. dissertation, University of North Caro-
    lina, 1959.

Lines, Stiles B. "Slaves and Churchmen: The Work of the
     Episcopal Church Among Southern Negroes, 1830-1860."
     Unpublished Ph.D. dissertation, Columbia University,
     1960.

Mocko, George Paul. "The Faith of American Slaves, 1830-
     1860." Unpublished S.T.M. thesis, Lutheran Theologi-
     cal Seminary, Gettysburg, Pa., 1971.

Ott, Philip Wesley. "The Mind of Early American Metho-
     dism: 1800-1844." Unpublished Ph.D. dissertation,
     University of Pennsylvania, 1968.

Purifoy, Lewis M., Jr. "The Methodist Episcopal Church,
     South, and Slavery, 1844-1865." Unpublished Ph.D.
     dissertation, University of North Carolina, 1965.

Rigell, William Richard. "Negro Religious Leadership on
     the Southern Seaboard: Maryland, Virginia, North
     Carolina, South Carolina, and Georgia, 1830-1861."
     Unpublished M.A. thesis, University of Chicago Di-
     vinity School, 1916.

Satterfield, James Herbert. "The Baptists and the Negro
     prior to 1863." Unpublished Ph.D. dissertation,
     Southern Baptist Theological Seminary, 1919.

Sigler, Phil Samuel. "The Attitudes of Free Blacks Towards
     Emigration to Liberia." Unpublished Ph.D. disserta-
     tion, Boston University, 1969.

Singleton, George Arnett. "Religious Instruction of the Negro
     in America Under the Slave Regime." Unpublished
     M.A. thesis, University of Chicago, 1929.

_____. "The Effect of Slavery Upon the Religion of the
     Negro." Unpublished B.D. thesis, University of Chi-
     cago Divinity School, 1930.

Smith, Cortland V. "Church Organization as an Agency of
     Social Control: Church Discipline in North Carolina,
     1800-1860." Unpublished Ph.D. dissertation, Univer-
     sity of North Carolina, 1966.

Taylor, Hubert V. "Slavery and the Deliberations of the
     Presbyterian General Assembly, 1833-1838." Unpublished
     Ph.D. dissertation, Northwestern University, 1964.

Thompkins, Robert E. "A History of Religious Education
    Among Negroes in the Presbyterian Church in the
    United States of America." Unpublished Ph.D. disser-
    tation, University of Pittsburgh, 1951.

Todd, Willie G. "The Slavery Issue and the Organization of
    a Southern Baptist Convention." Unpublished Ph.D.
    dissertation, University of North Carolina, 1964.

Williams, Thomas Leonard. "The Methodist Mission to the
    Slaves." Unpublished Ph.D. dissertation, Yale, 1943.

Appendix 1

STATISTICAL TABLES

TABLE I: Showing Results of Plantation Missions Among Slaves of the South, By the Methodist Episcopal Church, From 1829 to 1844, Previous to Organization of Methodist Episcopal Church, South.

Year	Missions	Members	Missionaries	Amount apportioned
1829	2	417	2	....
1830	3	1,077	3	$216.00
1831	4	1,357	4	727.67
1832	8	2,521	9	3,032.05
1833	15	3,350	17	6,565.00
1834	23	5,122	23	6,283.65
1835	17	5,021	20	5,266.42
1836	21	7,137	27	8,816.30
1837	26	12,643	29	11,339.35
1838	32	10,455	23	11,600.12
1839	61	19,188	73	16,704.80
1840	61	22,222	72	14,906.90
1841	59	20,608	68	17,977.53
1842	60	19,705	74	20,049.55
1843	61	18,547	73	23,350.33
1844	68	22,063	80	23,379.25
				$172,214.92

Source: J. C. Hartzell. Methodism and the Negro in the United States. New York: Hunt & Eaton, 1894, p. 16.

TABLE II: Showing Growth of Plantation Missions in
Methodist Episcopal Church, South, in Slave States, From
1845 to 1864.

Year	Missions	Members	Missionaries	Amount apportioned
1845	83	25,380	95	$33,399.96
1846	100	29,482	120	39,901.66
1847	103	30,835	120	35,815.13
1848	130	36,708	149	42,180.44
1849	108	29,817	122	43,995.72
1850	90	26,845	103	46,765.68
1851	96	27,515	108	63,455.50
1852	120	35,721	136	83,104.80
1853	149	43,222	164	82,132.04
1854	160	49,907	172	72,216.56
1855	174	49,983	190	83,103.20
1856	184	53,094	173	97,688.06
1857	208	55,032	206	107,362.74
1858	221	51,778	220	121,111.76
1859	287	56,468	288	130,076.88
1860	329	65,887	335	139,545.22
1861	329	66,559	327	98,510.06
1862	304	63,649	301	94,799.87
1863	270	49,494	267	153,320.48
1864	217	51,553	224	140,121.96
				$1,708,698.72

Source: J. C. Hartzell. Methodism and the Negro in the
United States. New York: Hunt & Eaton, 1894, p. 16.

290

APPENDIX 2

I have selected 23 of the more important figures
mentioned in the text for additional comment. The only
criterion which they all meet is that they were, in one
fashion or another, connected with either the white or the
black churches in the antebellum era. Individuals of whom
there is common knowledge, such as Frederick Douglass,
have been omitted, as have been many lesser names which
may have been mentioned in a peripheral way as our story
progressed.

ALLEN, RICHARD (1760-1831)

In the annals of American religious history, the name
of Richard Allen must henceforth be given a most prominent place. Born in Philadelphia, the slave of a Quaker
master, Allen was soon sold to a Mr. Stokely, near
Dover, Del. Through the preaching of Freeborn Garretson, Allen was converted at 17. After having purchased his freedom in 1783, Allen began traveling as a
Methodist exhorter and a year later attended the famous
Christmas Conference in Baltimore. In 1786 he came
to Philadelphia where he immediately began ministering
to the spiritually destitute of his brethren. On April 12,
1787, he was among those Philadelphia Negroes who
formed the Free African Society. With other black
Christians who had been rebuffed by the discrimination
in St. George's Methodist Church, Allen solicited support for an African Church. In 1794 Bethel Church was
dedicated with Allen as her pastor. Bishop Francis Asbury ordained Allen a deacon in 1799. When the African
Methodist Episcopal Church was organized in 1816,
Richard Allen became its first bishop. For the next 15
years he was the guiding light and the venerable patriarch of this growing denomination. At various times
throughout his life, Allen had been a shoemaker, teamster,

and labor contractor. He died, having kept the faith
and fought the good fight, on March 26, 1831.

ANDREW, JAMES OSGOOD (1794-1871)

As the central figure in the famous General Conference of 1844, Andrew's name has subsequently been associated with the slavery controversy which split the
Methodist Episcopal Church. The son of the first native
Georgian ever to enter the traveling ministry, Andrew
was born in Wilkes County, Georgia. Converted at 15,
licensed at 18, Andrew early exhibited concern for the
spiritual welfare of Negroes. In Georgia and the Carolinas he served numerous congregations, both large and
small. At the General Conference of 1832 Andrew was
elected to the office of bishop because he was a Southerner and did not own slaves. As a result of the death
of his first wife (1842) and his second marriage (1844),
Andrew became a slaveholder, although he wished to rid
himself of this burden by legal means. Southern pressure kept him from resigning his office, the result of
which was the division of the Methodists in 1844-45. At
the organizational conference of the Methodist Episcopal
Church, South, Bishop Andrew presided. In 1846 he
was duly recognized, along with Joshua Soule, as a bishop
of the Southern Methodists. In 1866 he resigned from the
office and retired from active work. He died five years
later.

BROWN, MORRIS (1770-1849)

The pastor of an African Methodist congregation in
Charleston, South Carolina, when the Denmark Vesey
conspiracy alarmed the South, Morris Brown was forced
to flee the South. He had been born among "the free
people of color" in Charleston and after having been appointed an elder in 1818 he was highly effective in establishing a foothold for the African Methodists behind
the cotton curtain. From 1823, when he came to Philadelphia, until 1832, when he was elevated to the episcopal chair, Brown did much to assist Richard Allen in
carrying on the work of the African Methodist Episcopal
Church. Although he could not write, Brown supported
Daniel Alexander Payne in his campaign to improve the
education of the church's clergy. In 1840 Brown helped

organize the Canadian Conference at Toronto.   He died
nine years later.

BRYAN, ANDREW (1737-1812)

Born a slave in 1737 at Goose Creek, South Carolina,
Bryan carried on the work of George Liele among the
black Baptists of the South. He began preaching to fellow slaves on his master's plantation and was ordained
by the Rev. Abraham Marshall in 1788. Bryan and his
small congregations in and about Savannah were often
persecuted for attempting to conduct their own religious
services. In 1794 they erected a church of their own
on property that Bryan possessed. Bryan was the
guiding force behind the growth of the First African
Baptist Church in Savannah. A prosperous man, he left
an estate estimated at between three and five thousand
dollars when he died in 1812. His wife and daughter,
whose freedom he had managed to purchase, survived
him.

CAPERS, WILLIAM (1790-1855)

The monument at Capers' gravesite in Charleston
gives eloquent testimony to the work of which he was
most proud. Outside of the dates of his birth and death,
the only inscription is--"He was the Founder of the Mission to the slaves on the plantations of the Southern
States." Of Huguenot ancestry, Capers was born about
twenty miles from Charleston. A sensitive and serious-
minded student, he entered the sophomore class of South
Carolina College in 1805. During the summer of 1808
he experienced conversion and within a few months was
licensed as an assistant in the Methodist itinerant ministry. Two years later he was ordained as a deacon in
the South Carolina Conference. Traveling extensively in
the Carolinas and Georgia, Capers soon became a popular
preacher and was known as a totally dedicated witness to
both blacks and whites. A slaveholder, Capers declined
the office of bishop in 1832 because of Northern opposition. His real work, he felt, was among the slaves on
the plantations, a cause that he first sought organized
support for in 1829. From 1840-44 Capers served as
Secretary of the Southern Missionary Department of the
Church. When the Methodists split, he became a bishop

of the Southern division in 1846. In the ensuing years
he traveled throughout the South promoting the general
welfare of the Southern Methodists and, in particular,
plantation missions. He died of a heart ailment in 1855.

COKER, DANIEL (d. 1825?)

As the leader of African Methodists in the Baltimore
area, Coker was a co-worker of Richard Allen in the
establishment of the A. M. E. Church. Coker's father
was a slave in Maryland and his mother was a white
English indentured serving-girl. Known as Isaac Wright
in his boyhood, Coker was counted a slave. He fled to
New York City where he joined the Methodist Episcopal
Church and was ordained a deacon by Bishop Francis Asbury. A group of white Baltimore citizens asked him to
come and establish a school for free Negro children.
When the A. M. E. Church was organized in 1816 in
Philadelphia, Daniel Coker was present as the chief
representative of Negro Methodists in Baltimore. Although his name was offered in nomination for the office
of bishop, Coker declined in favor of Richard Allen,
perhaps in part because of some prejudice pertaining to
Coker's lightness of skin. In 1820 Coker accompanied
a group of 86 Negro emigrants who were sailing for
Sierra Leone under the auspices of the American Colonization Society. Although no longer in official connection
with the A. M. E. Church, he hoped to do Christian mission work in West Africa.

GARNET, HENRY HIGHLAND (1815-1882)

One of the most outspoken black abolitionists and
clergymen of his time, Garnet began life as a slave in
Maryland. With his parents he escaped to Pennsylvania
in 1824. By 1826 young Henry was in New York City
attending the African Free School. Nine years later he
enrolled in the ill-fated Noyes Academy in Canaan, New
Hampshire. Garnet was licensed as a Presbyterian
minister shortly after graduating from the Oneida Institute in 1840. In 1843 Garnet delivered a blistering address to the Convention of Free Colored People in Buffalo, calling upon the slaves to take up arms. For the
next five years he served the Liberty Street Presbyterian
Church in Troy, New York. In 1852 he joined the United

Presbyterian Church of Scotland and was sent as a missionary to Jamaica. After three disappointing years, he
returned to New York City and assumed the pastorate of
the Shiloh Presbyterian Church. In 1864 he took charge
of the Fifteenth Street Presbyterian Church in Washington,
D.C. On February 12, 1865, Garnet had the honor of
preaching a sermon before the House of Representatives
in commemoration of the passage of the Thirteenth
Amendment. After the Civil War he was Recorder of
Deeds for a while and president of Avery College in
Pittsburg. In 1881 Garnet became the Minister to Liberia. But his time of service was cut short in 1882
when he died at Monrovia.

JASPER, JOHN (1812-1901)

After his striking conversion in a tobacco factory in
1839, Jasper began preaching in a vivid and free-wheeling
style that made him famous throughout the South. He
was reported to have been able to recite the Bible almost completely from memory. A true Baptist revivalist,
he shepherded congregations in Petersburg and Richmond,
Virginia. After the Civil War he gained an international
following for his Biblically inspired views on scientific
questions. "The Sun Do Move," in which he sought to
prove that Galileo was wrong, was his most famous
sermon. Whites flocked to hear him, many merely out
of curiosity, and blacks were inspired by his oratory.
One Negro follower reported that "it was ekul ter a revival ter se John Jasper moving like a King 'long de
street."

JONES, ABSALOM (1746-1818)

Ordained in 1795 to the diaconate by Bishop White,
Jones became the rector of the first Negro congregation
of the Protestant Episcopal Church. He was born a
slave in Delaware but at 16 he was taken to Philadelphia
to work in his master's store. Along with Richard Allen,
and other Philadelphia blacks, Jones helped to organize
the Free African Society. He became the spiritual leader
of those who left Old St. George's and wished to join with
the Protestant Episcopalians. As rector of St. Thomas'
African Episcopal Church, Jones served his people regularly and faithfully for 22 years. He was so industrious

that he was able not only to purchase his own freedom
(1784) but also that of his wife. As grand master of
the Masonic order, director of a black insurance company, and founder of a school for Negro children, Jones
took an active part in the affairs of Philadelphia.

JONES, CHARLES COLCOCK (1804-1863)

The labors of "the Apostle to the Negro Slaves" in
behalf of plantation missions are extensively examined
in this study. Born in Liberty County, Georgia, Jones
was briefly educated in a local academy before moving
to Savannah where he worked in a counting-house for six
years. After deciding to enter the ministry, he studied
first at Phillips Academy and then at Andover Seminary.
After completing his final year at Princeton Theological
Seminary, Jones served the First Presbyterian Church
of Savannah, Georgia. Then on December 2, 1832, he
became the first functioning missionary of the Association for the Religious Instruction of Negroes. For the
next 16 years, except for a two-year period when he
taught at Columbia Seminary, Jones preached to the
slaves in Liberty County. In 1848 he returned to Columbia Seminary; in 1850 he was appointed Secretary of the
Presbyterian Board of Domestic Missions. Ill health
brought about by overwork forced him to retire to Montevideo, his plantation, in 1853. Ten years later, during
the Civil War, he died. Something of Jones' character
is revealed by the fact that when the news of the secession of South Carolina reached Liberty County, he refused to let his wife Mary illuminate the mansion in
celebration. Besides his wife, Jones left two sons,
Joseph and Charles, Jr., who was an eminent historian
of Georgia. Jones was buried in an ancestral graveyard
not far from the small chapel in which he had preached
to the slaves for so many years.

LIELE, GEORGE (1751?-?)

The Richard Allen of black Baptists in South Carolina,
Liele was born a slave in Virginia but was soon taken
to Burke County, Georgia. He was allowed to preach to
his fellow slaves after his conversion in 1773. Active in
the Savannah region during the time of the British occupation, Liele was instrumental in gathering Negroes into

small Baptist congregations. He went to Kingston, Jamaica, in 1782, as the indentured servant of a British officer who had secured his release from prison during a period of persecution in Savannah. Together with his wife and four children, Liele lived out the rest of his days in the West Indies. He engaged in farming and in transporting cargo with horses and wagons. His real love, however, was the care of the small Negro Baptist congregations which he was instrumental in forming in Jamaica.

LOGUEN, JERMAIN WESLEY (1814-1872)

Born in Tennessee of a Negro mother who had been kidnapped in Ohio, Loguen was active in the antislavery movement and prominent in the African Methodist Episcopal Zion Church. When a young man, he escaped to Canada where he hired himself out as a farm laborer. He soon purchased a 200-acre farm on shares, but the venture failed and he drifted back to Rochester. Two years later Loguen entered Beriah Green's Oneida Institute. Licensed to preach in 1841, he was admitted to the A.M.E. Zion Church Annual Conference in 1843. After serving stations in Ithaca and Syracuse, he was appointed a presiding elder and moved to Troy, New York. Active in the Underground Railroad and on the antislavery lecture platform, Loguen fled to Canada after the passage of the Fugitive Slave Law in 1850. He was captured upon returning to Syracuse, but an outraged citizenry rescued him. In 1864 Loguen declined election to the office of bishop because he could not travel freely in the South. He was finally consecrated bishop on May 29, 1868.

M'TYEIRE, HOLLAND NIMMONS (1824-1889)

M'Tyeire will most probably be remembered as the principal agent in the establishment of Vanderbilt University. Born in Barnwell County, S.C., of Scotch-Irish parents, he early evidenced an aptitude for study. At 20 he graduated from Randolph-Macon College in Virginia. After tutoring for a while, he joined the clerical ranks of the Methodist Episcopal Church, South, and became pastor of the congregation in Williamsburg, Virginia. In 1848 he became the pastor of a church in Mobile, Alabama, and a year later he was appointed to the Louisiana Conference. In New Orleans M'Tyeire preached to a large Negro congregation and founded the New Orleans Christian Advocate in addition to his regular parish duties. The Methodist Episcopal Church, South, made him editor of its official church publication, the Christian Advocate, in 1858. In 1859 M'Tyeire published his influential Duties of Christian Masters. At the General Conference of 1866 he led a fight for lay representation and was elected bishop. In 1870 he was the chief agent in arranging for the formation of the Colored Methodist Episcopal Church.

MEADE, WILLIAM (1789-1862)

A leader of Episcopalians in Virginia, Meade was instrumental in winning Southerners over to the Evangelical or Low Church position. Of Irish descent, he was born in Frederick County, Virginia, the son of a Revolutionary aide to General Washington. In 1808 Meade graduated from the College of New Jersey and thereafter began private study in preparation for the Episcopal ministry. He was ordained a deacon in 1811 and a priest in 1814. In 1829 Meade became assistant bishop of Virginia. He worked hard to revive the Episcopal Church in the South and to awake Southerners to the great need of caring for the spiritual welfare of the slaves. From 1841 to 1862 Meade was the bishop of the diocese of Virginia. He presided over the formation of the Protestant Episcopal Church in the Confederate States on October 16, 1861.

PAUL, THOMAS (1773-1831)

A pioneer among free Negro Baptists of the North, Thomas Paul was born in Exeter, New Hampshire. Converted at an early age, he felt himself called to be a preacher. He was ordained in 1804 and immediately helped to organize the Joy Street Baptist Church in Boston, a congregation for which he labored nearly a quarter century. When Negro Baptists in the First Baptist Church of New York City sought to form a separate church, they asked Paul to come and assist them. The result was the formation of the Abyssinian Baptist Church in 1809. Paul went to Haiti under the auspices of the Baptist Missionary Society of Massachusetts for six months

in the early 1820s. Unable to speak French, he found
the work difficult and discouraging. He continued his
ministry in the North until his death in 1831.

PAYNE, DANIEL ALEXANDER (1811-1893)

An orphan by the age of 10, a school instructor by
19, a licensed preacher by 26, a bishop by 41, and a
college president by the age of 52, Daniel Alexander
Payne had, to put it mildly, a full and eventful life.
Born of free parents in Charleston, S.C., he devoted
his early life toward mastering all the essentials of a
good classical education. In 1826 he joined the Methodists and three years later began a small school for
teaching black children to read and write. Because of
a law passed in 1834 by the South Carolina legislature,
Payne was forced to abandon the work he loved most
dearly and go to the North. Upon graduating from the
Lutheran Theological Seminary in Gettysburg, Pennsylvania, Payne was ordained by the Franckean Synod.
Briefly in 1839 he served a Presbyterian Church at East
Troy, New York. Then in 1841, having come to Philadelphia, Payne joined Richard Allen's connection. A
year later he was received into the Philadelphia Conference and eventually became the pastor of the Israel
A.M.E. Church in Washington, D.C. Here he began
to work for the reform of the church and for higher educational standards for the A.M.E. clergy. In 1845 Payne
took charge of Bethel Church in Baltimore, a post he
left three years later when he became the official historian of the A.M.E. Church. Payne became a bishop
in 1852. Under his leadership the African Methodists
grew rapidly both in membership and denominational
maturity. On March 10, 1863, Payne purchased Wilberforce University in Ohio for the A.M.E. Church. After
his retirement from the college's presidential chair in
1876, Payne continued to write and speak in behalf of
the educational benefit of the church. A small man who
didn't look at all like a bishop, Payne was an amazingly
energetic and dedicated man. In the very year of his
death he participated in the Parliament of Religions at
the Columbian Exposition in Chicago. A fitting epitaph
for Payne was provided by Frederick Douglass, who said
of him that here was a "life without a flaw, and name
without a blemish."

PENNINGTON, JAMES W. C. (1809-1870)

Escaped slave, scholar, renowned pulpit and platform orator, and abolitionist, Pennington was perhaps
most well known as "the Fugitive Blacksmith." Born
into slavery on the Eastern Shore of Maryland, Pennington's early life was harsh and unrelenting. Even as a
skilled blacksmith he longed for freedom. After having
escaped into Pennsylvania at the age of 21, Pennington
was sent by a kindly Quaker to Long Island, New York.
He acquired enough education to teach in a Negro school
on Long Island and then in New Haven, Connecticut.
While in New Haven he studied theology and joined the
Congregational Church, serving twice as president of
the Hartford Central Association of Congregational Ministers. An effective platform speaker, Pennington traveled
in England and Europe in behalf of the antislavery cause.
Heidelberg University awarded him the Doctor of Divinity
degree. From 1847 to 1855 Pennington occupied the
pulpit of the First (Shiloh) Presbyterian Church in New
York City. As an author he contributed to Anglo-African
Magazine and, besides the narrative of his early life, is
most remembered for writing what was very likely the
first Negro history textbook. After 1855 he does not
seem to have had a regular charge. His effectiveness
was limited in his later years by the physical wastage
caused by liquor. He died while in Florida in search
of better health.

PLUMER, WILLIAM SWAN (1802-1880)

Correspondent and friend of Charles C. Jones, Plumer
was an eminent Presbyterian clergyman and author.
Born in Pennsylvania, he moved to Kentucky and then to
Ohio at an early age. His father owned a floating store
on the Ohio River. Plumer taught school for a while
and then entered Washington College in Lexington, Virginia. In 1826 he graduated from Princeton Theological
Seminary and engaged in missionary work in Virginia
and North Carolina. He served congregations in Petersburg and Richmond, Va., and in Baltimore, Md. In
1854 he began an eight-year professorship of pastoral
and didactic theology at the Western Theological Seminary at Allegheny, Pennsylvania. Meanwhile he continued to supply various Presbyterian churches. From
1867 to 1880 Plumer taught at Columbia Theological
Seminary at Columbia, South Carolina. The author of

numerous books and tracts, editor of The Watchman of the South, and popular preacher, Plumer did much to assist Jones in making Negro missions a cause that was to be championed by the entire Presbyterian communion.

RUFFNER, HENRY (1790-1861)

Born of German-Swiss parents, Ruffner was another one of the stalwart Presbyterian clergymen who showed concern for the spiritual welfare of the slaves. A graduate of Washington College, Lexington, Virginia, Ruffner devoted nearly three decades of his life toward the improvement of his alma mater. At various times he was both faculty member and president. In the debate over slavery, he advocated the restriction of slavery to the area east of the Blue Ridge. He hoped that it would be gradually abolished even there. In 1848 Ruffner left Washington College in order to recover his health, but after a few years he assumed the pastorate of a congregation in what is now Malden, West Virginia.

SMITH, WILLIAM ANDREW (1802-1870)

As an advocate of the Southern defense of slavery on Scriptural grounds, Smith was a man of power and influence in the Methodist Episcopal Church. Orphaned at 11, he achieved only a cursory education. In 1827 he was admitted to the Virginia Conference and subsequently served congregations in Petersburg, Lynchburg, Richmond, and Norfolk. In 1844 Smith was counsel to the Rev. F. A. Harding who had been suspended from the ministry because he had become a slaveholder by marriage. Smith also was a vocal supporter of Bishop James Andrew in the case that fully exposed the deep sectional divide within the Methodist communion. In 1846 Smith became president of Randolph-Macon College and Professor of Moral and Intellectual Philosophy. His lectures were published in 1856 as Lectures on the Philosophy and Practice of Slavery as Exhibited in the Institution of Domestic Slavery in the United States, with the Duties of Masters to Slaves. After the Civil War, Smith became pastor of a church in St. Louis. In 1868 he assumed the presidential chair of Central College in Fayette, Missouri. Ill health forced him to resign.

VARICK, JAMES (1750?-1828)

As the first bishop of the African Methodist Episcopal
Zion Church, Varick is an important but somewhat
elusive figure in the history of black Christianity. He
seems to have been born about 1750 near Newburgh,
New York. Although not present at the famous meeting
in 1796 when Negro members of the John Street Church
received permission from Bishop Asbury to begin holding
services by themselves, Varick's name soon appeared
as one of the leaders of the small African chapel. He
and Abraham Thompson were both appointed elder-elects
of the Zionite group in 1820 when, as a result of the
Stilwell controversy, the chapel was left without white
supervision. Varick was on the committee of Negro
Methodists which had the responsibility of drawing up a
new Discipline. When the first yearly conference of the
Zionites met on June 21, 1821, Varick was elected
District Chairman, an office similar to that of a Presiding Elder. In 1822 he became the first bishop of
the A.M.E. Zion Church. At his death in 1828, Varick
was succeeded by Christopher Rush, the historian of the
Zionite pioneer period.

WARD, SAMUEL R. (1817-1866?)

Born a slave in Maryland, Ward was brought by his
parents to New York City when he was nine years old.
His father gardened near Greenwich, New Jersey, and
taught Ward his most valuable lessons: the use of the
hoe, to spell in three syllables, to do elementary figures,
and to read the first chapter of the Gospel of John.
Ward attended the African Free School and, with the assistance of Gerrit Smith, the philanthropist, he was
trained in the classical curriculum at the Oneida Institute.
In 1839 he was licensed by the Congregational Church and
became a pastor among whites at South Butler, New York.
From 1846 to 1851 he served another white congregation
at Cortland. Ward was most renowned for his abolitionist activities. A large-framed and forceful orator,
he attracted attention wherever he went. In Western
and Central New York and in Canada he assisted fugitive
slaves. With Gerrit Smith and others, he was involved
in the famous "Jerry Rescue" case. In 1852 Ward went
to London on behalf of the Anti-Slavery Society of Canada.
While there he was befriended by John Chandler, a wealthy

Quaker, who offered him 58 acres in Jamaica. Ward
is perhaps the best example of how a black clergyman
associated with a white-controlled denomination managed
to speak out forcefully and effectively in behalf of the
rights of the Negro in America.

WILLIAMS, PETER, JR. (d. 1849?)

As rector of St. Phillip's Episcopal Church for Negroes in New York City, Peter Williams, Jr., was a
leader of many reform causes. His father, Peter
Williams, Sr., was a member of the John Street Church.
In return for performing the duties of a sexton, his
father was purchased and freed by the white Methodists.
Peter, Jr. assisted his father in maintaining a small
tobacco shop. Peter, Sr. supported the movement
towards religious freedom and laid the cornerstone of
the African chapel. Peter, Jr. was licensed by the
Episcopalians and appointed to preach at St. Phillip's
Church about 1820. He took an active part in abolitionist and reform societies. In 1834, under pressure
from Bishop Onderdonk, Williams resigned his executive
committee post in the American Anti-Slavery Society.
By 1840 the St. Phillip's congregation numbered some
350 communicants. Williams served these Negro
Episcopalians faithfully until about 1849.

INDEX

Liele, George   111, 216 n3
   biographical sketch of   296-97
Little, Malcolm   see   Malcolm X
Livingston College   145
Loguen, Jermain W.   87, 129, 136, 158, 159, 207 n28,
   223 n55
   biographical sketch of   297
Long, John Dixon   87, 98, 103
Lutherans   33-34, 51, 182 n41
Lynch, James   134

McKim (Garrison), Lucy   105
McNeilly, James   164
M'Tyeire, Holland   63, 66, 71-72, 76, 78-79, 94
   biographical sketch of   297-98
Malcolm X   68
Mallard, James H.   37, 184 n6
Mallard, Ralph Q.   64, 186-87 n28
Mann, Burell W.   147
Marriages, slave   71-78
Marshall, Andrew   113,114
Martin, J. Sella   165
Massey, J. H.   42
Mather, Cotton   32
Mays, Benjamin E.   107, 166
Mead, Sidney   176 n2
Meade, William   53, 62, 69-70
   biographical sketch of   298
Melden, Charles M.   165
Mercer, William   64
Methodist Episcopal Church, South   51, 73, 234 n6
Methodists, Negro
   in Charleston, South Carolina   20, 38-39, 41, 115
   proselytized by the Evangelicals before 1829   33-34
   numbers of, among the slaves   44, 51, 55-56, 289-90
   in Philadelphia   17, 116-20
   in Baltimore   120
   in New York City   120
   in Wilmington, Del.   120
   set aside as the Coloured Methodist Episcopal Church
      164, 234 n6
   See also African Methodist Episcopal Church (Bethelites);
      African Methodist Episcopal Zion Church (Zionites)
Methodists, white
   post-Revolutionary status of   25
   expansion of, into slave states   33-34, 185-86 n20

Pamphlet, Gowan 114
Parsons, C. G. 93
Patillo, Henry 183 n3
Paul, Nathaniel 148, 157
Paul, Thomas 120, 156
   biographical sketch of 298-99
Paxton, J. D. 89
Payne, Daniel Alexander
   on slave's ability to discern true Gospel 87
   joins the A. M. E. Church 131
   early life in the South 133
   enrolls at Gettysburg Lutheran Seminary 133
   election as bishop 133
   takes African Methodism to the South 134
   welcomes whites in A. M. E. Church 137
   fosters ministerial education 140-41
   opposed to "corn-field ditties" 141-42
   purchases Wilberforce University 143-45
   position of, on slavery 153
   refuses to join abolitionist campaign 156
   reaction of, to Fugitive Slave Act 159
   on future of the Negro Church 161
   on nature of African Methodism 169
   biographical sketch of 299
Pennington, James W. C. 91, 92, 140, 156-57, 164, 172-74
   biographical sketch of 300
Peter, Jesse 95, 111, 113
Pierce, George F. 73
Pinckney, Charles Cotesworth 41, 46, 62, 94
Pinckney, Henry L. 47
Plantation missionaries
   described as having a "low calling" 30, 36
   required to be white Southerners 41
   encounter hazards 42-43, 65
   adapt to religious instruction "without letters" 46, 65
   promise not to meddle in plantation affairs 46-47, 73
   claim antislavery debate threatened missions 48-50
   given competition by folk preachers 61-62, 93-94
   engage in a peripatetic ministry 63-64
   urged to avoid homiletical sophistry 67
   confuse temporal and spiritual goals 68-70
   complain of back-sliding and sexual sins among slaves
     70-72
   emphasize obedience to masters 62, 73-76
   urged to preserve a "mild dignity" among slaves 67-68,
     197 n36
   begin to preach on responsibilities of masters to slaves
     78-80